Webster's
Synonyms
Antonyms
and
Homonyms

Webster's Synonyms Antonyms and Homonyms

CRESCENT BOOKS
NEW YORK • AVENEL, NEW JERSEY

DEFINITIONS

Synonyms— Words that have the same meaning.
Example: big, large.

Antonyms— Words that have opposite meanings.
Example: large, small.

Note: Antonyms appear in parentheses ( ) following the synonyms.

Homonyms— Words that sound alike, but are spelled differently and have different meanings.
Example: one, won.

Note: Synonyms and Antonyms begin on page 1.
Homonyms begin on page 225.

SYNONYMS AND ANTONYMS

abandon—leave, forsake, desert, renounce, cease, relinquish, discontinue, cast off, resign, retire, quit, forego, forswear, depart from, vacate, surrender, abjure, repudiate. (*pursue, prosecute, undertake, seek, court, cherish, favor, protect, claim, maintain, defend, advocate, retain, support, uphold, occupy, haunt, hold, assert, vindicate, keep*)

abandoned—profligate, wicked, vicious, unprincipled, reprobate, incorrigible, sinful, graceless, demoralized, dissolute, depraved, bad, licentious, corrupt. (*virtuous, conscientious, correct, upright, worthy, righteous, self-controlled, high-principled, steady, good*)

abbreviate—shorten, reduce, abridge, contract, curtail, epitomize, condense, prune, compress. (*lengthen, prolong, extend, enlarge, produce, elongate, amplify, expand, dilate*)

abdicate—abandon, relinquish, resign, surrender, vacate. (*retain, maintain, claim, occupy, assert, grasp, seize, usurp*)

abet—aid, support, promote, countenance, uphold, assist, instigate, encourage, incite, advocate, sanction, subsidize, embolden. (*thwart, contradict, obstruct, oppose, baffle, confound, discourage, disapprove, disconcert, counteract, deter, dissuade, frustrate, impede, denounce, expose*)

abeyance—suspension, reservation, dormancy, expectation, intermission. (*revival, renewal, operation, resuscitation, action, enjoyment, possession, exercise, force*)

abhor—hate, abominate, detest, loathe, despise, dislike, eschew, nauseate. (*love, admire, enjoy, approve, affect, covet, relish, crave, desire*)

abide—dwell, stay, inhabit, continue, rest, tarry, lodge, reside, live, wait, sojourn, remain, expect, endure, tolerate, anticipate, confront, await, bear,

1

face, watch. (*deport, migrate, move, journey, proceed, resist, mislike, forefend, avoid, shun, reject, abandon, forfeit*)

ability—power, cleverness, faculty, skill, capacity, talent, expertness, aptitude, dexterity, efficiency, competency, qualification. (*weakness, incapacity, imbecility, inability, unreadiness, maladroitness*)

abject—degraded, outcast, miserable, vile, pitiable, worthless, despicable, groveling, fawning, squalid, base-minded, slavish, beggarly, servile, cringing, low, wretched, sordid. (*honorable, dignified, eminent, exalted, esteemed, worthy, venerable. noble, princely, illustrious, independent, self-assertive, self-reliant, vain, arrogant, insolent, haughty*)

abjure—renounce, deny, apostatize, discard, recant, disclaim, disavow, repudiate, revoke, retract, disown. (*profess, assert, demand, vindicate, claim, cherish, advocate, retain, acknowledge, appropriate, hug*)

able—strong, powerful, clever, skillful, talented, capable, fitted, efficient, effective, learned, gifted, masterly, telling, nervous, vigorous. (*weak, inefficient, unskillful, silly, stupid, incapable, ineffective, unqualified*)

abnormal—irregular, erratic, peculiar, unusual, exceptional, monstrous, aberrant, devious, divergent, eccentric, strange. (*typical, normal, regular, ordinary, usual, natural, customary, illustrative*)

abode—home, stay, place, residence, domicile, habitation, lodgings, berth, quarters: with the idea of permanence. (*halt, perch, tent, bivouac, caravansary: with the idea of transience*)

abolish—destroy, eradicate, invalidate, make void, obliterate, extirpate, abrogate, annul, subvert, cancel, revoke, quash, nullify, overthrow, annihilate, supersede, suppress, expunge. (*support, sustain, cherish, promote, continue, confirm, restore, repair, revive, reinstate, enact, institute, reenact*)

2

abominable—abhorrent, foul, accursed, detestable, hateful, horrible, loathsome, odious, offensive, execrable, nauseous, impure. (*delectable, desirable, admirable, enjoyable, lovable, charming, delightful, grateful, pure*)

abortion—failure, miscarriage, misadventure, downfall, mishap, misproduction, defect, frustration, blunder, mess. (*success, consummation, completion, achievement, realization, perfection, exploit, feat, development*)

abound—stream, swell, flow, increase, overflow, superabound, luxuriate, teem, swarm, flourish, prevail, be plentiful, wanton, revel, multiply. (*fall, waste, dry, lack, wane, evaporate, drain, die, decay, vanish, lessen, decrease*)

about—almost, with respect to, near, nearly, touching, concerning, surrounding, relative to, relating to, in relation to, approximately, touching, roughly, generally. (*afar, away or afar from, precisely, exactly*)

above—over, beyond, exceeding. (*below, within, beneath*)

abridge—abbreviate, diminish, shorten, lessen, curtail, restrict, contract, condense, epitomize, compress. (*amplify, expand, spread out*)

abrupt—sudden, steep, precipitous, craggy, coarse, curt, blunt, violent, harsh, unceremonious, rugged, rough. (*undulating, easy, gliding, polished, smooth, blending, courteous*)

absent—*a.* not present, gone away, elsewhere, inattentive, thoughtless, listless, pre-occupied. (*present, in this place, here, attentive*)

absent—*v.* keep away, depart, withdraw. (*be present, stay, remain*)

absolute—perfect, complete, unconditional, irrelative, irrespective, supreme, despotic, autocratic, certain, authoritative, unqualified, unequivocal, irresponsible, arbitrary. (*imperfect, incomplete,* *conditional, conditioned, contingent, relative, dependent, constitutional, dubious, accountable, responsible)*

absorb—swallow, drown, consume, imbibe, engross, drink in, suck up, engulf, monopolize, exhaust. *(eject, emit, exude, disgorge, dissipate, distract, distil, disperse)*

abstain—refrain, forbear, refuse, demur, avoid, cease, stop, keep back, desist, discontinue, withhold, scruple. *(indulge, exceed, reveal, wanton)*

abstemious—abstinent, moderate, self-denying, sober, temperate, sparing, frugal. *(sensual, self-indulgent, gluttonous, greedy, intemperate)*

abstract—separate, detach, part, eliminate, draw away, remove, take away, appropriate, purloin, steal, thieve, draw from. *(add, unite, conjoin, adduce, impose, restore, surrender, return)*

absurd—irrational, ridiculous, monstrous, senseless, asinine, stupid, chimerical, unreasonable, preposterous, silly, nonsensical, foolish. *(sensible, rational, reasonable, consistent, sound, substantial, logical, wise, sagacious, reflective, philosophical)*

abundant—plentiful, copious, plenteous, large, ample, overflowing, teeming, full, lavish, luxuriant, liberal, rich. *(rare, scarce, scant, deficient, short, insufficient, niggardly, sparing, dry, drained, exhausted, impoverished)*

abuse—*v.* injure, damage, spoil, maltreat, treat-ill, ill-use, ill-treat, revile, scandalize, disparage, reproach, upbraid, asperse, malign, slander, vituperate, prostitute, defame, pervert, misuse, misemploy, vilify. *(tend, protect, conserve, consider, regard, shield, cherish, praise, extol, laud, vindicate, panegyrize, respect)*

abuse—*n.* mistreatment, invective, ill treatment, opprobium, scurrility, vituperation, ribaldry, obloquy, reproach, insolence, misusage, ill-usage.

(good-usage, good-treatment, kindness, praise, deference, respect)

accelerate—hasten, urge, expedite, quicken, speed, urge on, press forward, hurry, promote, dispatch, facilitate. *(delay, obstruct, impede, clog, retard, hinder, shackle, drag)*

accent—stress, rhythm, pulsation, beat, emphasis. *(smoothness, inaccentuation, monotony, equableness, babble, flow)*

accept—welcome, hail, admit, recognize, avow, acknowledge, take, accede to, receive, assent to. *(refuse, decline, reject, disown, disavow, ignore, repudiate)*

acceptable—grateful, pleasant, welcome, agreeable, pleasurable, seasonable, gratifying. *(ungrateful, unwelcome, disagreeable, unpleasant)*

accessory—assistant, additive, additional, auxiliary, supplementary, conducive, accomplice, ally, associate, abettor, colleague, confederate, helper. *(essential, inherent, immanent, incorporate, superfluous, irrelevant, malapropos, obstructive, cumbersome, foe, antagonist, adversary, rival)*

accident—chance, fortuity, disaster, incident, adventure, casualty, hazard, contingency, calamity, misadventure, mishap. *(law, purpose, appointment, ordainment, provision, preparation)*

accommodate—convenience, oblige, adapt, supply, reconcile, suit, fit, adjust, furnish, serve, harmonize. *(inconvenience, disoblige, disturb, misfit, incommode, deprive, aggravate)*

accommodating—kind, unselfish, obliging, polite, considerate, yielding, conciliatory. *(disobliging, selfish, churlish, rude, imperious, dictatorial, exacting, inconsiderate, unaccommodating)*

accomplice—abettor, confederate, accessory, ally, associate, partner, colleague, coadjutor, assistant, *particeps criminis.* *(rival, foe, adversary, antagonist)*

accomplish—execute, perfect, perform, fulfil, do, carry out, attain, realize, consummate, achieve, finish, complete. (*fail, frustrate, defeat, disconcert, destroy, baffle, mar, spoil*)

accord—agree, consent, harmonize, tally, answer, comport, consist, conform, grant, concede, surrender, allow. (*disagree, differ, misfit, miscomport, misconform, withhold, deny, refuse*)

accordingly—agreeably, suitably, conformably, hence, consequently

account—*n.* narration, report, rehearsal, story, statement, narrative, recital, relation, description, motive, value, importance, advantage, ground, reason, profit. (*silence, suppression, project, misannouncement, of no account, attempt, without value, deed, project*)

account—*v.* deem, esteem, consider, regard, hold, judge, rate, estimate, value, reckon, explain, solve. (*disesteem, misestimate, mystify, underrate, undervalue, perplex, darken*)

accountable—responsible, liable, amenable, punishable, answerable, accredited, delegated, subordinate. (*autocratic, independent, irresponsible, absolute, supreme, despotic*)

accredit—believe, trust, entrust, delegate, depute, commission, authorize. (*disbelieve, distrust, suspect, recall, supersede, discard, dismiss*)

accumulate—collect, garner, grow, mass, heap, store, bring together, hoard, gather, agglomerate, husband, augment, amass, increase. (*dissipate, disperse, diminish, scatter, expend, waste*)

accumulation—heap, collection, store, mass, aggregation, hoard, pile. (*segregation, separation, unit, individual*)

accurate—careful, exact, faithful, precise, correct, close, truthful, strict, just, actual, nice. (*careless, inexact, faulty, incorrect, inaccurate, loose, defective*)

accuse—charge, incriminate, impeach, arraign, tax, taunt, censure, cite, summon, criminate. (*defend, vindicate, discharge, acquit, absolve, condone, pardon, exonerate, release*)

accustom—habituate, familiarize, form, inure, train, reconcile. (*disaccustom, dishabituate, estrange, wean, alienate*)

achieve—accomplish, do, gain, perform, execute, effect, fulfil, finish, attain, win. (*fail, lose, miss*)

achievement—exploit, feat, attainment, accomplishment, performance. (*failure, lack in completion*)

acknowledge—avow, admit, recognize, own, accept, profess, endorse, grant, concede, concern. (*disavow, disclaim, disown, repudiate, ignore, deny*)

acme—summit, zenith, climax, apex, pitch, culmination, meridian. (*base, floor, ground, foundation, nadir, depth, depression, foot, root*)

acquaint—advertise, inform, impart, make known, divulge, teach, notify, apprise, advise, tell. (*misinform, deceive, delude, mislead, misguide, hoodwink*)

acquaintance—knowledge, intimacy, familiarity, experience, companionship. (*ignorance, unfamiliarity, inexperience*)

acquiesce—assent, concur, repose, agree, yield, be resigned, comply. (*dissent, demur, object*)

acquit—discharge, exonerate, absolve, exculpate, release, dismiss, liberate, pardon. (*charge, accuse, impeach, constrain, implicate, bind, compel, condemn, oblige, sentence*)

acquittance—release, receipt, discharge. (*bond, claim, charge, obligation*)

across—athwart, against, transversely. Transverseness to a line of movement becomes opposition. (*lengthwise, along, concurrently, parallel*)

act—deed, performance, action, movement, proceeding, exercise, operation, play. (*inaction, rest, repose, cessation, suspension, quiet, immobility, inertia, quiescence*)

active—nimble, agile, lively, sprightly, brisk, quick, expert, dexterous, supple, wide-awake, prompt, busy, industrious, diligent. (*slow, inactive, indolent, sluggish, heavy*)

actual—developed, positive, unquestionable, demonstrable, certain, real, authentic. (*potential, undeveloped, hypothetical, supposititious, possible, virtual, theoretical, fabulous, fictitious, unreal*)

acute—pointed, penetrating, sagacious, perspicacious, keen, astute, piercing, sharp, shrewd, keen-sighted, severe, distressing. (*dull, blunt, obtuse, stupid, undiscerning, heavy, chronic, stolid*)

adapt—fit, accommodate, suit, adjust, conform, admeasure, harmonize, attune. (*misfit, misconform, misapply*)

add—adduce, adjoin, increase, extend, enlarge, sum up, cast up, subjoin, amplify, annex. (*deduct, subtract, dissever, abstract*)

addicted—given, accustomed, prone, inclined, disposed, habituated. (*unaddicted, disinclined, unaccustomed, indisposed, averse, free*)

addition—accession, enlargement, increase, extension, accretion, appendage. (*deduction, detraction, drawback, decrement, deterioration*)

address—*n.* tact, manners, speech, abode. (*awkwardness, unmannerliness*)

address—*v.* accost, greet, salute, approach, apostrophize, appeal, hail, woo, court. (*elude, avoid, shun, ignore, pass*)

adept—expert, adroit, handy, master, performer, professor, artist. (*awkward, clumsy, inexpert, tyro, novice, lubber, blunderer*)

8

adequate—equal, sufficient, fit, satisfactory, full, competent, capable, able. (*unequal, insufficient, incompetent, inadequate*)

adherence—adhesion, attachment, devotion, fidelity, cleaving to, constancy, endearment. (*separation, disunion, unfaithfulness, desertion, treachery*)

adherent—follower, supporter, ally, disciple, admirer, backer, aid, partisan. (*opponent, deserter, adversary, renegade, antagonist*)

adieu—good-bye (which is, "God be with ye"), farewell, leave-taking, parting, salutation, valediction. (*greeting, welcome, recognition, salutation*)

adipose—obese, corpulent, sebaceous, oleaginous, pinguetudinous. (*leathery, skinny, bony, thin, anatomical, mummified*)

adjacent—near, neighboring, contiguous, close, nigh, bordering, conterminous. (*remote, distant, separate*)

adjoin—annex, add, connect, append, supplement, attach, unite, border, neighbor, touch, abut, approximate, verge, trench. (*disjoin, dismember, disconnect, detach, disintegrate, disunite, part, separate, recede, return, diverge, be distant, removed, remote, incontiguous*)

adjourn—postpone, suspend, defer, prorogue, delay, protract, put off. (*expedite, despatch, urge, hasten, conclude, complete, seal, consummate, terminate*)

adjunct—addition, additament, attachment, appendage, auxiliary, appurtenance, aid, acquisition, advantage, help. (*essence, substance, body, clog, detriment, impediment, drawback, hindrance, obstruction, detraction*)

adjust—harmonize, collocate, arrange, localize, adapt, affix, right, suit, classify, set in order, reconcile, accommodate, compose. (*dislocate, dis-*

arrange, disturb, confound, dismember, disorder, confuse, discompose, derange)

administer—distribute, award, accord, dole, give, impart, afford, discharge, dispense, execute, perform, furnish, contribute, conduct. *(withdraw, withhold, refuse, retain, assume, resume, resign, deny, divert, appropriate, misadminister, betray, misconduct, mismanage)*

admirable—wonderful, excellent, surprising, astonishing, praiseworthy, pleasing. *(commonplace, mediocre, ridiculous, abominable, displeasing)*

admissible—allowable, permissible, probable, reasonable, just, proper, fair, right, qualified. *(unallowable, inadmissible, improper, unreasonable, absurd, preposterous, monstrous, unfair, wrong, unqualified, excluded)*

admit—receive, pass, permit, accept, grant, concede, allow, acknowledge, confess, own, avow, suffer. *(exclude, debar, disallow, reject, deny, discharge, dismiss, eject, extrude, repudiate, disavow, disown)*

admonish—remind, forewarn, advise, warn, dissuade, caution, counsel, reprove, censure, rebuke. *(encourage, instigate, abet, incite, urge, applaud, countenance)*

adopt—assume, select, affiliate, take, elect, arrogate, choose, endorse, avow, appropriate. *(reject, decline, repudiate, disavow, discard, renounce, abandon, disown, disclaim)*

adore—admire, hallow, glorify, praise, venerate, reverence, worship, idolize. *(abhor, despise, disesteem, abominate, execrate, blaspheme)*

adulation—flattery, compliment, sycophancy, courtship, incense, praise, blandishment, fawning, cringing. *(detraction, obloquy, defamation, calumny, traducement, sarcasm, ridicule, satire, bespatterment)*

advance—propel, elevate, promote, further, lend, propagate, progress, increase, prosper, rise. *(retard,* *hinder, withhold, withdraw, recall, depress, degrade, suppress, oppose, retreat, decrease)*

advantage—gain, success, superiority, help, assistance, benefit, good, avail, interest, utility, service, profit, acquisition. (*loss, disappointment, defeat, frustration, inferiority, obstacle, obstruction, difficulty, dilemma, disadvantage, drawback*)

adventurous—bold, brave, daring, enterprising, courageous, gallant, fearless, venturesome, rash, chivalrous, hazardous. (*timid, unenterprising, inadventurous, cowardly, nervous, hesitating, cautious*)

adversary—antagonist, foe, enemy, rival, assailant. (*accessory, abettor, aider, friend, helper, assistant, ally, accomplice*)

adversity—ill-luck, misfortune, misery, calamity, disaster, distress, unsuccess, failure, ruin, trouble, affliction, sorrow. (*good-luck, prosperity, happiness, success, advancement*)

advertent—attentive, regardful, mindful, watchful, thoughtful, observant, considerate. (*inattentive, inadvertent, casual, thoughtless, heedless, inobservant, inconsiderate*)

advertise—publish, inform, advise, circulate, announce, notify, proclaim, promulge. (*suppress, hush, conceal, ignore, hoodwink, misguide, mislead, misinform*)

advise—admonish, warn, deliberate, counsel, persuade, urge, prompt, instigate, incite, instruct, acquaint, inform. (*dissuade, deter, expostulate, remonstrate, prohibit, inhibit, restrain, curb, mislead, misadvise, hoodwink, deceive, delude, misinform*)

advocate—pleader, counsellor, upholder, propagator, promoter, supporter, countenancer, defender, maintainer. (*opponent, adversary, discountenancer, accuser, impugner, gainsayer*)

affable—courteous, accessible, condescending, conversible, gracious, sociable, gentle, complaisant, urbane, polite, easy, approachable. (*exclusive, discourteous, distant, inaccessible, unapproachable, inconversible, haughty, contemptuous, supercilious*)

affect—like, desire, favor, seek, assume, move, influence, concern, interest, feign, pretend. (*dislike, eschew, shun, repel, repudiate*)

affectation—pretence, artifice, hypocrisy, assumption, simulation, mannerism, euphuism, airs. (*genuineness, naturalness, unaffectedness, simplicity, artlessness*)

affection—influence, condition, state, inclination, bent, mood, humor, feeling, love, desire, propensity. (*insensibility, indifference, repugnance, disaffection, repulsion*)

affinity—relationship, relation, kindred, conformity, connection, alliance, similarity, analogy, homogeneity, harmony, correlativeness, sympathy, interdependence, interconnection, intercommunity. (*dissimilarity, discordance, disconnection, independence, antagonism, antipathy, repugnance, interrepulsiveness*)

affirm—assert, swear, testify, tell, aver, propound, asseverate, depose, state, declare, endorse, maintain. (*deny, dispute, doubt, demur, negative, contradict, gainsay, oppugn, impugn, oppose*)

affliction—trouble, trial, grief, pain, disease, misery, hardship, sorrow. (*consolation, relief, alleviation, assuagement, or, more positively: boon, blessing, gratification, pleasure*)

afford—produce, supply, give, yield, grant, confer, bestow, impart, administer, extend. (*withhold, deny, withdraw, retain, stint, grudge*)

affront—outrage, provocation, insult, ill-treatment, abuse, wrong, offense, indignity. (*homage, salutation, courtesy, apology, amends, compliment*)

afloat—adrift, abroad, at sea, abroach, loose, distracted, dazed. (*ashore, snug, tight, close, fast, collected, concentrated*)

afoot—working, launched, afloat, agoing, inaugurated, started, instituted, established. (*uncommenced, incomplete, projected, proposed, contemplated, designed*)

afraid—fearful, apprehensive, timid, timorous, cowardly, fainthearted, cautious, careful, frightened, alarmed, terrified, suspicious, distrustful, anxious. (*fearless, inapprehensive, unsolicitous, easy, indifferent, secure, confident, bold, hopeful, eager, reckless, audacious, venturesome*)

afresh—anew, again, frequently, repeatedly, intermittently. (*continuously, uniformly, uninterruptedly, unintermittently, connectedly*)

after—behind, following, succeeding. (*before, afore, introducing, preceding*)

again—anew, afresh, repeatedly, frequently. (*continuously, uniformly, uninterruptedly, unintermittently, once*)

against—over, opposite, abutting, opposing, resisting, despite, across, athwart, counter. (*with, for, accompanying, aiding, suiting, promoting*)

age—period, generation, era, epoch, date, century, antiquity, senility, eldership, seniority. (*youth, infancy, boyhood, childhood, moment, instant*)

agent—doer, performer, actor, force, means, instrument, influence, cause, promoter, operator. (*counteragent, counteractor, counteraction, opponent, neutralizer*)

aggravate—exasperate, provoke, wound, heighten, intensify, irritate, make worse, increase, enhance, embitter, magnify. (*soothe, conciliate, assuage, diminish, palliate, neutralize, soften, lessen, alleviate, attenuate, mitigate*)

agile—nimble, active, fleet, brisk, alert, featly, lithe, prompt, ready, quick, supple, swift, sprightly. (*slow, heavy, awkward, inert, clumsy, bulky, ponderous, elephantine*)

agitate—disturb, trouble, excite, ruffle, stir, fluster, oscillate, instigate, convulse, shake. (*calm, compose, allay, pacify, smooth*)

agony—pain, torture, torment, distress, woe, throe, suffering, pang, excruciation. (*assuagement, comfort, peace, ease, relief, gratification, enjoyment, rapture, ecstacy, composure*)

agree—suit, tally, accord, fit, harmonize, combine, assent, concur, acquiesce, admit, consent, conform, consort, comport, coincide. (*differ, disagree, revolt, protest, decline, refuse, dissent, demur*)

agreeable—obliging, pleasant, accommodating, grateful, acceptable, welcome, suitable, consistent, consonant, amiable, gratifying, pleasing, good-natured, complaisant. (*disobliging, unpleasant, unaccommodating, disagreeable, obnoxious, ungrateful, unwelcome, unacceptable, offensive*)

agreement—contract, compact, bond, concord, concurrence, conformity, harmony, unison, consonance, bargain, covenant, obligation, undertaking, treaty. (*as without legal force or bond: understanding, promise, parole*)

aid—help, assist, succor, support, befriend, cooperate, contribute, favor, foster, protect, abet, encourage, instigate, subsidize. (*oppose, resist, counteract, discourage, thwart, withstand, confront, deter, baffle*)

ailment—complaint, sickness, illness, disease. (*recovery, convalescence, sanity, health, robustness, vigor, salubriousness*)

aim—*n.* tendency, intent, aspiration, bent, drift, object, scope, goal, purpose, mark, end, design, intention. (*shunning, disregarding, disaffecting, overlooking, avoiding*)

aim—*v.* seek, level, propose, design, affect, intend, mean, purpose. (*shun, disregard, disaffect, ignore, overlook, avoid*)

akin—related, agnate, cognate, homogeneous, similar, consanguineous, congenial, allied, sympathetic. (*unrelated, unconnected, foreign, alien, heterogeneous, uncongenial, hostile, unallied, antagonistic, unsympathetic, dissimilar*)

alacrity—quickness, readiness, briskness, activity, cheerfulness, compliance, willingness, promptitude. (*slowness, reluctance, repugnance*)

alarming—terrible, fearful, frightful, portentous, ominous, threatening. (*soothing, assuring, encouraging, inviting, propitious, hopeful, alluring, enticing, attractive*)

alert—active, brisk, nimble, prepared, prompt, vigilant, ready, wakeful, watchful, on the watch, lively. (*slow, sleepy, lazy, absent, unready, oblivious, sluggish, inactive, unwatchful, dilatory, drowsy*)

alien—foreign, strange, undomesticated, inappropriate, irrelevant, impertinent. (*pertinent, essential, proper, appropriate, relevant, germane, akin, apropos, naturalized*)

alike—resembling, similar, together, twin-fellow, analogous, identical, equal, equivalent, same, homogeneous, akin, equally. (*unlike, heterogeneous, apart, dissimilar, variously, differently, unequally*)

alive—quick, living, breathing, warm, lively, vivacious, alert, existing, existent, safe, subsisting, active, brisk, animated. (*dead, departed, cold, lifeless, defunct, inanimate, dispirited, dull*)

allege—declare, affirm, assert, asseverate, depose, plead, cite, quote, assign, advance, maintain, say. (*contradict, gainsay, refute, deny, disprove, neutralize, quash, repel*)

allegiance—subjection, obedience, loyalty, fealty, homage. (*disloyalty, rebellion, resistance, disaffection, malcontentment, treason*)

alleviate—lighten, lessen, assuage, mitigate, soothe, moderate, relieve, remit, diminish. (*aggravate, enhance, increase, embitter, augment*)

alliance—compact, treaty, co-operation, union, connection, partnership, league, combination, coalition, confederation, friendship, relation, relationship. (*disunion, enmity, divorce, discord, disruption, antagonism, separation, estrangement, hostility*)

allot—assign, grant, award, give, apportion, deal, dispense, parcel, distribute, divide, mete out, portion out. (*refuse, withhold, retain, appropriate, resume, misapportion, misdeal*)

allow—concede, apportion, allot, assign, afford, tolerate, authorize, grant, remit, recognize, acknowledge, avow, confess, admit, permit, suffer, sanction, yield. (*withhold, withdraw, resume, refuse, deny, disallow, repudiate, protest, withstand, disapprove, resist, reject*)

alloy—admixture, deterioration, adulteration, drawback, diminution, decrement, impairment, debasement, depreciation, disparagement. (*purity, genuineness, enhancement, integrity*)

allude—point, indicate, suggest, hint, signify, insinuate, refer, imply, intimate. (*specify, demonstrate, declare, mention, state*)

ally—friend, companion, supporter, aider, abettor, accomplice, assistant, confederate, helper, associate, accessory, colleague, coadjutor. (*foe, enemy, opponent, adversary, baffler, counteractor, antagonist*)

aloud—audibly, loudly, clamorously, sonorously, vociferously, obstreperously. (*softly, silently, inaudibly, suppressedly*)

alter—substitute, change, vary, modify, exchange, diversify, remodel. (*retain, perpetuate, conserve, stereotype, arrest, solidify, stabilitate*)

alternative—choice, resource, opinion. (*compulsion, quandary, necessity, fix*)

altogether—collectively, combined, in one, totally, entirely, wholly, fully, completely, utterly, thoroughly. (*separately, individually, partially*)

amass—collect, accumulate, aggregate, heap, gather, store up, hoard, pile up. (*divide, dissipate, waste, scatter, disperse, parcel, portion, spend*)

amazement—astonishment, awe, wonder, bewilderment, surprise, stupefication, marvel. (*expectation, preparation, anticipation, familiarity, calmness, composure, coolness, self-possession*)

ambiguous—equivocal, vague, doubtful, enigmatical, uncertain, obscure, unintelligible, perplexing, indistinct, dubious. (*univocal, obvious, plain, clear, unambiguous, indisputable, necessary, unmistakable, unequivocal, lucid*)

ameliorate—improve, raise, better, advantage, promote, advance, amend, rectify, meliorate. (*debase, depress, deteriorate, injure, impair, vitiate, spoil, mar*)

amend—improve, mend, repair, correct, rectify, better, ameliorate, reform. (*deteriorate, degenerate, neglect, aggravate, tarnish, blemish, spoil, corrupt, vitiate, impair, mar*)

amiable—lovable, good, kind, benevolent, charitable, delectable, engaging, fascinating, agreeable, lovely, pleasing, charming, attractive. (*churlish, disagreeable, hateful, abominable, ill-natured, illconditioned, unamiable*)

amiss—wrong, untrue, wide, bad, false, defective, short, inappropriate, inopportune, injudicious, untimely, abortive. (*right, true, good, complete,* *effective, successful, satisfactory, consummate, expedient, appropriate, opportune)*

amnesty—pardon, acquittal, remission, condonation, oblivion, dispensation, absolution. *(penalty, retaliation, punishment, retribution, requital, visitation, infliction, exaction, trial, account)*

ample—large, bountiful, liberal, copious, spacious, roomy, diffusive, full, complete, sufficient, plentiful, abundant. *(narrow, niggardly, insufficient, stingy, scant, mean, stint, bare)*

amplify—enrich, enlarge, increase, augment, multiply, dilate, develop, swell, expatiate, expand, discuss, unfold, extend. *(retrench, amputate, curtail, condense, abbreviate, epitomize, gather, collect, sum)*

analogy—relation, resemblance, proportion, similarity, similitude, coincidence, affinity, comparison, parity. *(disproportion, dissimilarity, disharmony, irrelativeness, heterogeneousness, incongruity, inaffinity)*

analysis—dissection, separation, anatomy, segregation, decomposition, resolution, partition. *(composition, synthesis, aggregation, combination, coalition, amalgamation, coherence)*

anarchy—disorder, tumult, rebellion, riot, misgovernment, insubordination. *(order, subjection, government, organization, control, law)*

anatomy—dissection, division, segregation, analysis, resolution, dismemberment. *(synthesis, collocation, organization, union, construction, structure, form, body)*

ancient—old, antiquated, old-fashioned, antique, obsolete, old-time, aged, primeval, primordial, immemorial, time-honored. *(new, young, modern, juvenile, upstart, fresh, parvenu)*

anger—*n.* ire, incensement, vexation, grudge, pique, exasperation, indignation, enmity, displeasure, irritation, passion, spleen, gall, resentment, rage, animosity, fury, choler, wrath. (*peace, peacefulness, peaceableness, appeasement, forgiveness, good-will, patience, forbearance, reconciliation, conciliatoriness, mildness*)

anger—*v.* enrage, vex, kindle, fret, ruffle, chafe, infuriate, exasperate, provoke, irritate, incense, wound, inflame, embitter. (*to appease, compose, forbear, allay, soothe, calm, conciliate, heal*)

animosity—hatred, antipathy, dissension, aversion, acrimony, feud, strife, rancor, antagonism, bitterness, acerbity, hostility, enmity, malice, anger, malevolence, ill-will, malignity, feeling against. (*congeniality, companionship, friendship, sympathy, fellow-feeling, unanimity, harmony, concord, regard, alliance, kindliness*)

annex—add, attach, fasten, affix, subjoin, append, connect, unite. (*withdraw, detach, disconnect, separate, disengage, disunite, remove*)

annihilate—abolish, destroy, bring to naught, uproot, eradicate, nullify, exterminate, end, extinguish, demolish, obliterate, efface. (*keep, conserve, preserve, foster, tend, protest, cherish, develop, stabilitate, augment, cultivate, perpetuate*)

announce—declare, propound, give notice, enunciate, advertise, publish, report, notify, make known, give out, reveal, herald, proclaim, intimate, promulge. (*conceal, suppress, hush, stifle, withhold, shroud, bury, burke*)

annoy—tease, vex, irritate, disturb, affront, molest, pain, disquiet, incommode, tantalize, bother, weary, inconvenience, plague, discommode, harass, chafe, trouble. (*soothe, conciliate, appease, regard, quiet, accommodate, study, tend, foster, cherish, smooth, gratify*)

anomaly—irregularity, abnormity, exception, informality, peculiarity, eccentricity. (*conformity,* *regularity, illustration, conformance, exemplification, specimen)*

anonymous—nameless, unattested, authorless, unidentified, unauthenticated. *(authenticated, attested, identified, authorized, verified, signed)*

answer—reply, response, counter-argument, confutation, acceptance (as of a challenge), tally counterpart, solution, vindication, apology, exculpation, defense, rejoinder, repartee, retort. *(challenge, question, defiance, summons, interrogation, query)*

antecedent—prior, foregoing, previous, precursive, precedent, earlier, introductory, preliminary, former. *(posterior, later, subsequent, consequent, succeeding)*

anticipate—forestall, prejudge, expect, foretaste, apprehend, prevent, prearrange, prepare, meet, obviate, intercept, forecast. *(remember, recollect, remedy, recall, undo, cure, misapprehend)*

anticipation—prevention, expectation, forestallment, awaiting, preoccupation, preconception, foresight, forethought, foretaste, prelibation, preclusion, pregustation, antepast, forecast, provision. *(surprise, unpreparedness, unexpectedness, inexpectation, actual enjoyment, non-expectation, realization, consummation)*

anxiety—care, trouble, eagerness, disquiet, apprehension, carefulness, diffidence, solicitude, misgiving. *(carelessness, ease, confidence, contentment, acquiescence, contentedness, apathy, light-heartedness, nonchalance)*

anxious—solicitous, careful, uneasy, concerned, restless, watchful, disturbed, unquiet. *(without care, careless, inert, ease, unconcerned, calm, composed)*

apathy—indifference, insensibility, unfeelingness in company, insusceptibility, unconcern, sluggish-

ness, hebetude. (*anxiety, care, eagerness, interestedness, sensibility, susceptibility, sensitiveness, irritability, curiosity*)

ape—mimic, imitate, simulate, personate, represent. (*not to imitate, vary, modify, change*)

apiece—distributively, individually, separately, severally, analytically. (*collectively, together, accumulatively, indiscriminately, confusedly, synthetically*)

apology—defense, justification, plea, exculpation, excuse, vindication, acknowledgment, confession. (*charge, imputation, impeachment, offense, incrimination, injury. accusation, wrong, insult*)

appal—affright, alarm, terrify, scare, daunt, cow, shock, frighten, discourage, dishearten, horrify, dismay, astound. (*encourage, rally, assure, embolden, reassure*)

apparel—clothes, robes, vesture, vestments, raiment, garniture, habiliments, habit, dress, clothing, caparison, trappings, housings. (*nudity, divestiture, dishabille, tatters, rags*)

apparent—obvious, plain, conspicuous, manifest, appearing, unmistakable, clear, probable, seeming, presumable, likely, patent, ostensible, visible, evident, indubitable, notorious, certain. (*uncertain, dubious, inapparent, minute, unobservable, improbable, insupposable, hidden, real*)

appeal—accost, address, apostrophize, invite, cite, invoke, urge, refer, call upon, entreat, request, resort. (*deprecate, repudiate, protest, disavow, disclaim, defy, abjure*)

appearance—advent, coming, arrival, presence, apparition, aspect, manifestation, probability, likeness, exhibition, mien, manner, semblance, air, show, look, pretense, likelihood, presumption. (*departure, disappearance, unlikelihood, non-appearance, concealment, evanition*)

append—affix, supplement, subjoin, attach. (*separate, disengage, disconnect, detach*)

appetite—passion, desire, propensity, proclivity, inclination, propension, appetency, want, craving, disposition, tendency, proneness. (*repugnance, aversion, antipathy, loathing, indifference, apathy*)

applause—praise, plaudit, laudation, encomium, commendation, approbation, acclamation, approval, eulogy, acclaim. (*obloquy, condemnation, denunciation, dissatisfaction, contempt, censure, blame, vituperation, sibilation*)

applicable—available, ancillary, convenient, useful, pertinent, conducive, appropriate. (*useless, unavailable, inconducive, inapplicable, irrelevant*)

appoint—fix, determine, instal, allot, order, prescribe, institute, employ, apportion, apply, designate, assign, intrust, invest, ordain, arrange. (*reverse, cancel, recall, withdraw, reserve, withhold, retain, undo, suspend, disarrange, disappoint*)

apportion—assign, deal, allot, grant, share, divide, dispense, administer, distribute, appoint. (*reserve, retain, refuse, withhold, assume, resume, cancel, divert, suspend, reapportion, reappoint*)

appreciate—esteem, recognize, acknowledge, respect, value, prize, regard, reckon, estimate. (*undervalue, misconceive, misjudge, ignore, misappreciate*)

apprehend—comprehend, understand, take, expect, seize, conceive, arrest, fancy, dread, imagine, presume, anticipate, fear, conjecture. (*ignore, miss, lose, misconjecture, misconceive, misapprehend, misanticipate*)

approach—access, avenue, entrance, adit, vestibule, arrival, approximation, advent, nearing, admission, appropinquation, admittance, mode, path, way, advance, similarity. (*exit, egress, de-*

bouchure, outlet, departure, recession, distance, diversity, disparity)

approve—like, comment, sanction, praise, support, second, promote, encourage, authorize. *(disapprove, dislike, censure, blame, disown, disavow)*

approximate—approach, resemble, border, abut, near, trench. *(separate, differ, vary, recede, diverge, deviate)*

apt—fit, apposite, clever, meet, liable, becoming, appropriate, ready, fitting, suitable, pertinent, qualified, prompt, adapted, likely. *(unfitted, ill-timed, awkward, unlikely, inapt)*

arbitrary—tyrannical, despotic, harsh, dictatorial, imperious, unforbearing, overbearing, selfish, absolute, irresponsible, tyrannous, domineering, peremptory. *(mild, modest, lenient, considerate, obliging, limited, equitable, constitutional)*

arbitrate—settle, adjust, compose, decide, determine, accommodate, adjudicate. *(dispute, claim, appeal, misdetermine, litigate, contend, misjudge)*

ardent—longing, passionate, aspiring, warm, eager, fervent, excited, fiery, glowing, zealous, fervid, fierce, keen, vehement, hot, affectionate, impassioned, burning, heated. *(cool, cold, indifferent, dispassioned, apathetic, passionless, unimpassioned, phlegmatic, platonic)*

argue—discuss, debate, prove, question, evidence, establish, imply, sift, dispute, persuade, controvert, contend, demonstrate, reason. *(dictate, assert, propound, command)*

argument—reasoning, controversy, evidence, discussion, topic, dispute. *(assertion, assumption, without proof or evidence)*

arid—dry, parched, sterile, unproductive. *(moist, dewy, watered, fertile, luxuriant, exuberant, verdant, blooming, productive)*

aright—right, well, rightly, correctly, truly, properly, uprightly, unexceptionably, justly, suitably, appropriately. (*wrongly, awry, incorrectly, improperly, defectively, erroneously*)

arouse—stir, excite, disturb, animate, wake up, stimulate, alarm, provoke, cheer. (*allay, assuage, mitigate, pacify, compose, moderate, still, quiet*)

arraign—summon, accuse, censure, indict, charge, impeach. (*acquit, condone, discharge, release*)

arrange—order, put in order, group, array, place, adjust, range, locate, dispose, assort, deal, sort, parcel, classify. (*derange, disarrange, confuse, disturb, disperse, jumble, disorder*)

array—*v.* vest, deck, equip, decorate, rank, adorn, dress, accoutre, invest, attire, place, arrange, draw up, marshal, set in order, dispose. (*disarray, disarrange, confuse, jumble, divest, denude, strip*)

array—*n.* arrangement, order, disposition, sight, exhibition, show, parade. (*disarray, disorder, confusion, confusedness, jumble*)

arrest—seize, take, stop, capture, withhold, restrain, hold, detain, apprehend. (*release, dismiss, liberate, free, discharge, expedite*)

arrive—reach, attain, come to, enter, get to, land. (*embark, depart, start*)

arrogance—haughtiness, contemptuousness, overbearingness, hauteur, browbeating, loftiness, self-conceit, stateliness, vainglory, insolence, self-importance, assumption, discourtesy. (*bashfulness, servility, considerateness, deference, courtesy, modesty, shyness, diffidence, politeness*)

artful—cunning, designing, maneuvering, sharp, knowing, subtle, sly, crafty, wily, shrewd. (*simple, undesigning, artless, open, innocent, unsophisticated*)

artificial—invented, fabricated, fictitious, constructed, manufactured, pretended, simulated, false, assumed, concocted, contrived, deceptive, artful, affected, unnatural, constrained. (*natural, inartificial, genuine, spontaneous, transparent, artless, unaffected*) (See artful)

ascertain—prove, verify, find out, discover, confirm, detect, determine, learn, discern. (*guess, conjecture, surmise, suppose, presume*)

ascribe—assign, attribute, impute, refer, render, allege, charge. (*deny, refuse, exclude, dissociate, disconnect, dissever*)

aspiration—longing, desire, aim, wish, craving, ambition, endeavor, hope, appetition, effort, eagerness. (*apathy, indifference, aimlessness, dullness, inertia, callousness, carelessness, aversion, avoidance, rejection, repudiation*)

assembly—meeting, concourse, assemblage, multitude, group, synod, conclave, conference, convocation, unison, company, congregation, collection, crowd, gathering, convention, aggregate. (*dispersion, dissipation, disunion, disruption*)

assent—coincidence, agreement, concert, acknowledgment, consent, acquiescence, approval, concurrence, approbation, compliance. (*dissent, disagreement, difference, disavowal, repudiation, declension, disclaimer, protest*)

assign—attribute, apportion, allege, refer, specify, consign, intrust, commit, point out, allot to, adduce, advance, appoint, convey. (*withhold, withdraw, resume, retain, refuse, disconnect, dissociate*)

assist—help, succor, aid, support, relieve, befriend, second, co-operate with, back, benefit, further. (*hinder, resist, oppose, antagonize, counteract, clog, prevent*)

assistant—helper, aider, attendant, coadjutor, auxiliary, ally, associate, contributer, partner, confederate. (*hinderer, opposer, rival, foe, antagonist*)

association—union, connection, conjunction, consortment, companionship, alliance, familiarity, community, membership, society, company, denomination, partnership, fellowship, fraternity, friendship. (*disunion, disconnection, estrangement, separation, severance, independence, avoidance, disruption, dismemberment, solitude, individuality*)

assortment—collection, disposition, distribution, class, quantity, selection, stock, miscellany, lot, variety. (*misarrangement, disarrangement, displacement, misplacement*)

assume—take, appropriate, arrogate, wear, exhibit, postulate, suppose, presume, usurp, claim, pretend, feign, affect. (*waive, allow, doff, render, surrender, concede, grant, demonstrate, abandon, argue, prove*)

assure—advise, advertise, promise, inform, rally, console, encourage, countenance, aid, support, convince, uphold, certify. (*misinform, misadvise, mislead, deceive, discomfit, disconceit, deter, discourage, warn, dissuade, unsettle, intimidate*)

astonish—startle, surprise, confound, amaze, astound, fill with wonder, stupefy, alarm, terrify, electrify, scare, dumbfounder. (*rally, encourage, assure, embolden*)

astray—loose, abroad, missing, about, at large, wrong, erring, wandering. (*right, close, at home, safe*)

athletic—strong, vigorous, powerful, stalwart, brawny, muscular, ablebodied, lusty, sinewy, robust. (*weak, puny, effeminate, nerveless, strengthless, unbraced*)

atrocious—monstrous, nefarious, wicked, outrageous, villainous, enormous, shameful, heinous, cruel, flagrant, facinorous, flagitious. (*laudable, noble, honorable, generous, humane, admirable, chivalrous*)

attach—fasten, apply, append, add, fix, subjoin, annex, unite, conciliate, tie, connect, conjoin, attract, win, bind. (*unfasten, loose, disunite, untie, disconnect, detach, alienate, estrange, repel*)

attack—*v.* assail, assault, invade, encounter, charge, besiege, impugn, contravene. (*defend, resist, repel, protest, withstand on one's own part, or for another, support, aid, shield, uphold, vindicate, shelter*)

attack—*n.* invasion, assault, onset, aggression, onslaught. (*defense, resistance, repulse, protection, aid, vindication, support, maintenance, shelter*)

attain—reach, extend, master, arrive at, compass, earn, win, achieve, accomplish, get, obtain, acquire, gain, secure, grasp. (*lose, fail, forfeit, miss, abandon, resign*)

attempt—try, endeavor, strive, undertake, seek, essay, attack, violate, force. (*disregard, abandon, pretermit, dismiss, neglect, shun, drop*)

attend—listen, heed, notice, observe, wait on, serve, mind, watch, accompany, consort, follow, imply, involve. (*wander, disregard, leave, forsake, abandon, desert, exclude, neutralize*)

attention—observation, notice, regard, watchfulness, heed, consideration, circumspection, study, vigilance, care. (*disregard, inadvertence, remission, indifference, carelessness, abstraction, distraction, absence*)

attest—vouch, aver, assert, certify, witness, vouch for, affirm, testify, evidence, support, confirm, suggest, prove, involve, demonstrate, establish, imply, bespeak. (*deny, controvert, contradict, contravene, disprove, disestablish, exclude, neutralize, upset, oppugn, refute*)

attire—robes, garment, clothing, vestments, habiliment, habit, raiment, clothes, garb, apparel, accoutrements, livery, uniform, costume. (*nudity,* *divestment, exposure, denudation, bareness, disarray, dishabille, tatters, rags, patches, shreds)*

attract—influence, induce, dispose, incline, tempt, prompt, allure, charm, fascinate, invite, entice. *(repel, deter, indispose, disincline, estrange, alienate)*

attractive—winning, alluring, tempting, inviting, engaging, captivating, fascinating, enticing, interesting, charming, pleasant, beautiful, agreeable. *(unattractive, repugnant, repulsive, uninteresting, disagreeable, unpleasant, deformed, ugly, deterrent, loathsome, forbidding)*

attribute—*v.* refer, assign, associate, apply, ascribe, charge, impute, connect. *(divorce, disconnect, dissociate, dissever)*

attribute—*n.* property, quality, characteristic, attainment, sign, mark, indication, manifestation. *(Its correlative, viz. essence, nature, substance, etc., or, spuriously, affectation, misnomer, semblance, assumption, mask, veil)*

attrition—sorrow, repentance, affliction, penitence, compunction, remorse, self-reproach. *(impenitence, callousness, obduracy, reprobation, relentlessness)*

audacious—insolent, adventurous, presumptuous, valiant, rash, bold, daring, reckless, enterprising. *(timid, cowardly, cautious, inadventurous, unventuresome, unenterprising)*

audacity—boldness, rashness, temerity, recklessness, hardihood. *(caution, self-preservation, timidity, calculation, forethought, foresight, diffidence, inadventurousness)*

augment—increase, enlargement, amplification, enrichment, supply, enhancement, addition, acquisition, improvement. *(deduction, detraction, diminution, contraction, withdrawal, reservation, expenditure, loss, waste, detriment, deterioration, impoverishment, reduction, curtailment)*

augury—prophecy, prediction, divination, conjecture, omen, prognostication. (*experience, science, observation*)

august—majestic, dignified, stately, noble, pompous, imposing, grand, solemn, exalted. (*mean, undignified, unimposing, common, vulgar, despicable, paltry, unnoticeable, beggarly, commonplace*)

auspicious—propitious, lucky, favorable, encouraging, satisfactory, successful, hopeful, promising, happy, golden, fortunate, opportune, prosperous. (*unpropitious, unfavorable, discouraging, unsatisfactory, inauspicious, unpromising, abortive, hopeless*)

austere—hard, rigid, stern, severe, morose, unrelenting, unyielding, strict, rigorous, harsh, sour, relentless. (*mild, affable, kindly, tender feeling, bland, indulgent, genial*)

authentic—genuine, veritable, reliable, real, original, trustworthy, not spurious, true, legitimate, certain, accepted, current, received. (*unreliable, spurious, false, apocryphal, disputed, exploded, rejected, counterfeit, unfounded, unauthorized, baseless, fabulous, fictitious*)

authoritative—decisive, sure, conclusive, authentic, powerful, firm, potent, dictatorial, imperious, arbitrary, arrogant, imperative, dogmatic, commanding. (*weak, inconclusive, vague, indeterminate, indefinite, vacillating, undecisive, bland, conciliatory, affable, lenient, persuasive*)

authority—ground, justification, authenticity, genuineness, conclusiveness, decisiveness, control, direction, jurisdiction, government, regulation, power, right, rule, sway, sufferance, supremacy, dominion. (*groundlessness, spuriousness, indecision, inconclusiveness, inoperativeness, incompetency, weakness, usurpation, wrong*)

autocratic—independent, arbitrary, despotic, irresponsible, absolute. (*dependent, subordinate, responsible, constitutional, limited*)

auxiliary—helpful, abetting, aiding, accessory, promotive, conducive, assistant, ancillary, assisting, subsidiary, helping. (*unassisting, unconducive, unpromotive, redundant, superfluous, obstructive, retardative, irrelevant, cumbersome*)

avail—suffice, hold, stand, endure, answer, tell, profit, help, benefit, advantage, service, use, utility. (*fail, fall, disappoint, betray*)

available—useful, appropriate, convertible, attainable, handy, conducive, applicable, procurable, advantageous, helpful, profitable, suitable, serviceable. (*useless, inappropriate, inapplicable, unprocurable, inconducive, irrelevant, inoperative, unavailable*)

avarice—greed, cupidity, rapacity, penuriousness, niggardliness, miserliness, stinginess, covetousness, acquisitiveness, griping, greediness. (*largeheartedness, unselfishness, liberality, bountifulness, profuseness, squander, prodigality, extravagance, waste*)

aver—assert, asseverate, affirm, depose, avouch, protest, oblige, declare. (*deny, contradict, contravene, disavow, disclaim, repudiate, gainsay, oppugn*)

avidity—cupidity, avarice, desire, greed, longing, rapacity, eagerness. (*coldness, indifference, apathy, insensibility, antipathy, nausea, aversion, repugnance, loathing*)

avoid—quit, shun, abandon, desert, forsake, relinquish, fly, eschew, elude, dodge, escape, shirk. (*seek court, approach, accost, address, affect*)

award—assign, apportion, attribute, accord, grant, distribute, divide, allot, give, determine, decree, order, adjudge. (*refuse, withhold, withdraw, retain, misappropriate, misapportion*)

aware—conscious, sensible, informed, certified, assured, known, apprised, cognizant. (*unconscious, insensible, ignorant, unaware, uninformed*)

awful—fearful, direful, appalling, terrible, alarming dreadful, horrible, solemn, portentous, horrific. (*innocuous, informidable, unimposing, unastonishing, commonplace, unnoticeable, unalarming, alluring*)

awkward—ungainly, clownish, clumsy, maladroit, unhandy, uncouth, rough, boorish, bungling, gawky. (*neat, clever, dexterous, skilful, adroit, handy*)

axiom—self-evident truth, aphorism, truism, apophthegm, maxim. (*nonsense, absurdity, stultiloquy, absurdness*)

B

babble—prate, prattle, dribble, chatter, gabble, twaddle, blab, cackle. (*enunciate, vociferate, hush, suppress*)

babel—hubbub, confusion, clamor, jargon, din, discord, clang. (*elocution, articulation, monotony, distinctness, consecutiveness, intonation, enunciation, unisonousness*)

baffle—frustrate, counteract, estop, disconcert, elude, mock, thwart, confound, defeat, perplex, restrain, upset, foil, mar, balk, neutralize, dodge, counterfoil. (*point, aid, abet, enforce, promote, assist, advance, encourage*)

bait—morsel, snare, decoy, enticement, allurement, inducement. (*warning, scarecrow, dissuasive, deterrent, prohibition, intimidation, threat*)

balance—weigh, poise, pit, set, counterpoise, counteract, neutralize, equalize, estimate, redress, adjust. (*upset, tilt, cant, subvert, mispoise, overbalance*)

balderdash—gasconade, flummery, rhodomontade, bombast, fustian, froth. (*sense, wisdom, logic, reason, sobriety, truthfulness*)

balk—estop, bar, thwart, frustrate, foil, stop, prevent, hinder, neutralize, nullify, mar, counteract, disappoint, defeat, baffle. (*aid, abet, promote, advance, encourage, instigate*)

banish—expel, abandon, dispel, eject, extrude, exclude, relegate, expatriate, repudiate, disclaim. (*cherish, foster, protect, consider, encourage, locate, retain, entertain, domiciliate, domesticate, harbor*)

banquet—feast, festivity, treat, entertainment, festival, carousal, carouse, regalement, cheer. (*fast, abstinence, starvation*)

banter—badinage, chaff, mockery, derision, ridicule, irony, jeering, raillery. (*discussion, discourse, argument*)

bargain—transaction, negotiation, business, profit, speculation, higgling, gain, hawking, chaffer, haggling. (*loss, misprofit*)

base—vile, dishonorable, low, sordid, ignoble, worthless, mean, infamous, shameful, grovelling, disingenuous, disesteemed, cheap, corrupt, deep. (*lofty, exalted, refined, noble, esteemed, honored, valued, pure, correct, shrill*)

bashful—modest, diffident, shy, retiring, reserved. (*bold, impudent, forward, unreserved, pert, conceited, ostentatious, egotistic*)

battle—fight, conflict, contest, combat, engagement, encounter, action. (*peace, truce, pacification, arbitrament, council, mediation*)

bawl—shout, vociferate, halloo, roar, bellow. (*whisper, mutter, babble, mumble*)

beach—shore, coast, strand, seacoast, seaboard, seashore. (*sea, ocean, deep, main*)

beaming—shining, gleaming, bright, radiant, beautiful, transparent, translucid. (*dull, opaque, dingy, beamless, wan, matt*)

bear—carry, lift, transport, convey, maintain, uphold, suffer, undergo, support, tolerate, waft, yield, sustain, hold, harbor, entertain, fill, enact, endure, admit, produce, generate. (*drop, refuse, decline, resign, expel, eject, resist, repel, protest, resent, reject*)

beat—strike, pound, batter, surpass, thrash, cudgel, overcome, defeat, conquer, worst, whack, belabor, vanquish. (*defend, protect, shield, fall, shelter, surrender, stroke, caress, pat*)

beauty—loveliness, grace, fairness, seemliness, comeliness, picturesqueness, exquisiteness, adornment, embellishment. (*foulness, ugliness, deformity, hideousness, bareness, unattractiveness*)

because—owing, consequently, accordingly. (*irrespectively, independently, inconsequently, unconnectedly*)

beck—nod, sign, signal, symbol, token, indication, authority, orders, instruction, subserviency, influence, call, command, control, mandate. (*independence, unsubservience*)

becoming—beseeming, neat, fit, proper, decorous, comely, seemly, befitting, graceful, decent, suitable, improving. (*unbeseeming, unseemly, uncomely, unbecoming, unbefitting, ungraceful, indecent, unsuitable, unimproving, derogatory*)

befitting—fitting, decent, becoming, suitable, appropriate, proper, consistent, expedient, desirable. (*obligatory, compulsory, unbefitting, indecent, unbecoming, unsuitable, inappropriate, incompatible, inexpedient, improper*)

before—precedently, anteriorly, antecedently. (*after, afterwards, subsequently, posteriorly, later, behind*)

beg—ask, request, entreat, supplicate, beseech, implore, pray, petition, crave. (*insist, exact, extort, require, demand*)

beggarly—miserable, poor, stinted, wretched, niggardly, stingy, scant, illiberal. (*noble, princely, stately, prodigal, sumptuous, liberal, profuse, gorgeous, magnificent*)

begin—initiate, commence, prepare, start, originate, arise, inaugurate. (*achieve, complete, terminate, conclude, consummate, finish, close, end*)

beginning—commencement, start, origin, rise, initiation, preparation, preface, prelude, inauguration, inception, threshold, opening, source, outset, foundation. (*end, close, termination, conclusion, consummation, completion*)

behavior—conduct, bearing, demeanor, proceeding, comportment, action, manner, deportment. (*misdemeanor, misbehavior, misconduct*)

belief—assent, faith, trust, credence, avowal, assurance, admission, conviction, opinion, permission, creed, reliance, concession, confidence. (*dissent, unbelief, distrust, denial, misgiving, disavowal, rejection, disbelief*)

belonging—related, connected, appertaining, cognate, congenial, obligatory, accompanying. (*unrelated, unconnected, irrelevant, impertinent, alien, uncongenial, discretional, optional, uninvolved, unimplied, independent*)

bend—curve, deviate, incline, tend, swerve, diverge, mold, persuade, influence, bias, dispose, direct, lower, subordinate to, lean, deflect, bow, condescend, yield, stoop, submit. (*proceed, continue, extend, advance, stand, stiffen, break, crush, resist*)

benediction—blessing, commendation, approval, benison, gratitude, thankfulness, thanksgiving. (*curse, malediction, disapproval, censure, obloquy, execration, ingratitude*)

benefactor—friend, supporter, contributor, upholder, well-wisher, favorer, welldoer, patron.

(*foe, opponent, disfavor, antagonist, rival, back-friend, oppressor*)

beneficial—profitable, salutary, advantageous, wholesome, salubrious. (*prejudicial, noxious, hurtful, unprofitable, detrimental*)

benefit—boon, behoof, service, utility, avail, use, good, advantage, profit, favor, blessing. (*evil, loss, disadvantage, detriment, damage, calamity, bereavement, injury, privation*)

bequeath—give, grant, leave by will, devise, will, bestow, impart, demise, leave. To *n.* legacy, inheritance. (*withhold, alienate. To n. Disinheritance, transference, abalienation, dispossession*)

bereavement—destitution, affliction, deprivation, loss. (*gift, blessing, donation, benefaction, compensation, reparation, restoration, reinstatement, substitution, restitution, consolation*)

besotted—intoxicated, steeped, stupefied, drunk, drenched, doltish, gross, prejudiced. (*sober, temperate, clear, unbiased, unprejudiced, enlightened, refined*)

bespeak—betoken, foreorder, forestall, provide, prearrange, indicate, evidence. (*belie, resign, countermand*)

betimes—early, beforehand, prepared, readily. (*behindhand, slowly, sluggishly, belatedly*)

betray—deceive, delude, dupe, circumvent, ensnare, dishonor, manifest, indicate, reveal. (*protect, preserve, guard, conserve, foster, cherish, fence, conceal, cover, suppress*)

better—meliorate, improve, amend, emend, ameliorate, rectify, reform. (*make worse*)

beware—care, refrain, consider, heed, look, fear, avoid. (*ignore, overlook, neglect, incur, brave, dare*)

bewilder—daze, dazzle, confound, mystify, puzzle, embarrass, astonish, perplex, confuse, mislead. (*guide, inform, lead, instruct, enlighten, edify*)

bewitch—enchant, fascinate, charm, captivate, entrance. (*exorcise, disillusionize, disenchant*)

bid—tell, request, instruct, direct, order, proffer, charge, command, propose, offer. (*forbid, deter, prohibit, restrain*)

bide—wait, remain, tarry, stay, await, expect, anticipate, continue, bear, abide, endure. (*quit, depart, migrate, move, resist, resent, repel, abjure, protest, rebel*)

big—large, great, wide, huge, bulky, proud, arrogant, pompous, fat, massive, gross. (*little, small, narrow, minute, slight, lean, affable, easy, unaffected*)

binding—restrictive, obligatory, restraining, stringent, styptic, costive, astringent. (*loosening, opening, enlarging, distending*)

birth—parentage, extraction, nativity, family, race, origin, source, rise, lineage, nobility. (*death, extinction, plebeianism*)

bitter—harsh, sour, sharp, tart, acrimonious, sarcastic, severe, sad, afflictive, intense, stinging, pungent, acrid, cutting. (*sweet, mellow, pleasant, affable, kindly, genial, light, mitigated, trivial*)

blacken—bespatter, befoul, bedaub, defame, decry, calumniate, dishonor, asperse, traduce, vilify, slander, malign. (*vindicate, clear, eulogize*)

blackguard—scoundrel, rascal, rapscallion, blackleg, villain. (*gentleman*)

blame—censure, chide, rebuke, reproach, vituperate, dispraise, disapprove, condemn, reprehend, reprobate, reprove. (*acquit, exculpate, exonerate, encourage, praise, approve*)

bland—soft, mild, gentle, complaisant, courteous, affable, gracious, tender, benign. (*harsh, abrupt, rough*)

blast—blight, shrivel, destroy, wither. (*restore, expand, swell*)

blast—breeze, efflation, explosion, blight, burst, blaze, frustration, destruction, squall, gale, tempest, hurricane, afflation. (*zephyr, gentle breeze, neutralization*)

bleak—blank, bare, open, cold, exposed, stormy, nipping. (*warm, sheltered, verdant, luxuriant, zephyrous, balmy, halcyonic*)

blemish—spot, blur, blot, flaw, speck, fault, imperfection, stain, daub, tarnish, defacement, discoloration, disfigurement, disgrace, dishonor, defect. (*purity, unsulliedness, honor, intactness*)

blend—mix, harmonize, unite, combine, fuse, merge, amalgamate, mingle, commingle, coalesce. (*run, separate, divide, dissociate, confound*)

bless—felicitate, endow, enrich, gladden, rejoice, cheer, thank. (*deprive, sadden, impoverish, ignore, curse, anathematize*)

blind—sightless, unseeing, eyeless, depraved, undiscerning, ignorant, prejudiced, uninformed, unconscious, unaware. (*farsighted, penetrating, sensitive, keen, discriminating, clear-sighted, pure-minded, aware, conscious*)

blink—wink, ignore, connive, overlook. (*notice, visit, note, mark*)

bliss—blessedness, joy, ectasy, rapture. (*condemnation, accursedness, suffering, misery, woe*)

blithe—light, merry, joyous, happy, bright, elastic, gladsome, bonny, vivacious, lively, cheerful, blithesome, gay. (*heavy, dull, dejected, sullen*)

blockhead—dolt, dunderhead, jolterhead, dunce, ninny, numskull, dullard, simpleton, booby, loggerhead, ignoramus. (*sage, adept, luminary, schoolman, philosopher, savant*)

blooming—flourishing, fair, flowering, blossoming, young, beautiful. (*fading, waning, blighted, old, blasted, paralyzed, superannuated, unsightly, deformed*)

blot—obscure, tarnish, spoil, sully, spot, discolor, pollute, obliterate, erase, blur, stain, blotch, smear, smutch. (*elucidate, clear, absterge, perpetuate, cleanse, manifest, conserve*)

blow—puff, blast, breath, stroke, infliction, wound, disappointment, affliction, knock, shock, calamity, misfortune. (*assuagement, consolation, relief, comfort, blessing, sparing*)

bluff—bare, open, bold, abrupt, frank, plain-spoken, blunt, surly, rude, blustering, swaggering, brusque, hectoring, coarse, discourteous, rough, bullying. (*undulating, inclined, inabrupt, courteous, polished, reserved*)

blunder—error, mistake, misunderstanding, fault, oversight, inaccuracy, delusion, slip. (*accuracy, truthfulness, exactness, correctness, faultlessness, ratification, atonement, foresight, prevention, hit, success, achievement, correction*)

blush—bloom, color, carnation, complexion, aspect, shame, confusion, guiltiness, self-reproach. (*innocence, purity, guiltlessness, unconsciousness, boldness, effrontery*)

boast—vaunt, brag, swagger, swell, bluster, vapor, triumph, glory

body—substance, mass, whole, substantiality, collectiveness, assemblage, collection, matter, association, organization. (*spirit, soul, individual*)

boggle—halt, hesitate, dubitate, falter, blunder, blotch, botch, spoil, mar. (*encounter, face, advance, refine, clear, work, perfect, complete, beautify*)

bold—courageous, fearless, adventurous, brave, self-confident, forward, intrepid, dauntless, valiant, daring, audacious, lionhearted, doughty. (*timid, fearful, inadventurous, shy, bashful, retiring*)

bombast—rhodomontade, braggadocio, gasconade, bluster, inflatedness, pomposity, exaggerativeness, fustian. (*truthfulness, moderation, refrain, veracity, modesty, temperateness, humility*)

bond—tie, fastening, chain, association, manacle, fetter, compact, obligation, security. (*freedom, option, discretion, honor, parole*)

bondsman—slave, serf, prisoner, captive, vassal. (*freeman, yeoman, gentleman, lord, master*)

bonny—fair, pretty, pleasant, lively, cheerful, shapely, buxom. (*dull, unseemly, ill-favored, deformed*)

border—limit, boundary, brink, rim, verge, brim, edge, edging, band, hem, enclosure, confine. (*land, tract, interior, substance, space, center*)

border on—be contiguous to, be adjacent to, conterminous with, adjoin, adjacent to. (*remote from, away from*)

botch—patch, cobble, blunder, clump, disconcert, spoil, jumble, mess, bungle, mar, blacksmith. (*finedraw, trim, harmonize, mend, beautify, embroider, manipulate, handle, manage*)

bother—fuss, worry, pester, excitement, stir, plague, vex, annoy, tease, confusion, vexation, flurry, trouble. (*calm, composure, orderliness, peace, quiet*)

boundless—unbounded, immeasurable, infinite, unlimited, illimitable, unmeasurable. (*narrow, restricted, limited, confined, circumscribed*)

bounty—liberality, bounteousness, benevolence, munificence, donation, gift, generosity, charity, benignity. (*illiberality, closeness, hardness, churlishness, stinginess, niggardliness*)

brag—boast, vaunt, swagger, bully. (*cringe, whine, whimper*)

branch—member, bifurcation, bough, limb, off-spring, shoot, spray, sprig, twig, ramification, off-shoot, relative, scion. (*trunk, stock, stem, race, family, house*)

break—fracture, rupture, shatter, shiver, destroy, tame, curb, demolish, tear asunder, rend, burst, sever, smash, split, subdue, violate, infringe. (*heal, piece; conjoin, protect, conserve, encourage, rally, observe, obey*)

breath—respiration, inspiration, expiration, inhalation, exhalation. (*cessation, passing, departure, perishing, dying, death*)

breeding—nurture, education, training, discipline, instruction, manners, air, demeanor, decorum. (*ill-manners, ill-training, ill-behavior, ignorance*)

brevity—shortness, closeness, conciseness, succinctness, terseness, compendiousness, pointedness, abbreviation, abridgment. (*length, protraction, elongation, extension, prolixity, diffuseness, interminableness, tediousness*)

bright—shining, brilliant, burnished, luminous, lucid, sparkling, limpid, clever, happy, witty, joyous, cheerful, radiant. (*opaque, dull, dead, muddy, stupid, slow, sullen, dejected, cheerless, joyless, imbecile*)

brilliant—flashing, radiant, shining, lustrous, glorious, luminous, effulgent, beaming, sparkling.

bring—fetch, procure, convey, carry, bear, adduce, import, produce, cause, induce. (*export, remove, abstract, subtract, prevent, exclude, debar, transport*)

brisk—quick, lively, vivacious, active, alert, nimble, sprightly, spirited, animated, prompt, effervescent. (*slow, heavy, dull, inactive, indolent, sluggish, unenergetic, stagnant*)

broad—wide, extensive, expansive, ample, liberal, comprehensive, unreserved, indelicate, coarse, generic. (*narrow, restricted, confined, limited, bigoted, prejudiced, illiberal, narrow-minded, reserved, veiled, enigmatical, shrouded, shaded, refined, delicate, sketchy, specific, pointed.*)

brotherhood—fraternity, association, fellowship, society, sodality.

brutal—savage, inhuman, rude, unfeeling, merciless, ruthless, brutish, barbarous, sensual, beastly, ignorant, stolid, dense, cruel, violent, vindictive, bloodthirsty, intemperate. (*humane, civilized, generous, intelligent, polished, chivalrous, conscientious, self-controlled*)

bubble—trifle, toy, fancy, conceit, vision, dream, froth, trash. (*acquisition, prize, treasure, reality, substance, verity, jewel, good, advantage*)

bugbear—hobgoblin, goblin, gorgon, ghoul, spirit, spook, specter, ogre, scarecrow.

building—edifice, architecture, construction, erection, fabric, structure. (*ruin, dilapidation, dismantlement, demolition*)

bulk—mass, whole, entirety, integrity, majority, size, magnitude, extension, body, volume, bigness, largeness, massiveness, dimension. (*tenuity, minority, dismemberment, disintegration, diminution, portion, contraction, section, atom, particle*)

bungler—botcher, clown, lubber, fumbler, novice. (*adept, adroit, master, artist, workman, proficient, professor*)

buoyant—sprightly, spirited, vivacious, lively, light, floating, hopeful, cheerful, elastic, joyous. (*heavy, depressed, cheerless, joyless, dejected, moody, desponding*)

burden—load, weight, incubus, obstruction, oppression, grief, difficulty, affliction. (*ease, lightness, airiness, expedition, facility, acceleration, abjugation, liberation, light-heartedness, alleviation, assuagement, mitigation, consolation, disburdenment*)

burn—ignite, kindle, brand, consume, cauterize, rage, glow, smoulder, blaze, flash, cremate, incinerate. (*extinguish, stifle, cool, wane, subside, glimmer, lower, pale*)

bury—inter, inhume, conceal, repress, suppress, obliterate, cancel, entomb, compose, hush. (*disinter, exhume, bruit, excavate, expose, resuscitate, publicate, aggravate*)

business—occupation, profession, vocation, transaction, trade, calling, office, employment, interest, duty, affair, matter, concern. (*stagnation, leisure, inactivity*)

bustle—business, activity, stir, commotion, energy, excitement, haste, hurry, eagerness, flurry. (*idleness, vacation, inactivity, indolence, indifference, unconcernedness, coolness, calm, stagnation, quiet, desertion*)

busy—industrious, diligent, assiduous, engaged, occupied. (*idle, slothful, lazy, indolent, unoccupied*)

but—save, except, barring, yet, beside, excluding, still, excepting, notwithstanding. (*with, including, inclusive, nevertheless, however, notwithstanding*)

C

calamity—disaster, misfortune, mishap, catastrophe, misadventure, trouble, visitation, affliction, reverse, blight. (*God-send, blessing, boon*)

calculate—estimate, consider, weigh, number, count, apportion, proportion, investigate, reckon, rate, compute. (*guess, conjecture, hit, chance, risk, stake, miscalculate*)

calculation—estimation, consideration, balance, apportionment, investigation, reckoning, computation, anticipation, forethought, regard, circumspection, watchfulness, vigilance, caution, care. (*in-*

considerateness, inconsideration, incaution, indiscretion, miscalculation, misconception, exclusion, exception, omission, carelessness, supposition)

caliber—gauge, diameter, ability, capacity, force, strength, power, quality, character.

called—named, designated, denominated, yclept, termed. (*unnamed, undesignated, misnamed, misdesignated*)

calm—smooth, pacify, compose, allay, still, soothe, appease, assuage, quiet, tranquilize. (*stir, excite, agitate, disconcert, ruffle, lash, heat, discompose*)

calumny—slander, defamation, detraction, libel, traducement, back-biting, opprobrium, aspersion. (*vindication, clearance, eulogy, panegyric*)

cancel—efface, blot out, annul, expunge, nullify, quash, rescind, repeal, revoke, abrogate, obliterate, discharge, erase, abolish, countervail. (*enforce, enact, re-enact, confirm, perpetuate, contract*)

candid—fair, honest, open, sincere, frank, artless, impartial, plain, straightforward, aboveboard, transparent, unreserved, ingenious. (*unfair, close, mysterious, reserved, shuffling, disingenuous, insincere, jesuitical*)

candidate—aspirant, petitioner, canvasser, applicant, claimant, solicitor. (*waiver, decliner, abandoner, resigner, abjurer, noncompetitor*)

canvass—question, investigate, challenge, test, dispute, solicit, sift, examine, discuss, apply for, request. (*pretermit, allow, ignore, disregard, admit, pass, misexamine, misinvestigate*)

capacity—space, size, volume, tonnage, calibre, ability, faculty, capability, cleverness, talents, magnitude, parts, competency, comprehensiveness, accommodation. (*narrowness, restriction, incapacity, coarctation, contractedness*)

capital—chief, excellent, important, cardinal, principal, consummate, high. (*inferior, unimportant, subordinate, minor, defective, mean*)

capricious—wayward, uncertain, fanciful, freakish, fitful, fickle, changeful, whimsical, humorsome, inconstant, crotchety. (*firm, unchanging, inflexible, decided, unswerving, constant*)

captivated—taken, charmed, smitten, fascinated, enslaved, captured, enthralled. (*free, unaffected, uninfluenced, unscathed, insensible, insensitive*)

care—attention, pains, anxiety, concern, trouble, circumspection, regard, solicitude, caution, prevention, custody, preservation, thrift, heed, foresight, wariness, economy, prudence. (*inattention, neglect, disregard, carelessness, indifference, temerity, remissness, improvidence, unguardedness, incaution*)

career—course, success, walk, line, progress, history, way of life, passage, race. (*misproceeding, misdeportment, unsuccess, miscarriage*)

caress—endearment, blandishment, wheedling, fondling, stroking. (*vexation, irritation, annoyance, teasing, persecution, provocation*)

caricature—mimicry, parody, travesty, burlesque, extravagance, exaggeration, hyperbole, monstrosity, farce. (*portraiture, representation, resemblance, justice, fidelity, truthfulness*)

carnival—revel, rout, festivity, masquerade. (*fast, mortification, lent, retirement*)

carpet—table, board, consideration, consultation. (*shelf, rejection, disposal, oblivion*)

carriage—transportation, conveyance, bearing, manner, conduct, demeanor, walk, gait, mien, behavior, deportment, vehicle. (*misconveyance, miscarriage, misconduct, misconsignment*)

case—occurrence, circumstance, contingency, event, plight, predicament, fact, subject, condition, instance. (*hypothesis, supposition, fancy, theory, conjecture*)

cast—hurl, send down, throw, fling, pitch, impel, project, construct, mold, frame. (*raise, elevate, recover, erect, accept, approve, retain, carry, ignore, miscalculate, misprovide, break, dissipate, dismember, dislocate*)

cast—mould, stamp, kind, figure, form, aspect, mien, air, style, manner, character. (*malformation, deformity, abnormity*)

caste—order, class, rank, lineage, race, blood, dignity, respect. (*degradation, taboo, disrepute, abasement, reproach*)

casual—accidental, occasional, incidental, contingent, unforeseen, fortuitous. *regular, ordinary, systematic, periodic, certain, fixed*)

catastrophe—revolution, disaster, calamity, misfortune, misadventure, reverse, blow, visitation. (*blessing, victory, triumph, felicitation, achievement, ovation, success, godsend*)

cause—source, origin, producer, agent, creator, purpose, inducement, reason, account, principle, motive, object, suit, action. (*effect, result, accomplishment, end, production, issue preventive*)

cease—intermit, stop, desist, abstain, discontinue, quit, refrain, end, pause, leave off. (*ceaseless, never-ending, everlasting, constant, incessant*)

celebrated—famed, renowned, illustrious, eminent, glorious, famous, noted, distinguished, notable, exalted. (*unrenowned, obscure, undistinguished, unknown, disgraced, mean*)

celebrity—fame, honor, glory, star, reputation, distinction, renown, notability, eminence, notoriety. (*obscurity, meanness, ingloriousness, ignominy, disgrace, contempt, cipher, nobody*)

celestial—heavenly, ethereal, atmospheric, supernal, angelic, radiant, eternal, immortal, seraphic, divine, godlike, elysian. (*earthly, terrestrial, terrene, sublunary, human, mortal, hellish, infernal*)

censure—blame, stricture, reproach, reprobate, inculpate, reprove, condemn, reprehend, chide, berate, scold, upbraid, disapproval, remonstrance, rebuke, reprimand, dispraise. (*praise, eulogy, approbation, encouragement, commendation*)

ceremonial—official, ministerial, functional, pompous, imposing, sumptuous, scenic. (*ordinary, private, unimposing, unostentatious, undramatic*)

certain—true, fixed, regular, established, incontrovertible, undoubtful, indubitable, infallible, unmistakable, sure, unfailing, real, actual, undeniable, positive, convinced, assured. (*uncertain, dubious, exceptional, irregular, casual, occasional, questionable, doubtful, vacillating, undecided, uncertain*)

certify—acknowledge, aver, attest, vouch, avow, avouch, testify, protest, declare, demonstrate, prove, evidence, inform, assure. (*disprove, disavow, misinform, misadvise*)

challenge—defy, summon, dare, question, investigate, brave, canvass. (*pass, allow, grant, concede*)

chance—accident, fortuity, hazard, haphazard, fortune, random, casualty, befallment, luck. (*law, rule, sequence, consequence, causation, effectuation, intention, purpose, design, certainty*)

changeless—regular, settled, steady, firm, stationary, consistent, resolute, reliable, undeviating, uniform, immutable, immovable. (*irregular, unsettled, unsteady, wavering, fluctuating, capricious, irresolute, vacillating, variable, mutable, plastic*)

character—symbol, letter, nature, type, disposition, genius, temperament, cast, estimation, repute,

46

office, reputation, part, capacity, class, order, sort, stamp, kind, quality, species, sign, tone, mark, figure, record. (*vagueness, anonymousness, non-description, disrepute*)

characteristic—distinction, peculiarity, diagnosis, idiosyncrasy, specialty, individuality, personality, singularity. (*nondescription, abstractedness, generality, miscellany*)

charitable—kind, benign, benevolent, beneficent, liberal, considerate, forgiving, compassionate, placable, inexacting, inextreme. (*uncharitable, unkind, harsh, selfish, churlish, illiberal, censorious, unforgiving, uncompassionate, implacable, extreme, exacting, retaliative, revengeful*)

charm—bewitch, enchant, fascinate, lay, soothe, mesmerize, delight, enrapture, transport, entice, allure, entrance, captivate, subdue. (*disenchant, disillusionize, excite, rouse, disturb, annoy, irritate, alarm, terrify, repel, disgust*)

charm—spell, incantation, enchantment, fascination, attraction, allurement. (*disenchantment, repulsion, fear*)

chaste—pure, modest, uncontaminated, spotless, immaculate, undefiled, virtuous, incorrupt, simple, unaffected, nice. (*impure, corrupt, meretricious, gaudy, flashy, overdecorated*)

cheap—common, inexpensive, uncostly, mean, vile, worthless, low-priced. (*rare, costly, worthy, expensive, honorable, noble, high*)

cheat—*v.* overreach, fleece, silence, trick, gull, cozen, juggle, defraud, swindle, dupe, beguile, deceive, deprive, hoodwink, prevaricate, dissemble, shuffle, inveigle. (*enlighten, guide, remunerate, compensate, undeceive, disabuse*)

cheat—*n.* deception, fraud, imposition, trick, artifice, illusion, impostor, swindle, finesse, deceit, lie, fiction. (*truth, reality, verity, fact, certainty, genuineness, verification, honesty, authenticity*)

cheer—hope, happiness, comfort, hospitality, plenty, conviviality. (*dejection, sullenness, gloom, starvation, niggardliness, dearth, inhospitableness, churlishness, unsociableness*)

cheerful—lively, gay, bright, happy, bonny, merry, joyful, pleasant, buoyant, sunny, enlivening, in good spirits, sprightly, blithe, joyous. (*lifeless, dull, gloomy, unhappy, dejected, depressed, sullen, joyless, melancholy, depressing, dispiriting*)

childish—weak, silly, puerile, infantine, imbecile, foolish, trifling, paltry, trivial. (*strong, resolute, manly, wise, judicious, sagacious, chivalrous, profound, polite*)

chivalrous—courageous, generous, knightly, gallant, heroic, adventurous, valiant, spirited, handsome, high-minded. (*unhandsome, dirty, sneaking, pettifogging, scrubby, dastardly, recreant, ungenerous, ungentlemanly*)

choice—option, adoption, selection, election, preference, alternative. (*compulsion, necessity, rejection, refusal, unimportance, indifference, refuse*)

chuckle—grin, crow, cackle. (*cry, wail, grumble, whimper, whine*)

cipher—nonentity, dot, nothing, trifle, button (*fig.*), straw, pin, rush, mole-hill. (*somebody, bigwig, something, notability, celebrity, triton, colossus, star*)

circumstance—detail, feature, point, event, occurrence, incident, situation, position, fact, topic, condition, particular, specialty. (*deed, case, transaction*)

civil—well-mannered, political, courteous, wellbred, complaisant, affable, urbane, polite, obliging, accommodating, respectful. (*disobliging, unaccommodating, disrespectful, boorish, clownish, churlish, uncivil*)

claim—*v.* demand, ask, require, insist, pretense, right, privilege, title, request, maintain. (*forego, waive, disclaim, abjure, disavow, abandon, concede, surrender, repudiate*)

claim—*n.* assertion, vindication, pretension, title, right, privilege, arrogation, demand. (*waiving, abjuration, disclaimer, surrender*)

claimant—assertor, vindicator, appellant, litigant. (*relinquisher, resigner, conceder, waiver, renouncer, abjurer*)

classification—order, species, nature, character, cast, stamp, group, kind, section, sect, category, assortment, designation, description, genus. (*individuality, specialty, isolation, alienation, division, distinction, singularity, exclusion, heterogeneity*)

clause—portion, paragraph, stipulation, provision, article, condition, chapter, section, passage. (*document, instrument, muniment*)

clear—*v.* clarify, disencumber, disentangle, disembarrass, vindicate, liberate, set free, release, exonerate, exculpate, justify, retrieve, acquit, absolve, whitewash, extricate, eliminate. (*befoul, contaminate, pollute, clog, encumber, embarrass, involve, implicate*)

clear—*a.* open, pure, bright, transparent, free, disencumbered, disentangled, disengaged, absolved, acquitted, serene, unclouded, evident, apparent, distinct, manifest, conspicuous, unobstructed, plain, obvious, intelligible, lucid. (*thick, muddy, foul, opaque, encumbered, entangled, condemned, convicted, turbid, dubious, indistinct, unintelligible*)

clever—able, ready, talented, quick, ingenious, dexterous, adroit, expert, gifted, quick-witted, skillful, well-contrived. (*weak, dull, stupid, slow, ill-contrived, doltish, uninventive, awkward, clumsy, bungling, botched*)

cling—fasten, hold, adhere, embrace, stick, cleave, hang, twine, hug. (*drop, recede, secede, apostatize, abandon, relax, forego, swerve, surrender*)

cloak—conceal, disguise, mask, veil, hide, cover, palliate, screen, mitigate, extenuate. (*exhibit, propound, promulge, portray, aggravate, expose, demonstrate, reveal*)

close—narrow, limited, restricted, condensed, packed, secret, compressed, solid, firm, compact, reserved, niggardly, shut, fast, dense. (*wide, open, ample, spacious, airy, unconfined, dispersed, rarefied, subtle, vaporous, patent, public, advertised, openhanded, liberal, frank*)

clownish—rustic, boorish, bucolic, foolish, awkward, clumsy, cloddish, untutored, rude. (*polite, civil, urbane, affable, graceful, polished, refined, courtly, high-bred, intelligent, educated*)

clumsy—awkward, inexpert, uncouth, maladroit, botching, bungling, unskillful, unwieldy, unhandy, ill-shaped. (*neat, workmanlike, artistic, handy, skillful, clever, expert, adroit, dexterous*)

coarse—common, ordinary, indelicate, vulgar, gross, unrefined, immodest, rough, rude, unpolished. (*fine, refined, gentle, polished, delicate, choice*)

cognizance—notice, observation, recognition, knowledge, experience. (*inadvertence, neglect, ignorance, inexperience, oversight, connivance*)

coherent—consecutive, consistent, complete, sensible, compact, logical, close. (*inconsecutive, rambling, disunited, inconsistent, discursive, loose, silly, illogical, aberrant*)

coincidence—chance, fortuity, casualty, concurrence, correspondence, contemporaneousness, commensurateness, harmony, agreement, consent. (*design, purpose, adaptation, asynchronism, anachronism, disharmony, incommensurateness, discordance, variation, difference*)

colleague—helper, companion, associate, ally, confederate, coadjutor, partner, assistant, adjutant, assessor. (*co-opponent, co-rival, counter-agent, co-antagonist, competitor, colluctator*)

collect—collate, gather, glean, sum, infer, learn, congregate, assemble, convoke, convene, muster, amass, garner, accumulate. (*classify, arrange, distribute, dispose, dispense, divide, sort, deal*)

collection—assembly, assemblage, store, gathering, collation. (*dispersion, distribution, dispensation, division, arrangement, disposal, classification*)

color—hue, tint, complexion, pretense, speciousness, tinge, garbling, falsification, distortion, perversion, varnish. (*achromatism, paleness, nakedness, openness, genuineness, transparency, truthfulness*)

combination—union, association, consortment, concert, confederacy, alliance, league, coalition, cabal, synthesis, co-operation. (*division, disunion, disruption, dissolution, dispersion, analysis, opposition, resistance, inter-repellence*)

comfortable—snug, satisfied, pleasant, agreeable, cozy, commodious, convenient, consoled. (*uncomfortable, dissatisfied, troubled, miserable, wretched, cheerless, unhappy, disagreeable, forlorn*)

commerce—trade, traffic, merchandize, barter, exchange, business, communication, dealing, intercourse. (*stagnation, exclusion, inactivity, interdict, embargo, dullness*)

commodious—ample, easy, convenient, spacious, suitable, comfortable. (*inconvenient, incommodious, narrow, ill-contrived, incommensurate, discommodious*)

common—ordinary, familiar, habitual, everyday, frequent, coarse, vulgar, low, mean, universal. (*unusual, exceptional, scarce, rare, uncommon, re-*

fined, partial, infrequent, sporadic, egregious, excellent)

community—aggregation, association, commonwealth, co-ordination, society, sympathy, order, class, brotherhood, fraternity, polity, unity, nationality, similarity, homogeneity. *(segregation, secession, independence, dissociation, disconnection, rivalry, hostility, animosity, estrangement, dissimilarity, contrariance, heterogeneity)*

company—aggregation, association, union, sodality, order, fraternity, guild, corporation, society, community, assemblage, assembly, crew, posse, gang, troop, audience, congregation, concourse. *(rivalry, opposition, disqualification, antagonism, counter-agency, competition, counter-association)*

compass—encompass, surround, enclose, environ, circumscribe, embrace, achieve, effect, effectuate, consummate, complete, circumvent. *(expand, dispand, unfold, amplify, display, dismiss, liberate, discard, fail, bungle, botch, misconceive, mismanage, miscontrive)*

compatible—consistent, consentaneous, harmonious, co-existent, correspondent, congruous, accordant, agreeable, congenial, consonant. *(incompatible, impossible, insupposable, inconsistent, discordant, hostile, adverse, antagonistic, incongruous, destructive, inter-repugnant, contradictory)*

compel—force, oblige, drive, constrain, necessitate, make, coerce, bind. *(persuade, convince, coax, allure, egg, induce, tempt, seduce, acquit, cozen, liberate, release)*

compensation—remunerative, equivalent, wages, pay, allowance, restoration, restitution, satisfaction, atonement, expiation, indemnification, amercement, damages. *(deprivation, injury, nonpayment, gratuity, donation, fraudulence, damage)*

competition—rivalry, emulation, race, two of a trade. (*association, colleagueship, alliance, joint-stock, copartnership, confederation*)

complacement—pleased, satisfied, content, pleasant, affable, kind, mannerly, acquiescent, amiable. (*dissatisfied, irritated, churlish, unmannerly, morose, austere, grudging*)

complaint—murmur, discontent, repining, grievance, annoyance, remonstrance, expostulation, lamentation, sickness, disease. (*congratulation, rejoicing, approbation, complacency, boon, benefit, applause, jubilee, health, sanity*)

complement—completion, fulfilment, totality, ·supply, counterpart, correlative. (*deficiency, deficit, insufficiency, abatement, detraction, defalcation, diminution, drawback*)

complete—full, perfect, finished, adequate, entire, consummate, total, exhaustive, thorough, accomplished. (*incomplete, partial, imperfect, unfinished, inadequate*)

complexion—face, aspect, color, look, feature, appearance, character, hue, interpretation, indication. (*unindicativeness, concealment, reticence, inexpression, heart, core*)

complicated—confused, intricate, involved, perplexed, entangled. (*clear, simple, uninvolved, lucid, unraveled*)

compliment—homage, courtesy, flattery, praise. (*insult, discourtesy, contempt*)

complimentary—commendatory, laudatory, panegyrical, eulogistic, encomiastic, lavish of praise. (*disparaging, condemnatory, damnatory, denunciatory, reproachful, abusive, objurgatory, vituperative, defamatory*)

composition—compound, conformation, structure, mixture, combination, compromise, adjustment, settlement, commutation. (*analysis, segregation, examination, criticism, discussion, disturbance, aggravation, perpetuation*)

comprehend—comprise, embody, grasp, understand, conceive, apprehend, enclose, include, involve, embrace. (*exclude, except, misunderstand*)

comprehensive—wide, ample, general, extensive, large, broad, all, embracing, generic, significant, capacious, inclusive, compendious, pregnant. (*narrow, restricted, shallow, exclusive, adversative, exceptive*)

compromise—arbitrate, adjust, compose, settle, endanger, implicate, involve. (*aggravate, excite, foster, perpetuate, exempt, enfranchise, disengage, extricate, exonerate*)

conceal—hide, secrete, disguise, keep secret, dissemble, screen, suppress. (*reveal, manifest, exhibit, avow, confess, expose, promulgate, publish, divulge*)

concentrate—assemble, converge, muster, congregate, convene, draw, conglomerate, condense, localize, centralize. (*disperse, scatter, dismiss, decentralize*)

concerning—about, of, relating, regarding, touching, in relation to, respecting, with respect to, with regard to, with reference to, relative to. (*omitting, disregarding*)

concert—union, combination, concord, harmony, agreement, association, co-operation. (*dissociation, counteraction, opposition*)

condescension—affability, graciousness, favor, stooping. (*haughtiness, arrogance, pride, superciliousness, disdain, scorn*)

condition—state, case, mood, term, mode, qualification, requisite, stipulation, predicament, proviso, situation, circumstances, plight. (*relation, dependence, situation, circumstances, concession, fulfilment, adaptation*)

conditionally—provisionally, relatively, provided, hypothetically, contingently. (*absolutely, unconditionally, categorically, positively*)

conducive—contributive, promotive, subsidiary, causative, effective, productive. (*preventive, counteractive, contrariant, repugnant, destructive*)

conduct—lead, bring, carry, transfer, direct, guide, control, manage, administer. (*mislead, miscarry, mismanage, misconduct, misadminister*)

confer—compare, collate, discuss, deliberate, converse, consult, give, present. (*dissociate, contrast, hazard, conjecture, withhold, withdraw*)

confession—creed, catechism, articles, doctrine, tenets, profession, declaration, subscription. (*heresy, apostasy, protest, condemnation, refutation, index, renunciation, abjuration*)

confidant—confessor, adviser, confederate. (*traitor, betrayer, rival*)

confident—positive, assured, sure, certain, impudent, bold, sanguine. (*See certain*)

confidential—private, secret, trustworthy, intimate. (*public, open, patent, official, treacherous, insidious*)

confirm—strengthen, stabilitate, establish, substantiate, settle, prove, fix, perpetuate, sanction, corroborate, ratify. (*weaken, shake, upset, cancel, abrogate, repeal, annul, confute, refute*)

confront—oppose, face, encounter, resist, intimidate, menace. (*rally, encourage, abet, countenance*)

confused—abashed, embarrassed, perplexed, disconcerted, disorganized, promiscuous, chaotic, complex, involved, disarranged, disordered. (*unabashed, unembarrassed, systematic, unconfused, organized, arranged*)

congress—parliament, council, conclave, assembly, synod, legislature, convention. (*cabal, conclave, mob*)

conjecture—guess, divination, hypothesis, theory, notion, surmise, supposition. (*computation, calculation, inference, reckoning, proof, deduction*)

connection—junction, conjunction, union, association, concatenation, relation, affinity, relevance, intercourse, communication, kinsman, relationship, kindred. (*disconnection, disjunction, dissociation, independence, irrelevance, disunion*)

conquer—subdue, vanquish, surmount, overcome, overpower, overthrow, defeat, crush, master, subjugate, prevail over. (*fail, fall, retreat, succumb, fly, submit, surrender, lose, forfeit, sacrifice, resign, cede*)

conscious—aware, cognizant, sensible. (*unaware, unconscious, insensible*)

consecutive—orderly, arranged, coherent, continuous. (*disordered, undigested, incoherent, rambling, inconsequent, inconsecutive, discursive*)

consent—submit, agree, acquiesce. (*resist, disagree, dissent, decline, refuse*)

consequence—effect, issue, result, inference, coherence, deduction, conclusion, outcome, importance, note, moment, dignity. (*cause, causation, antecedence, premise, origin, datum, postulate, axiom, unimportance, insignificance, inconsequence, inconsecutiveness, irrelevance, meanness, paltriness*)

consider—attend, revolve, meditate, think, reflect, investigate, regard, observe, judge, opine, infer, deduce, weigh, cogitate, deliberate, ponder, deem. (*disregard, ignore, pretermit, despise, guess, conjecture, hazard*)

considerate—thoughtful, attentive, forbearing, unselfish, judicious, serious, prudent, circumspect, reflective, careful, cautious. (*thoughtless, inconsiderate, inattentive, rude, overbearing, selfish, injudicious, rash, careless*)

consistency—consistence, congruity, composition, substance, material, amalgamation, compound, mass, density, solidity, closeness, compactness, coherence, uniformity, harmony, analogy, proportion. (*volatility, vaporousness, subtility, tenuity, sublimation, incoherence, inconsistency, incongruity, disproportion, contrariety, contradiction*)

consistent—congruous, accordant, consonant, agreeing, compatible, harmonious. (*incongruous, at variance with, not agreeing with, incompatible, inharmonious*)

conspicuous—visible, easily seen, prominent, distinguished, manifest, eminent, famous, noted, salient, observable, noticeable, magnified. (*invisible, inconspicuous, inobservable, noticeable, microscopic*)

constant—uniform, regular, invariable, perpetual, continuous, firm, fixed, steady, immutable, faithful, true, trustworthy. (*irregular, exceptional, variable, casual, accidental, incidental, broken, interrupted, inconsistent, fickle, untrustworthy, faithless, treacherous, false*)

constitution—temperament, frame, temper, character, habit, nature, government, polity, state, consistence, composition, substance, organization, structure, regulation, law. (*accident, habituation, modification, interference, anarchy, despotism, tyranny, rebellion, revolution, dissipation, disorganization, demolition, destruction*)

construction—composition, fabrication, explanation, rendering, erection, fabric, edifice, reading, understanding, interpretation, view. (*dislocation,* *dismemberment, demolition, displacement, misplacement, misconstruction, misunderstanding, misconception, misinterpretation)*

consult—interrogate, canvass, question, deliberate, confer, advise with, regard, consider, ask advice of, care for, promote. *(resolve, explain, expound, direct, instruct, dictate, counteract, contravene)*

consumption—decline, decay, expenditure, waste, decrement, lessening, decrease. *(growth, development, enlargement, augmentation)*

contact—touch, contiguity, continuity, apposition, adjunction. *(proximity, adjacence, interruption, disconnection, separation, distance, isolation, non-contact)*

contagious—catching, epidemic, infectious, pestilential, communicated, transferred, transmitted, infectious. *(sporadic, endemic, preventive, antipathetic)*

contaminate—defile, taint, corrupt, sully, befoul, soil. *(purify, cleanse, lave, clarify, sanctify, chasten)*

contemplate—meditate, behold, observe, ponder, study, purpose, design, intend, project. *(ignore, overlook, waive, abandon)*

contemptible—despicable, mean, vile, pitiful, disreputable, paltry, trifling, trivial. *(important, grave, weighty, honorable, respectable, venerable)*

content—full, satisfied, pleased, gratified, contented, willing, resigned. *(unsatisfied, dissatisfied, unwilling, reluctant, discontented)*

contentious—litigious, perverse, wayward, splenetic, cantankerous, exceptious. *(pacific, obliging, considerate, obsequious, accommodating, easy)*

contingent—dependent, incidental, resultant, co-efficient, hypothetical, uncertain, conditional. *(positive, absolute, independent, unmodified, unaffected, uncontrolled, irrespective)*

continually—constantly, persistently, always, ever, perpetually, unceasingly, repeatedly, frequently, continuously. (*casually, occasionally, contingently, sometimes, rarely, fitfully, intermittently*)

contract—*v.* abridge, abbreviate, narrow, lessen, reduce, compress, decrease, retrench, curtail, form, agree. (*expand, amplify, dilate, elongate, reverse, cancel, abandon*)

contract—*n.* covenant, agreement, compact, bond, pact, stipulation, bargain. (*promise, assurance, parole*)

contradict—oppose, dissent, negative, controvert, deny, disprove, confute, refute, gainsay, contravene. (*state, propound, maintain, argue, confirm, affirm, endorse*)

contrary—opposed, opposite, repugnant, antagonistic, adverse, incompatible, inconsistent. (*agreeing, consentaneous, compatible, kindred, coincident, consistent*)

contribute—conduce, add, subscribe, give, co-operate, assist, tend, supply. (*refuse, withhold. misconduce, misapply, contravene*)

contrive—plan, design, arrange, fabricate, adapt, manage, scheme, devise, concert, adjust. (*hit, hazard, run, chance, venture, bungle, over-vault, over-do*)

control—check, curb, moderate, repress, guide, regulate, restrain, coerce, manage, administer, govern. (*neglect, abandon, license, liberate, mismanage, misconduct*)

convenient—handy, apt, adapted, fitted, suitable, helpful, commodious, useful, timely, seasonable, opportune. (*inconvenient, awkward, obstructive, useless, superfluous, unseasonable, untimely, inopportune*)

conventional—customary, usual, ordinary, stipulated, prevalent, social. (*unusual, unsocial, legal,* *compulsory, statutable, immutable, natural, invariable)*

conversant—familiar, acquainted, proficient, experienced, versed, learned. (*unfamiliar, unacquainted, ignorant, unversed, unlearned, strange, inconversant*)

convertible—identical, commensurate, conterminous, equivalent, equipollent. (*variant, incommensurate, unequivalent, contrary, contradictory, contrariant*)

conviction—assurance, persuasion, belief. (*doubt, misgiving, disbelief*)

co-operate—assist, abet, contribute, concur, work together, help, conspire. (*thwart, oppose, counteract, rival*)

copy—imitation, portraiture, fac-simile, counterfeit, duplicate, image, likeness, transcript. (*original, prototype, model, example, pattern*)

cordial—warm, earnest, sincere, reviving, invigorating, affectionate, hearty. (*cold, distant, formal, ceremonious*)

corner—cavity, hole, nook, recess, retreat. (*coin, abutment, prominence, salience, angle, protrusion, elbow, protection, convexity*)

corpulent—stout, burly, fat, portly, gross, lusty, plethoric, fleshy. (*lean, thin, attenuated, slight, emaciated*)

correct—*a.* true, exact, faultless, accurate, proper, decorous, right. (*false, untrue, incorrect, faulty, wrong*)

correct—*v.* chasten, punish, rectify, amend, reform, emend, redress, set right, improve. (*spare, falsify, corrupt*)

correction—amendment, discipline, emendation, chastisement, punishment. (*deterioration, debasement, retrogradation, reward, recompense*)

correspond—match, tally, fit, answer, agree, suit, harmonize. (*vary, differ, disagree, jar, clash*)

correspondence—fitness, agreement, adaptation, congruity, answerableness, match, congeniality, communication, letter, writing, despatches. (*conversation, colloquy, confabulation, reservation, withdrawal, withholding, non-intercourse, difference, repugnance*)

corrupt—defiled, polluted, vitiated, decayed, depraved, putrid, rotten, infected, tainted, profligate, contaminated. (*pure, uncorrupt, undefiled*)

corruption—decomposition, decay, putrescence, adulteration, depravity, rottenness, defilement, deterioration, perversion, debasement, taint, contamination, putrefaction. (*vitality, organization, purity, purification, amelioration*)

cost—*v.* require, consume, absorb. (*bring, produce, yield, afford, fetch, return*)

cost—*n.* expenditure, outlay, disbursement, payment, compensation, price, worth, expense, charge, outgoings. (*receipt, income, emolument, return, profit, perquisite, revenue*)

costly—valuable, expensive, high-priced, rich, precious, sumptuous. (*valueless, cheap, low-priced, mean, worthless, beggarly, paltry*)

council—cabinet, bureau, chamber, consultation, conclave, parliament, congress, synod, company, assembly, meeting, conference, convention, convocation. (*league, conspiracy, cabal, intrigue, mob, multitude, crowd*)

counsel—advice, instruction, monition, admonition, warning, recommendation. (*misguidance, misinstruction, betrayal*)

count—compute, reckon, enumerate, estimate, number, sum, calculate. (*hazard, conjecture, guess, lump, confound*)

countenance—*v.* help, aid, abet, favor, sanction, patronize, support, encourage. (*oppose, confront, discourage, discountenance, browbeat*)

countenance—*n.* aid, encourage, support. (*discountenance*)

counteract—counterinfluence, counterfoil, foil, baffle, neutralize, oppose, rival, thwart, hinder. (*aid, help, abet, promote, conserve, co-operate, subserve*)

counterpart—match, fellow, tally, brother, twin, copy, correlative, complement, supplement. (*opponent, counter-agent, reverse, obverse, opposite, antithesis, contrast, contradiction*)

countryman—rustic, clown, boor, compatriot, swain, yeoman, husbandman, farmer, agriculturist, laborer, peasant, fellow-countryman, fellow-subject, fellow-citizen, subject, citizen, inhabitant, native. (*oppidan, townsman, cockney, foreigner, alien, stranger*)

couple—bracket, link, conjoin, unite, splice, buckle, button, clasp, pair, yoke, connect, tie, brace. (*loose, part, isolate, separate, detach, divorce, uncouple, unclasp, untie*)

courage—bravery, boldness, valor, pluck, fortitude, resolution, gallantry, fearlessness, intrepidity. (*timidity, cowardice, pusillanimity, poltroonery, dastardliness*)

course—order, sequence, continuity, direction, progress, line, way, mode, race, career, road, route, series, passage, succession, round, manner, plain, conduct, method. (*disorder, discursion, solution, interruption, deviation, hindrance, error, conjecture, hazard, speculation, caprice*)

courtly—dignified, polished, refined, aristocratic, high-bred, mannerly. (*undignified, rough, unpolished, coarse, unrefined, plebeian, awkward, boorish, rustic, unmannerly*)

covetous—acquisitive, avaricious, greedy, grasping, rapacious. (*unselfish, liberal, self-sacrificing, profuse, bountiful, charitable*)

coward—craven, dastard, recreant, poltroon, renegade. (*champion, hero, daredevil, desperado*)

coxcomb—fop, dandy, puppy, prig, pedant. (*genius, savant, authority, celebrity, philosopher, sage*)

coy—shy, reserved, bashful, shrinking, retreating, modest. (*bold, forward, rompish, hoydenish*)

crabbed—sour, morose, cross-grained, petulant, churlish, irritable, crusty. (*pleasant, open, easy, genial, conversable, warm, cordial, hearty*)

craft—art, artifice, cunning, guile, stratagem, maneuver, wiliness, trickery, duplicity, chicanery, intrigue, underhandedness, dodge. (*openness, fairness, candor, honesty, frankness, sincerity, artlessness, ingenuousness, straightforwardness*)

cram—stuff, choke, squeeze, ram, pack, gorge. (*disgorge, vent, discharge, unload, unpack, eviscerate, empty, eliminate*)

crash—jar, clang, clash, resonance. (*murmur, whisper, babble, rumbling, reverberation, din*)

cream—marrow, pith, gist, acme. (*refuse, offal, dregs, dross, garbage*)

credential, or **credentials**—missive, diploma, title, testament, seal, warrant, letter, vouchers, certificates, testimonials. (*self-license, self-constitution, self-appointment, autocracy*)

credit—relief, trustworthiness, reputation, security, honor, praise, merit, confidence, faith. (*disbelief, distrust, untrustworthiness, shame, insecurity, disgrace, censure*)

creed—belief, catechism, articles, confession, subscription. (*protest, abjuration, recantation, retractation, disbelief, non-subscription*)

criminal—illegal, felonious, vicious, culpable, wrong, iniquitous, sinful, immoral, guilty, nefarious, flagitious. (*lawful, virtuous, right, just, innocent, moral, meritorious, creditable, honorable, praiseworthy, laudable*)

critical—nice, delicate, exact, fastidious, discriminating, censorious, accurate, dubious, precarious, ticklish, crucial, important, momentous, hazardous. (*inexact, popular, loose, easy, undiscriminating, safe, determined, decided, settled, retrieved, redressed*)

criticism—stricture, censure, animadversion. (*approval, praise*)

cross-grained—perverse, wayward, peevish, morose, cantankerous, ill-conditioned. (*genial, pleasant, agreeable, jolly, obliging, accommodating*)

crude—raw, undigested, unconsidered, half-studied, harsh, unshaped, unchastened, unfinished, unrefined, ill-prepared. (*well-prepared, well-digested, well-considered, well-studied, ripe, well-adapted, well-proportioned, well-expressed, classical, finished, refined, artistic, elaborate, highly-wrought*)

cruel—savage, barbarous, pitiless, inexorable, unrelenting, ruthless, truculent, hard-hearted, harsh, unmerciful, brutal, inhuman, maleficent, malignant. (*humane, forbearing, generous, merciful, forgiving, benevolent, beneficent*)

crush—pulverize, triturate, pound, bray, crumble, overpower, demolish. (*consolidate, compact, cake, solidify, compress, amalgamate, upraise, stabilitate, aggrandize*)

cuff—slap, box, smack, punch, pummel, hustle buffet. (*cudgel, flagellate, thrash, cane, strap, lash, whip*)

cultivate—promote, foster, study, improve, fertilize, till, advance, refine, improve, civilize, nourish, cherish. (*neglect, desert, abandon, stifle, prevent, discourage, abolish, blight, blast, paralyze, eradicate, extirpate, uproot*)

cupidity—avarice, acquisitiveness, covetousness, stinginess. (*prodigality, extravagance, liberality*)

cure—remedy, alleviation, restorative, heal-all, amelioration, reinstatement, restoration, renovation, convalescence. (*aggravation, confirmation, complaint, disease, ailment, inoculation, contagion, corruption*)

curiosity—inquisitiveness, interest, wonder, marvel, interrogativeness, rarity, phenomenon, celebrity, oddity, lion. (*indifference, heedlessness, disregard, abstraction, absence, weed, drug, dirt, cipher, bagatelle, song*)

curious—inquiring, inquisitive, scrutinizing, prying, meddling, singular, searching, interrogative, peeping, peering, rare, unique, odd, recondite. (*indifferent, uninquiring, incurious, uninterested, trite, common, superficial*)

current—running, prevalent, ordinary, present, popular, general, floating, exoteric, vulgar. (*rejected, obsolete, exploded, confined, private, secret, esoteric*)

custody—keeping, guardianship, conservation, care. (*neglect, betrayal, exposure, abandonment, desertion, liberation, jeopardy, discharge*)

cynical—sarcastic, snarling, snappish, sneering, cross-grained, currish, carping. (*genial, lenient, complaisant, urbane*)

D

daft—silly, innocent, idiotic, lunatic, light-headed, cracked. (*sane, sound, sensible, practical, rational, shrewd, deft*)

dainty—choice, rare, refined, tasty, exquisite, luxurious, epicurean. (*common, coarse, unrelishing, nasty, dirty, omnivorous, greedy, gluttonous*)

damp—cool, blunt, dishearten, quench, slack, moderate, humid, wet, moist, discourage, discountenance, repress. (*urge, inflame, incite, fan, excite*)

dapper—spruce, neat, natty, smart. (*slovenly, awkward, unwieldy, untidy*)

daring—adventurous, dashing, bold, courageous, venturesome, dauntless, foolhardy, fearless, brave, intrepid, valorous. (*cautious, timid, inadventurous*)

dark—black, dusky, sable, swarthy, opaque, obscure, enigmatical, recondite, abstruse, unintelligible, blind, ignorant, besotted, benighted, dim, shadowy, inexplicable, secret, mysterious, hidden, murky, nebulous, cheerless, dismal, dim, gloomy, sombre, joyless, mournful, sorrowful. (*white, fair, light, radiant, bright, lucid, crystalline, transparent, plain, intelligible, enlightened, glaring, dazzling, illumined, festive, luminous*)

dash—hurl, cast, throw, subvert, detrude, drive, rush, send, fly, speed, dart, scatter, strike, course. (*raise, reinstate, erect, creep, crawl, lag, hobble*)

daunt—terrify, scare, frighten, cow, dishearten, appall, intimidate, confront. (*countenance, encourage, rally, inspirit*)

dawdle—lag, dally, idle. (*haste, speed, dash, rush, work, fag*)

dead—defunct, deceased, departed, gone, inanimate, lifeless, insensible, heavy, unconscious, dull, spiritless, cheerless, deserted, torpid, still. (*vital, living, animate, vivacious, susceptible, alive, joyous, stirring, thronged, bustling*)

deadly—mortal, fatal, malignant, baleful, pernicious, noxious, venomous, destructive, baneful, implacable. (*vital, life-giving, healthful, wholesome, nutritious*)

deaf—surd, hard of hearing, disinclined, averse, inexorable, insensible, rumbling, inaudible, heedless, dead. (*acute, listening, disposed, interested, attentive, willing, susceptible, sensible, alive*)

dear—high-priced, costly, expensive, beloved, precious, loved. (*cheap, inexpensive, misliked, vile*)

death—departure, demise, decease, dissolution, mortality, fall, failure, termination, cessation, expiration, release, exit. (*birth, rise, life, growth, vigor, animation, spirit, activity, operation, action, commencement, vitality, auspices, inauguration*)

debatable—dubious, doubtful, inestimable, uncertain, problematical, floating, unsettled, disputable. (*certain, sure, unquestionable, indisputable, self-evident, incontestible*)

debauch, debauchery—riot, revel, excess, orgies, gluttony. (*meal, moderation, frugality, asceticism, abstinence, fast, maceration*)

debt—debit, liability, default, obligation, claim, score, something due. (*liquidation, assets, credit, trust, grace, favor, obligation, accommodation, gift, gratuity*)

decay—decline, wane, sink, dwindle, rot, wither, perish, waste, ebb, decrease. (*rise, grow, increase, flourish, luxuriate, vegetate, expand, enlarge*)

decay—declension, waning, sinking, wasting, decrease, corruption, decadence, putrefaction, rottenness, dry rot, consumption, decline. (*rise, growth, birth, increase, fertility, exuberance, luxuriance, prosperity*)

deceit—cheat, imposition, trick, fraud, deception, double dealing, delusion, circumvention, guile, beguilement, treachery, sham, insidiousness, indirection, duplicity, cunning, artifice. (*enlighten-*

ment, instruction, guidance, reality, verity, fair dealing, honesty, openness)

deceitful—deceptive, delusive, fraudulent, fallacious. (*open, fair, honest, truthful, veracious*)

deceive—trick, cheat, beguile, delude, gull, dupe, take in, overreach, mislead, betray, ensnare, entrap, circumvent. (*enlighten, advise, illumine, guide, disabuse, undeceive, deliver*)

decide—determine, fix, settle, adjudicate, terminate, resolve. (*waver, raise, moot, drop, doubt waive, suspend, misjudge, misdetermine*)

decipher—read, spell, interpret, solve, unravel, explain, unfold. (*cipher, symbolize, impuzzle, mystify, enigmatize*)

declaration—avowal, exhibition, manifestation, statement, ordinance, assertion, affirmation, profession. (*denial, concealment, suppression*)

decompose—analyze, segregate, individualize, resolve, dissolve. (*compound, concoct, mix, organize, compose*)

decorum—seemliness, propriety, dignity, order, decency, good manners, good behavior, modesty. (*unseemliness, impropriety, disturbance, disorder*)

decrease—diminish, lessen, subside, abate, lower, decline, retrench, curtail, reduce, wane. (*increase, grow, amplify, expand, augment, extend, enlarge*)

decrepit—infirm, weak, crippled, superannuated, effete, broken down, enfeebled, tottering, aged. (*strong, robust, agile, youthful, active*)

dedicate—devote, consecrate, offer, set, apportion, assign, apply, separate, hallow, set apart. (*alienate, misapply, desecrate, misappropriate, misconvert, misuse*)

deed—act, action, commission, achievement, perpetration, instrument, document, muniment, exploit, feat. (*omission, failure, abortion, false-witness, innocent, cancelling, disproof, invalidation, retractation, impossibility, non-performance, recall, reversion, undoing*)

deep—profound, subterranean, submerged, designing, abstruse, recondite, learned, low, sagacious, penetrating, thick, obscure, mysterious, occult, intense, heartfelt. (*shallow, superficial, artless, undesigning, familiar, commonplace*)

deface—mar, spoil, injure, disfigure, deform, damage, mutilate, destroy. (*decorate, adorn, embellish*)

default—lapse, forfeit, omission, defect, delinquency, absence, want, failure. (*maintenance, appearance, plea, satisfaction, forthcoming, supply, presence*)

defeat—*n.* frustration, overthrow, discomfiture. (*victory, triumph, success*)

defeat—*v.* conquer, overcome, worst, beat, baffle, rout, overthrow, vanquish, frustrate, foil. (*secure, promote, insure, speed, advance, establish, aid*)

defect—shortcoming, omission, fault, imperfection, flaw, blemish, want. (*supply, sufficiency, emendation, compensation, virtue, ornament, complement*)

defective—faulty, imperfect, insufficient, deficient, wanting, short. (*correct, complete, sufficient, full, ample, abundant, satisfactory*)

defense—resistance, protection, vindication, plea, justification, excuse, rampart, bulwark, apology, shelter, excuse. (*abandonment, surrender, betrayal, exposure*)

defer—delay, postpone, waive, adjourn, prorogue, put off, retard, procrastinate, protract, hinder, prolong. (*expedite, hasten, quicken, press, urge, hurry, overdrive, dispatch*)

deference—respect, consideration, condescension, contention, regard, honor, veneration, submission, reverence, obedience, homage, allegiance. (*disrespect, contumely, contumacy, disregard, slight, impudence, disobedience, non-allegiance, defiance, attention*)

definite—clear, specified, determined, definitive, restricted, specific, certain, ascertained, precise, exact, fixed, limited, bounded, positive. (*vague, unspecified, undetermined, indefinite, obscure, confused, intermingled*)

definition—determination, limitation, specification, restriction. (*confusion, vagueness, acceptation, description, explanation, misconception, misstatement*)

defray—meet, liquidate, pay, settle, bear, discharge, quit. (*dishonor, repudiate, dissatisfy, misappropriate, embezzle*)

defy—scorn, challenge, provoke, despite, brave. (*see* **dare**)

degree—grade, rank, stage, step, extent, measure, mark, rate, position, quality, class, station, range, quantity, amount, limit, order. (*space, mass, magnitude, size, numbers*)

deliberate—*v.* consider, meditate, consult, weigh, reflect, ponder, debate, perpend. (*shelve, burke, discard, hazard, chance, risk*)

deliberate—*a.* grave, purposed, intentional, designed, determined, resolute, earnest, unbiased, unprejudiced. (*playful, jocose, facetious, irresolute, unresolved, undetermined, dubious, compulsory, suggested, dictated, instigated, biased, prejudiced*)

delicious—exquisite, luxurious, delightful, dainty, choice. (*coarse, common, unsavory, unpalatable, nauseous, loathsome*)

delight—enjoyment, pleasure, happiness, transport, ecstasy, joy, gratification, gladness, rapture, bliss. (*pain, suffering, sorrow, trouble, misery, displeasure, dissatisfaction, disappointment, discomfort, dejection, depression, distress, melancholy, discontent*)

delinquent—criminal, culprit, offender. (*worthy, paragon, pattern*)

deliver—liberate, free, save, utter, set free, surrender, yield, transmit, concede, give up, rescue, pronounce, hand, give, entrust, consign. (*confine, capture, suppress, retain, betray, withdraw, assume, appropriate, misdeliver*)

democratic—popular, leveling, radical, subversive, unlicensed, anarchical, destructive, republican. (*regal, imperial, aristocratic, oligarchical, constitutional, conservative, tyrannical, despotic, autocratic*)

demonstrate—prove, show, exhibit, manifest, evince, illustrate. (*disprove, conceal, misdemonstrate, misexemplify*)

demure—sedate, staid, grave, modest, downcast, sober, dispassionate, prudish, discreet. (*lively, vivacious, facetious, wanton, wild, noisy, boisterous, rompish, hoydenish, indiscreet*)

denomination—name, designation, description, kind, class, order, appellation. (*non-description, misnomer*)

dense—slow, thick, stupid, stolid, solid, stout, compact, consolidated, condensed, close, thick-set. (*quick, clever, intelligent, rare, rarefied, uncompacted sparse*)

deny—refuse, reject, withhold, negative, contradict, gainsay, disclaim, disavow, disown, oppose. (*grant, accept, concede, admit, affirm, confirm, afford, yield, indulge*)

department—section, division, portion, function, office, branch, province, line. (*institution, establishment, art, science, literature, service, state, whole, organization, community, society, body*)

dependent—hanging, resting, contingent, trusting, relying, subject, relative. (*independent, irrelative, irrespective, absolute, free*)

depression—lowering, degradation, debasement, dejection, discouragement, hollow, valley, dip. (*raising, elevation, exaltation, promotion, preferment, amelioration, encouragement, rallying, rising, eminence, mound, prominence*)

deprive—strip, bereave, despoil, rob, divest, dispossess, abridge, depose, prevent, hinder. (*invest, endow, compensate, enrich, supply, present, reinstate, indemnify*)

derision—scorn, contempt, mockery, irony, sarcasm, contumely, disrespect. (*respect, regard, admiration, reverence*)

descendant—offspring, progeny, stock, scion, seed, branch, issue, house, family, lineage. (*author, founder, parent, ancestor, progenitor, stock, root, source, origin*)

describe—draw, delineate, portray, explain, illustrate, define, picture, depict, represent, relate, narrate, recount. (*confound, confuse, mystify, misrepresent, caricature, distort*)

desert—wild, waste, wilderness, solitude, void. (*inclosure, field, pasture, garden, oasis*)

design—*v.* contemplate, purpose, intend, plan, prepare, project. (*hit, risk, guess, conjecture, chance, fluke, misconceive, miscontrive*)

design—*n.* contemplation, purpose, intention, plan, preparation, draft, delineation, sketch, drawing, artifice, cunning, artfulness, guile, contrivance, intent, project, scheme. (*execution, performance, result, issue, construction, structure, candor, fairness, openness, artlessness, sincerity, simplicity, change, accident*)

desirable—expedient, advisable, valuable, acceptable, proper, judicious, beneficial, profitable, good, enviable, delightful. (*undesirable, unadvisable, inexpedient, objectionable, improper, injudicious, unprofitable, evil*)

desire—longing, affection, propension, craving, concupiscence, appetency. (*loathing, hate, repugnance, disgust, aversion, abomination, horror*)

despair—hopelessness, despondency, desperation. (*hopefulness, elation, anticipation, hilarity, confidence, sanguineness, expectation*)

desperate—wild, daring, audacious, determined, reckless, abandoned, rash, furious, frantic, despairing, regardless, mad, desponding, hopeless, inextricable, irremediable. (*cool, calm, cautious, timid, shy, irresolute, remediable, hopeful, promising, propitious*)

despotic—autocratic, domineering, arbitrary, arrogant, imperious, self-willed, irresponsible, absolute, cruel, tyrannical. (*limited, constitutional, humane, merciful*)

destination—purpose, intention, design, consignment, object, end, fate, doom, arrival, application, use, scope, appointment, point, location, goal, aim. (*operation, tendency, exercise, action, movement, design, initiation, project, effort*)

destiny—fate, decree, lot, fortune, predestination, necessity, doom, end. (*will, volition, choice, deliberation, freedom, free will*)

destroy—demolish, annihilate, subvert, ruin, overthrow, undo, waste, consume. (*restore, reinstate, repair, fabricate, make, construct, create*)

destructive—detrimental hurtful, noxious, injurious, deleterious, baleful, baneful, ruinous, subversive. (*wholesome, conservative, preservative, beneficial, reparatory, subsidiary, restorative*)

detraction—diminution, deterioration, depreciation, slander, backbiting, derogation. (*augmenta-

tion, improvement, enhancement, eulogy, compliment, flattery)

detriment—loss, harm, hurt, injury, deterioration, impairment, disadvantage, prejudice, damage, inconvenience. (*enhancement, improvement, remedy, reinstatement, repair, augmentation*)

detrimental—injurious, hurtful, pernicious. (*beneficial, profitable, augmentative*)

develop—educe, enucleate, eliminate, enunciate, lay open, disclose, unravel, unfold, clear, amplify, expand, enlarge. (*envelop, wrap, obscure, mystify, conceal, narrow, restrict, contract, condense, compress, involve*)

device—artifice, expedient, design, plan, stratagem, project, symbol, emblem, show, invention, contrivance, cognizance. (*fairdealing, openness, miscontrivance, abortion, fortune, luck, hazard, hit, incognito*)

devil—satan, lucifer, fiend, arch-fiend, foul fiend, demon. (*archangel, angel, seraph, cherub*)

devise—contrive, plan, maneuver, concert, manage. (*miscontrive, mismanage*)

devoid—void, wanting, destitute, unendowed, unprovided. (*furnished, supplied, replete, provided, gifted*)

devotion—piety, devoutness, religiousness, dedication, self-abandonment, consecration, ardor, self-surrender, self-sacrifice, love, attachment. (*impiety, profanity, selfishness, aversion, alienation, antipathy, indifference, apathy*)

devour—eat, consume, swallow, gorge, gobble, bolt, absorb. (*disgorge, vomit*)

dictate—prompt, suggest, enjoin, order, direct, prescribe, decree, instruct, propose, command. (*follow, repeat, obey, echo, answer*)

dictation—imperative, imperious, domineering, arbitrary. (*condescending, affable, indulgent, mod-*

est, unassuming, suppliant, supplicatory, precatory, persuasive, insinuating)

die—expire, depart, perish, decline, decease, disappear, wither, languish, wane, sink, fade, decay, cease. (*begin, originate, rise, live, develop, grow, strengthen, flourish, luxuriate, vegetate*)

difference—separation, destruction, dissimilarity, unlikeness, disagreement, dissonance, discord, contrariety, dissent, distinction, dissimilitude, estrangement, variety. (*community, consociation, condonation, similarity, likeness, agreement, sympathy, consonance, harmony, consentaneousness, reconciliation, uniformity, identity*)

difficult—hard, intricate, involved, perplexing, enigmatical, obscure, trying, arduous, troublesome, uphill, unmanageable, unamenable, reserved, opposed. (*easy, plain, straight, simple, lucid, categorical, tractable, amenable, unreserved, favorable*)

digest—sort, arrange, dispose, order, classify, study, ponder, consider, prepare, assimilate, incorporate, convert, methodize, tabulate. (*displace, confound, complicate, derange, disorder, discompose, eject, refuse, reject, disturb*)

dilemma—fix, hobble, quandary, doubt, difficulty, scrape. (*extrication, rebutment, freedom, advantage, superiority, escape, solution, retort*)

diligence—care, assiduity, attention, application, heed, industry. (*indifference, carelessness, neglect, inattention, heedlessness, desultoriness, inertness, idleness*)

dingy—dull, dusky, rusty, bedimmed, soiled, tarnished, dirty, dim, colorless, obscure, dead, sombre. (*bright, burnished, glossy, high-colored, radiant, luminous, gleaming, lustrous*)

diplomacy—embassage, ministry, ambassadorship, representation, tact, contrivance, management, negotiation, out-witting, circumvention.

(*cancel, recall, conge, miscontrivance, mismanagement, mal-administration, over-vaulting, self-entanglement, self-defeat, self-stultification*)

diplomatic—judicious, knowing, wise, prudent, well-contrived, clever, astute, politic, discreet, well-planned, well-conceived, sagacious, well-managed. (*injudicious, bungling, stultifying, ill-managed, undiplomatic*)

direction—course, tendency, inclination, line, control, command, bearing, superscription, order, address. (*misdirection, deviation, miscontrol, misinstruction, aberration*)

directly—straightly, straight-away, immediately, undeviatingly, at once, promptly, quickly, instantly. (*indirectly, by-and-by, interveniently*)

disability—disqualification, impotency, unfitness, incapacity, forfeiture, incompetency. (*qualification, recommendation, fitness, deserving, merit*)

disappoint—betray, deceive, frustrate, baffle, delude, vex, mortify, defeat, foil. (*realize, justify, verify, fulfil, encourage, satisfy, gratify*)

discernible—visible, conspicuous, manifest, palpable, apparent, plain, perceptible, evident. (*invisible, inconspicuous, obscure, indiscernible; impalpable, microscopic, minute*)

discipline—order, strictness, training, government, instruction, drilling, control, coercion, punishment, organization. (*disorder, confusion, rebellion, mutiny, encouragement, reward, disorganization*)

discomfort—disquiet, vexation, annoyance, trouble, unpleasantness, disagreeableness. (*comfort, ease, pleasantness, agreeableness*)

disconcert—abash, confuse, confound, upset, baffle, derange, discompose, thwart, disturb, defeat, fret, interrupt, vex, ruffle, disorder, unsettle, frustrate, discomfit. (*encourage, rally, countenance, aid, concert, concoct, arrange, order, prepare, scheme, contrive, hatch, design*)

discourtesy—see **courtesy**

discreet—discerning, wise, prudent, circumspect, cautious, wary, regulative, sensible, judicious. (*undiscerning, blind, foolish, imprudent, indiscreet, unrestrained, reckless, injudicious, silly*)

discrimination—penetration, sagacity, acuteness, nicety, shrewdness, judgment, discernment, insight, distinction. (*dullness, confusedness, indiscriminateness, shortsightedness, hebetude, indiscernment*)

disease—complaint, disorder, illness, indisposition, distemper, ailment, malady, sickness. (*health, convalescence, sanity, salubrity*)

disgust—nausea, loathing, abomination, aversion, dislike, repugnance, abhorrence, distaste. (*desire, liking, partiality, predilection, relish, fondness, longing, avidity*)

dismal—dreary, ominous, foreboding, lonesome, cheerless, gloomy, sad, depressed, lugubrious, funereal, sorrowful, melancholy, tragic, blank. (*gay, propitious, promising, cheerful, lively, elated, joyous, laughable, ridiculous, comic*)

dispatch—expedite, send, accelerate, hasten, execute, conclude. Used also in the sense of kill. (*retard, detain, obstruct, impede*)

dispel—disperse, scatter, dissipate, drive away, dismiss. (*collect, recall, summon, convene, congregate, conglomerate, mass, accumulate*)

disperse—dispel, scatter, disseminate, separate, break up, spread abroad, deal out, distribute, dissipate. (*collect, summon, recall, gather, concentrate, meet*)

dispute—argue, question, canvass, contest, contend, challenge, debate, controvert, controversy, difference, gainsay, impugn, quarrel, altercation. (*waive, concede, allow, forego*)

dissemble—disguise, conceal, repress, smother, restrain, cloak. (*exhibit, manifest, protrude, vaunt, pretend, simulate, feign, assume, expose, profess, proclaim*)

disseminate—spread, propagate, preach, proclaim, publish, promulgate, scatter, circulate. (*repress, suppress, stifle, discountenance, extirpate, eradicate*)

dissolute—abandoned, profligate, loose, licentious, wanton, vicious. (*upright, conscientious, strict, self-controlled, correct*)

distance—interval, removal, separation, interspace, remoteness, absence, space, length. (*proximity, nearness, adjacency, contiguity, neighborhood, propinquity, contact, presence*)

distinct—separate, independent, unconnected, detached, disjoined, unlike, definite, obvious, different, dissimilar, clear, conspicuous, plain, perspicuous. (*united, consolidated, conjoined, one, obscure, dim, confused, indistinct*)

distinction—difference, separation, dignity, eminence. (*unity, identity, debasement, insignificance, degradation*)

distinguish—discern, descry, perceive, characterize, make famous, know, discriminate, see, discover, separate, divide, dissimilate, differentiate. (*miss, overlook, confound, confuse*)

distinguished—illustrious, noted, celebrated, conspicuous, eminent, marked, famous. (*obscure, inconspicuous, hidden, not famous*)

distress—harass, embarrass, trouble, grieve, annoy, vex, mortify, pain, disturb, afflict, worry. (*soothe, compose, please, gratify, gladden, console, elate, comfort*)

disturb—derange, discompose, disorder, discommode, plague, confuse, rouse, agitate, annoy, trouble, interrupt, incommode, worry, vex, molest, disquiet. (*order, collocate, arrange, pacify, soothe, quiet, compose, leave*)

diversion—detour, divergence, deviation, recreation, amusement, pastime, sport, enjoyment. (*continuity, directness, procedure, business, task, work, study, labor, avocation*)

divide—separate, dissect, bisect, portion, part, divorce, segregate, sever, sunder, deal out, disunite, keep apart, part among, allot, distribute, multiply. (*unite, collocate, classify, convene, congregate, conglomerate, conglutinate, commingle, join, consociate, co-ordinate*)

divorce—separate, disconnect, dissever, divert, alienate. (*conjoin, unite, connect, apply, reconcile, reunite*)

do—work, act, accomplish, execute, achieve, transact, finish, enact, perform, produce, complete. (*undo, mar, neglect, omit*)

docile—compliant, amenable, easily managed, yielding, gentle, quiet, pliant, tractable, teachable, tame. (*intractable, stubborn, obstinate, self-willed, dogged*)

dogmatic—doctrinal, theological, imperious, dictatorial, authoritative, arrogant, magisterial, self-opinionated, positive. (*practical, active, moderate, modest, diffident, vacillating*)

doleful—dolorous, rueful, melancholy, piteous, somber, sorrowful, woebegone, dismal. (*merry, joyful, gay, blithe, beaming*)

dominion—power, authority, rule, tyranny, despotism, government, control, empire, sway, realm, territory, jurisdiction. (*weakness, submission, subjugation, inferiority, servitude*)

dormant—sleeping, slumbering, latent, undeveloped, quiescent, inert. (*vigilant, wakeful, active, operative, developed, energetic*)

doubt—dubiousness, dubitation, scruple, hesitation, suspense, distrust, suspicion, perplexity, uncertainty, ambiguity, difficulty, indecision. (*certainty, clearness, precision, determination, decision, conviction, satisfaction*)

drain—draw, strain, drip, percolate, drop, exhaust, empty, dry. (*replenish, fill, supply, pour, moisten, drown, inundate, drench, swill*)

draw—drag, pull, attract, induce, haul, entice, inhale, sketch, delineate, describe. (*push, carry, propel, throw, repel, drive, compel, impel, thrust*)

dreadful—fearful, shocking, monstrous, dire, terrible, frightful, terrific, horrible, alarming, awful. (*encouraging, inspiriting, assuring, promising, hopeful*)

dreamy—fanciful, visionary, speculative, abstracted, absent, foggy. (*collected, earnest, attentive, awake, active, energetic, practical*)

dregs—refuse, sediment, offal, lees, off-scouring, dross, trash. (*cream, flower, pink, pickings, bouquet, sample*)

dress—garniture, preparation, arrangement, clothing, habiliments, accoutrements, vestments, uniform, raiment, apparel, attire, clothes, array, garments, livery, costume, garb, investiture. (*nudity, disorder, disarrangement, undress, deshabille*)

drift—tendency, direction, motion, tenor, meaning, purport, object, intention, purpose, scope, aim, result, issue, inference, conclusion, end, course. (*aimlessness, pointlessness, vagueness, unmeaningness, indefiniteness, confusedness, aberrancy*)

drink—imbibe, swallow, quaff, absorb, drain, draught. (*disgorge, replenish, pour, exude, water, moisten*)

drivel—fatuity, nonsense, trifling, snivel, babble, (*soundness, coherence, substance, solidity*)

droll—whimsical, comical, odd, queer, amusing, laughable, funny, comic, fantastic, farcical. (*sad, lamentable, tragic, lugubrious, funereal*)

drop—ooze, emanate, distil, percolate, fall, decline, descend, faint, droop. (*evaporate, rally, rise, soar, ascend, recover*)

drown—sink, immerse, swamp, overwhelm, engulf, deluge, inundate, submerge. (*dry, drain, expose, air, ventilate*)

dry—arid, parched, moistureless, juiceless, barren, tame, sarcastic, vapid, lifeless, dull, tedious, uninteresting, monotonous. (*moist, fresh, juicy, lively, entertaining*)

dull—stupid, stolid, doltish, insensible, callous, heavy, gloomy, dismal, cloudy, turbid, opaque, dowdy, sluggish, sad, tiresome, commonplace, dead. (*sharp, clever, lively, animated, sensible, cheerful, exhilarating, bright, transparent, brilliant, burnished*)

durable—lasting, permanent, stable, persistent, abiding, constant, continuing. (*evanescent, transient, impermanent, unstable*)

duty—obligation, part, business, responsibility, allegiance, function, office, province, calling, trust, commission, service. (*freedom, exemption, immunity, license, dispensation, desertion, dereliction*)

dwindle—pine, waste, diminish, decrease, fall off, decline, melt. (*expand, enlarge, increase, grow, flourish, augment, develop*)

E

early—soon, betimes, forward, shortly, quickly, ere long, anon, matutinal, beforehand. (*late, tardily, backward, vespertinal, belated*)

earn—merit, acquire, achieve, obtain, win, gain, deserve, realize. (*forfeit, forego, waste, lose, spend, squander*)

earnest—eager, serious, intent, determined, strenuous, solemn, grave, warm, fervent, intense, ardent. (*indifferent, idle, playful, desultory, irresolute, unearnest, sportive, jesting, flippant*)

easy—quiet, comfortable, manageable, indulgent, facile, lenient, unconstrained, gentle, not difficult, unconcerned, self-possessed. (*uneasy, disturbed, uncomfortable, difficult, unmanageable, hard, exacting, anxious, awkward, embarrassed*)

economy—administration, dispensation, management, rule, arrangement, distribution, husbanding. (*maladministration, waste, misrule, mismanagement, disorder, prodigality*)

ecstasy—rapture, inspiration, fervor, frenzy, transport, emotion, joy, delight, enthusiasm, happiness. (*indifference, coolness, dullness, weariness, tedium, bore, fidget, misery*)

edifice—structure, building, tenement, fabric. (*ruin, heap, demolition, dismantlement*)

educate—instruct, nurture, discipline, train, teach, develop, ground, school, initiate. (*miseducate, misinstruct, misnurture*)

effective—powerful, conducive, operative, cogent, telling, able, potent, talented, efficacious, efficient, serviceable, effectual. (*weak, ineffective, inconducive, inoperative, futile, nugatory*)

effort—trial, attempt, endeavor, exertion. (*failure, misadventure, unsuccess, frustration, futility, inactivity, ease, facility, spontaneity*)

egotism—conceit, vanity, self-assertion, self-conceit, self-praise, self-exaltation, conceitedness. (*considerateness, deference, self-abnegation*)

ejaculation—exclamation, utterance, cry. (*obmutescence, silence, speechlessness, dumbfoundedness, oration, speech, drawl*)

elastic—ductile, extensile, alterable, resilient, modifiable, flexible, buoyant, springy. (*tough, unchangeable, rigid, unflexible, inelastic, crystallized, dull, inert*)

elated—cheered, joyed, inspirited, overjoyed, proud, inflated. (*depressed, dispirited, disappointed, abashed, confounded, humiliated, disconcerted, dejected*)

elegance—beauty, grace, refinement, symmetry, gracefulness, taste. (*deformity, awkwardness, inelegance, disproportion, ungracefulness, coarseness, rudeness*)

elegant—graceful, lovely, well formed, well made, symmetrical, accomplished, polished, refined, handsome. (*inelegant, deformed, unsymmetrical, ill-proportioned, ungraceful, coarse, rude*)

elementary—physical, material, natural, elementary, primary, rudimental, simple, inchoate, component, constituent, ultimate. (*immaterial, incorporeal, impalpable, compound, collective, aggregate, developed, organized*)

eligible—capable, suitable, worthy, desirable, preferable, choice, prime. (*undesirable, worthless, unprofitable, ordinary, indifferent, ineligible*)

elude—escape, avoid, baffle, shun, eschew, evade, parry, fence, mock, frustrate. (*encounter, meet, confront, court, dare, defy*)

embalm—conserve, preserve, treasure, store, enshrine, consecrate. (*expose, desecrate, abandon, vulgarize*)

embarrass—entangle, disconcert, trouble, perplex, confuse, hamper, clog, distress, puzzle, encumber. (*extricate, liberate, expedite, facilitate, accelerate, assist, disencumber*)

embezzle—appropriate, confuse, falsify, peculate, misappropriate. (*square, balance, clear*)

embody—express, methodize, systematize, codify, incorporate, aggregate, integrate, compact, introduce, enlist, combine. (*eliminate, segregate, analyze, dissipate, disintegrate, dismember, colliquate, disband, disembody*)

embrace—clasp, comprehend, include, hug, comprise, contain, close, embody, incorporate. (*exclude, reject, except*)

emergency—crisis, conjuncture, pitch, embarrassment, strait, necessity, exigency, casualty, difficulty. (*rescue, deliverance, solution, subsidence, provision, anticipation, arrangement*)

emotion—passion, feeling, excitement, agitation, perturbation, trepidation, tremor. (*indifference, insensibility, impassiveness, imperturbability, stoicism*)

emphatic—earnest, forcible, strong, energetic, impressive, positive, important, special, egregious, consummate. (*mild, unemphatic, cool, unimpassioned, unimportant, ordinary, unnoticeable, commonplace*)

employ—use, apply, economize, occupy, engage, engross. (*discard, dismiss, misuse, misemploy*)

empower—enable, commission, encourage, qualify, delegate, warrant, sanction, direct, authorize. (*hinder, prevent, discourage, disable, disqualify*)

empty—vacant, void, unencumbered, unobstructed, unoccupied, waste, uninhabited, unfrequented, devoid, vacuous, destitute, unfilled, unfurnished, untenanted, evacuated, deficient, weak, silly, idle, senseless. (*full, occupied, encumbered, obstructed, cultivated, colonized, inhabited, informed, well-instructed, experienced, sensible, significant, forcible, important, substantial*)

enamor—captivate, fascinate, enslave, charm, endear, bewitch, enchain. (*repel, disgust, estrange, disenchant, horrify*)

enclose—shut, encircle, environ, include, circumscribe, envelop, wrap, afforest. (*open, disclose, exclude, bare, disencircle, expose, develop, disafforest, disenclose*)

encourage—embolden, rally, enhearten, cheer, incite, stimulate, foster, cherish, promote, urge, impel, advance, countenance, forward, reassure, animate, inspirit, prompt, abet. (*deter, discourage, dissuade, dispirit*)

endanger—imperil, expose, peril, jeopardize, hazard, risk. (*cover, defend, protect, shield, screen*)

endear—attach, conciliate, gain. (*estrange, alienate, embitter*)

endless—interminable, illimitable, unending, unceasing, boundless, deathless, imperishable, everlasting, perpetual, eternal, infinite. (*terminable, limited, temporary, brief, transient, periodic, ephemeral, fugitive, finite*)

endowment—gift, provision, benefit, benefaction, capacity, attainment, qualification. (*impoverishment, spoliation, disendowment, incapacity, poverty, lack*)

enforce—urge, compel, require, exact, exert, strain. (*relax, waive, forego, remit, abandon*)

engage—promise, undertake, vouch, employ, occupy, hire, gain, attract, enlist, stipulate, pledge, agree, buy, adopt, involve. (*decline, refuse, withdraw, dismiss, discard, extricate, disengage*)

enigmatical—puzzling, perplexing, obscure, mystic. (*lucid, explanatory, plain, self-evident*)

enlarge—amplify, expand, augment, broaden, swell, stretch out, extend, stretch, dilate, increase. (*narrow, lessen, contract, restrict, diminish, curtail, reduce*)

enlighten—illumine, edify, instruct, illuminate, inform, teach. (*mislead, darken, confound, obscure, mystify, perplex*)

enlist—enter, register, enroll, incorporate, embody. (*withdraw, erase, expunge, dismiss, disband, disembody*)

enmity—discord, hate, hostility, malevolence, maliciousness, aversion, malignity, ill-feeling, animosity, opposition, bitterness, acrimony, asperity. (*friendship, love, affection, esteem, friendliness, cordiality*)

enormous—huge, immense, gigantic, colossal, elephantine, vast, gross, monstrous, prodigious. (*diminutive, insignificant, trivial, venial, average, ordinary, regular*)

enough—sufficient, ample, plenty, abundance. (*bare, scant, insufficient, inadequate, short*)

ensue—follow, accrue, supervene, befall. (*precede, threaten, premonish, forewarn*)

ensure—fix, determine, secure, seal. (*imperil, hazard, jeopardize, forfeit*)

enterprising—active, bold, daring, adventurous, speculative, dashing, venturesome. (*inactive, timid, inadventurous, cautious*)

entertain—harbor, maintain, conceive, foster, receive, recreate, amuse. (*eject, exclude, deny, debar, annoy, weary, bore, tire.*)

enthusiasm—excitement, frenzy, sensation, inspiration, transport, rapture, warmth, fervor, fervency, zeal, ardor, vehemence, passion, devotion. (*coldness, callousness, indifference, disaffection, repugnance, alienation, contempt*)

entire—whole, complete, unimpaired, total, perfect, all, full, solid, integral, undiminished. (*partial, broken, impaired, incomplete*)

entitle—qualify, empower, fit, enable, name, style, denominate, designate, characterize. (*disqualify, disentitle, disable, not designate, not characterize*)

entreat—implore, obsecrate, beg, beseech, importune, crave, solicit, supplicate, pray, ask, urge, petition. (*command, insist, bid, enjoin*)

enumerate—specify, name, number, recount, detail, reckon, compute, calculate, call over. (*confound, miscount, misreckon*)

ephemeral—transient, evanescent, fleeting, fugacious, fugitive, momentary. (*abiding, persistent, permanent, perpetual, eternal, perennial, immortal*)

equable—uniform, regular, proportionate, even, smooth, easy. (*irregular, desultory, variable, fitful, disjointed, uneasy*)

equal—uniform, commensurate, co-ordinate, adequate, alike, equivalent, even, equable, sufficient, impartial, co-extensive, smooth. (*unequal, incommensurate, inco-ordinate, inadequate, disparate, variable*)

equitable—fair, just, proportionate, impartial, upright, proper, reasonable, even-handed, honest. (*unfair, unjust, disproportionate, partial*)

erase—obliterate, efface, expunge, blot, cancel. (*mark, write, delineate*)

erect—elevate, raise, establish, plant, uplift, construct, build, found, institute, set up. (*lower, supplant, subvert, depress, remove, destroy, demolish*)

erratic—desultory, aberrant, abnormal, flighty, changeful, capricious. (*regular, normal, methodical, calculable, unalterable, steady, undeviating*)

error—fault, mistake, blunder, falsity, deception, fallacy, untruth, hallucination. (*correction, correctness, truth, accuracy, soundness, rectification*)

escape—elude, decamp, abscond, fly, flee, evade, avoid. (*incur, confront, encounter, meet, suffer*)

essential—innate, inherent, requisite, necessary, vital, immanent, indispensable, leading. (*acci-*

dental, qualitative, quantitative, promotive, regulative, induced, imported, adventitious, ascititious, redundant, superfluous)

establish—plant, fix, settle, found, demonstrate, organize, confirm, institute, prove, substantiate. (*supplant, unsettle, break up, disestablish, misstate, confute, refute, upset, subvert, presume, suppose, guess, conjecture, surmise*)

esteem—price, value, consider, deem, judgé, believe, estimate, think, regard, affect, appreciate, revere, honor, respect, admire, venerate, prize, love, like. (*disregard, disconsider, disaffect, dislike, undervalue, underrate, decry, deprecate*)

eternal—infinite, endless, everlasting, deathless, imperishable, never-dying, ceaseless, ever-living, perpetual, undying, unceasing. (*ephemeral, transient, temporal, fleeting, evanescent, sublunary*)

etiquette—manners, breeding, fashion, conventionality. (*boorishness, rudeness, misobservance, singularity, non-conformance*)

evaporate—melt, colliquate, liquefy, vaporize, disappear, dissolve, exhale, distil. (*consolidate, compact, solidify, indurate, crystallize*)

event—occurrence, circumstance, episode, adventure, issue, accident, result, fact, incident. (*cause, antecedent, operation, inducement, contribution, convergence, predisposition, tendency*)

eventful—remarkable, memorable, signal, important, marked, noted, critical, stirring, notable. (*ordinary, unmarked, unimportant, eventless, uninteresting, characterless, trivial*)

evidence—manifestation, attraction, averment, testimony, disposition, declaration, appearance, sign, token, proof, indication, exemplification, illustration. (*surmise, conjecture, counter-evidence, disproof, refutation, concealment, suppression, misindication, fallacy*)

evident—plain, visible, conspicuous, manifest, indisputable, obvious, clear, palpable, incontrovertible. (*doubtful, obscure, questionable, uncertain, dubious*)

evil—ill, noxious, deleterious, wrong, bad, mischievous, hurtful, sinful, unhappy, adverse, unpropitious, wicked, corrupt, harmful, unfair, notorious, miserable, sorrowful. (*wholesome, beneficial, right, virtuous, holy, pure, happy, fortunate, felicitous, joyous, welcome, grateful, good*)

exactly—precisely, accurately, correspondently. (*loosely, inadequately, incorrectly, differently, otherwise*)

exaggerate—amplify, enlarge, heighten, magnify, overstate, overdraw, strain, over-paint, overestimate. (*disparage, attenuate, palliate, understate, underestimate, lenify, mitigate, soften, qualify, modify*)

examine—weigh, ponder, investigate, perpend, test, scrutinize, criticize, prove, study, discuss, inquire, search, overhaul, explore, inspect. (*discard, conjecture, guess, slur, misconsider, misinvestigate*)

example—sample, specimen, pattern, model, copy, illustration, instance, issue, development. (*stock, material, substance, law, rule, character, principle, system, quality, case*)

except—exclude, save, bar, segregate, negative. (*count, include, reckon, state, classify, propound, affirm, admit*)

exceptional—rare, peculiar, uncommon, irregular, unusual, abnormal. (*common, regular, normal, usual, ordinary*)

excessive—enormous, undue, exorbitant, overmuch, superabundant, superfluous, unreasonable, immoderate, inordinate, extravagant. (*insufficient, scant, inadequate*)

excuse—exculpate, absolve, pardon, forgive, overlook, condone, remit, indulge, justify, vindicate, defend, acquit, mitigate, extenuate, release, exempt, exonerate. (*charge, inculpate, condemn, sentence, exact, strain, accuse*)

execrable—detestable, loathsome, accursed, cursed, villainous, diabolical, hateful, abominable, damnable. (*desirable, eligible, respectable, laudable*)

exemplary—laudable, praiseworthy, conspicuous, honorable, wary, meritorious, worthy, excellent. (*detestable, objectionable, exceptionable*)

exempt—free, irresponsible, unamenable, clear, liberated, privileged, absolved. (*subject, responsible, liable, amenable*)

exercise—exertion, use, practice, application, training, employment, drill. (*rest, ease, relaxation, recreation*)

exhaust—empty, spend, consume, debilitate, waste, void, drain, weaken, weary. (*fill, replenish, augment, invigorate, refresh*)

existence—being, entity, creature. (*nonenity, non-existence, chimera*)

expand—swell, dilate, spread, extend, open, diffuse, develop, unfold, enlarge, amplify. (*contract, curtail, attenuate, restrict, condense*)

expect—Anticipate, await, forecast, forebode, wait for, rely on, look for, foresee. (*welcome, hail, recognize, greet, realize*)

expediency—utility, advantage, interest. (*inexpediency, disadvantage, inutility, detriment*)

expend—spend, disburse, lay out, waste, consume, use. (*save, husband, economize*)

expense—price, cost, charge, payment, expenditure, outlay. (*income, profit, receipt*)

experience—*v.* try, feel, undergo, encounter, endure. (*evade, escape, miss, lose*)

experience—*n.* experiment, trial, test, proof, habit, knowledge.

explain—expound, teach, illustrate, clear up, interpret, elucidate, decipher. (*mystify, obscure, darken, bewilder, misinterpret*)

explanation—exposition, explication, interpretation, sense, description. (*mystification, obscuration, confusion, misinterpretation*)

explicit—plain, detailed, inobscure, declaratory, categorical, stated, distinctly stated, express, definite, determinate. (*implicit, implied, hinted, suggestive, obscure*)

expression—countenance, look, indication, phrase, term, face, feature, lineament. (*falsification, misstatement, solecism, enigma, suppression*)

exquisite—choice, rare, refined, delicate, perfect, matchless, intense, consummate, delicious. (*common, coarse, ordinary*)

extend—prolong, stretch, expand, enlarge, increase, augment, reach, spread, amplify, avail, apply. (*curtail, contract, restrict, narrow, limit, recur, return, miss, fail*)

extent—degree, distance, quantity, space, size. (*diminution, restriction, limitation*)

extinguish—abolish, destroy, extirpate, eradicate, kill, quench, annihilate, put out. (*implant, replenish, cherish, promote, invigorate, propagate, establish, confirm, secure*)

extortionate—hard, close-fisted, severe, rigorous, exorbitant, preposterous, monstrous, exacting. (*liberal, indulgent, bountiful, reasonable, fair, moderate*)

extraordinary—unwonted, uncommon, peculiar, unusual, unprecedented, wonderful, marvelous, prodigious, monstrous, remarkable, strange, preposterous. (*wonted, common, usual, ordinary, frequent, unremarkable, unimportant*)

extravagant—wild, monstrous, preposterous, absurd, prodigal, wasteful, reckless, excessive, lavish, profuse, abnormal. (*sound, sober, consistent, rational, fair, economical, frugal, careful, regular, usual*)

extreme—terminal, final, remote, utmost, farthest, last, extravagant, immoderate, most violent, distant, ultimate. (*initial, primal, moderate, judicious*)

F

fable—apologue, fiction, parable, allegory, romance, invention, fabrication, untruth, novel, falsehood. (*history, narrative, fact*)

facetious—witty, funny, humorous, jocular, waggish, playful, droll, jocose. (*heavy, matter-of-fact, dull, grave, serious, lugubrious, sombre, saturnine*)

facile—docile, tractable, manageable, indulgent, weak, irresolute, easy, affable, flexible, characterless, pliable. (*sturdy, obstinate, determined, resolute, pig-headed, crusty, inflexible, self-willed, independent, self-reliant*)

facility—ease, address, readiness, quickness, adroitness, dexterity, pliancy. (*labor, awkwardness, difficulty*)

fact—truth, deed, occurrence, certainty, circumstance, event, reality. (*fiction, supposition, falsehood, unreality, lie, delusion, chimera, invention, romance*)

fade—fall, fail, decline, sink, droop, dwindle, vanish, change, pale, bleach, set, etiolate. (*rise, increase, grow, bloom, flourish, abide, stand, last, endure*)

fag—work, toil, slave, drudge. (*bask, idle, lounge, dawdle, strike*)

faint—weak, languid, fatigued, unenergetic, timid, irresolute, feeble, exhausted, half-hearted, obscure, dim, pale, faded, inconspicuous. (*strong, vigorous, energetic, fresh, daring, resolute, prominent, marked, conspicuous, glaring*)

fair—open, clear, spotless, unspotted, untarnished, reasonable, unblemished, serene, beautiful, just, honorable, equitable, impartial. (*lowering, dull, foul, disfigured, ugly, unfair, dishonorable, fraudulent*)

faithful—true, firm, attached, loyal, accurate, close, consistent, correspondent, exact, equivalent, staunch, incorruptible. (*false, fickle, capricious, wavering, inaccurate, untrue, faithless, inexact*)

fallacy—sophistry, error, blunder, misconception, bugbear, fiction, delusion, chimera. (*truth, verity, fact, logic, argument, soundness, proof, postulate, axiom*)

false—untrue, erroneous, fallacious, sophistical, spurious, deceptive, fabrication, counterfeit, mendacious, sham, mock, bogus, unfaithful, fib, falsity, fiction, dishonorable, faithless. (*true, correct, sound, conclusive, authentic, real, genuine, candid, honorable, faithful*)

falsify—mistake, misinterpret, misrepresent, belie, betray, garble, cook. (*verify, correct, rectify, certify, check, justify, exhibit, publicate, expose, declare*)

falter—halt, hesitate, hobble, slip, dubitate, stammer, demur, waver, flinch, vacillate. (*proceed, run, speed, flow, discourse, determine, persevere, resolve, career*)

familiar—household, common, free, frank, affable, every-day, well-acquainted, accustomed, conversant, intimate. (*uncommon, rare, strange, extraordinary, unaccustomed, unacquainted, new, inconversant, unfamiliar*)

famous—renowned, glorious, celebrated, illustrious, far-famed. (*unknown, obscure, unsung, inglorious*)

fanciful—grotesque, chimerical, unreal, imaginary, quaint, eccentric, freakish, humorous, erroneous, capricious, whimsical, erratic, absurd, fitful. (*natural, literal, regular, real, sober, ordinary, truthful, accurate, correct, orderly, calculable*)

fancy—thought, belief, idea, supposition, imagination, caprice, notion, conceit, vagary, inclination, whim, humor, predilection, desire. (*object, subject, fact, reality, order, law, truth, system, verity, aversion, horror*)

fashion—form, shape, guise, style, appearance, character, figure, mould, mode, custom, practice, usage, manner, way, ceremony. (*person, work, dress, speech, formlessness, shapelessness, derangement, eccentricity, strangeness, outlandishness*)

fast—firm, secure, fixed, constant, steadfast, stable, unyielding, unswerving, rapid, accelerated, wild, reckless, dissipated, gay. (*loose, insecure, slow, tardy, steady, sober, virtuous*)

fastidious—critical, over-nice, over-refined censorious, punctilious, particular, squeamish, dainty. (*easy, indulgent, uncritical, coarse, omnivorous*)

fat—corpulent, fleshy, brawny, pursy, rich, luxuriant, portly, stout, fertile, unctuous, obese, oleaginous. (*lean, slender, attenuated, emaciated, barren, poor, scant, marrowless, exsanguineous, anatomical*)

fatal—calamitous, deadly, destructive, mortal, lethal. (*beneficial, wholesome, nutritious, vitalizing, salubrious, restorative, slight, superficial, harmless.*)

fate—necessity, destiny, lot, end, fortune, doom. (*will, choice, decision, freedom, independence*)

fault—defect, error, imperfection, flaw, misdeed, failure, omission, want, drawback. (*sufficiency, correctness, completeness, perfection*)

favor—permission, grace, concession, predilection, gift, civility, benefit, kindness, good-will, regard, condescension, preference, boon, countenance, patronage. (*refusal, denial, prohibition, disfavor, withdrawal, withholding, frown, disapproval, injury, discountenance*)

favorable—permissive, indulgent, propitious, concessive, partial, fond, liberal, advantageous, auspicious, friendly. (*reluctant, unpropitious, unfavorable, impartial*)

fear—apprehension, solicitude, alarm, fright, dread, terror, trepidation, dismay, consternation, misgiving, horror, timidity, awe. (*assurance, confidence, courage, fearlessness, trust, boldness*)

feeble—wretched, weak, poor, frail, debilitated, dull, forceless, puny, nerveless, enfeebled, enervated, faint, infirm, incomplete, vain, fruitless, scanty, pitiable. (*strong, robust, active, effective, successful, abundant*)

feeling—touch, sensation, contact, pathos, tenderness, impression, consciousness, sensibility, emotion, sentiment, passion, sensitiveness. (*insensibility, callousness, imperturbability, inexcitability, coldness, insensateness*)

felicitous—happy, timely, successful, opportune, joyous. (*unfortunate, unhappy, untimely, unsuccessful, disastrous, inopportune, sad*)

feminine—delicate, womanly, tender, modest, soft. (*robust, manly, indelicate, rude, rough, unfeminine*)

fertile—rich, luxuriant, teeming, productive, exuberant, causative, conducive, pregnant, fraught, prolific, fecund, fruitful, ingenious, inventive. (*poor, sterile, barren, unproductive, ineffective, incon-*

ducive, *fruitless, inoperative, uninventive, unimagi-*
native)

fickle—fanciful, fitful, capricious, irresolute,
changeable, vacillating, mutable, unreliable, veer-
ing, shifting, variable, restless, inconstant, unstable. (*sober, orderly, reliable, well-regulated, cal-*
culable, trustworthy, steady, uniform)

fiction—invention, fabrication, creation, figment,
fable, falsehood, romance, myth. (*fact, truth,*
verity, reality)

fidelity—fealty, attachment, truthfulness, allegiance, accuracy, closeness, exactness, faithfulness,
integrity, loyalty, honesty. (*treachery, disloyalty,*
disaffection, untruthfulness, inaccuracy, inexactness,
infidelity)

fiery—hot, vehement, ardent, fervent, fierce,
passionate, irascible, choleric, excited, enkindled,
glowing, fervid, impassioned, irritable, hot-brained.
(*cold, icy, indifferent, phlegmatic, passionless, unim-*
passioned, mild, quenched, extinguished, tame)

fight—battle, contention, struggle, conflict, combat, contest, action, engagement, encounter.
(*pacification, reconciliation)*

figure—aspect, shape, emblem, type, image,
condition, appearance, form, symbol, metaphor,
likeness, delineation, illustration. (*misrepresenta-*
tion, deformity, disfigurement)

fill—replenish, content, supply, satisfy, gorge,
glut, occupy, appoint, stuff, store, rise, swell, glow,
expand, increase. (*exhaust, deprive, drain, dis-*
satisfy, stint, vacate, misappoint, subside, shrink,
ebb, evaporate, diminish)

final—terminal, last, latest, ·conclusive, definite,
developed, ultimate, decisive. (*initiative, open,*
unconcluded, progressive, continuous, current, in-
cipient, inaugural, inchoate, rudimental, nascent)

find—meet, confront, ascertain, experience, perceive, discover, furnish, invent. (*miss, elude, overlook, lose, withhold, withdraw, miscontrive*)

fine—thin, minute, slender, delicate, pure, smooth, filmy, gauzy, keen, artistic, choice, finished, high, grand, noble, sensitive, refined, generous, honorable, excellent, superior, pretentious, handsome, pretty, beautiful, showy, elegant, ostentatious, presumptuous, nice, casuistical, subtle. (*coarse, large, rough, blunt, rude, unfinished, mean, petty, illiberal, unimposing, paltry, modest, unaffected, affable, categorical, plain-spoken, unanalytical, unreflective, indissective*)

finical—affected, over nice, dandyish, dallying, foppish, spruce, factitious, euphuistic. (*unaffected, effective, practical, energetic, real, genuine, natural, outspoken, blunt, coarse, rude*)

finish—complete, perfect, accomplish, conclude, achieve, end, shape, terminate. (*begin, commence, start, undertake, fail, miscontrive, mismanage, botch, mar*)

first—leading, primary, pristine, original, foremost, primitive, principal, primeval, highest, chief, earliest, onmost. (*subsequent, secondary, subordinate, subservient, lowest, unimportant, last, hindmost*)

fit—decent, befitting, meet, apt, fitting, adapted, seemly, appropriate, becoming, decorous, qualified, congruous, peculiar, particular, suitable, prepared, adequate, calculated, contrived, expedient, proper, ripe. (*awkward, ungainly, misfitting, ill-suited, unseemly, inappropriate, unsuitable, unprepared, inadequate, miscalculated, miscontrived, inexpedient, improper, unfit*)

fix—place, settle, fasten, link, locate, attach, consolidate, tie, plant, root, establish, secure, determine, decide. (*displace, unsettle, disarrange, re-*

move, uproot, transfer, transplant, disestablish, weaken, shake, reverse, disturb, change, unfix)

flat—dull, tame, insipid, vapid, spiritless, level, horizontal, absolute, even, downright, mawkish, tasteless, lifeless. (*exciting, animated, interesting, thrilling, sensational*)

flexible—pliant, lithe, supple, elastic, easy, indulgent, ductile, flexible, yielding, pliable. (*tough, rigid, inelastic, inflexible, hard, inexorable.*)

flimsy—gauzy, poor, thin, transparent, trifling, trivial, puerile, inane, slight, superficial, weak, shallow. (*solid, sound, irrefragable, substantial, cogent*)

flippant—pert, forward, superficial, thoughtless, saucy, malapert. (*flattering, servile, obsequious, accurate, considerate, deferential, complimentary, respectful*)

flock—herd, congregate, throng, assemble, crowd. (*disperse, scatter, separate, segregate*)

flood—deluge, inundation, abundance. (*drought, drain, ebb, scarcity, subsidence*)

florid—rubicund, flowery, sanguine, ornate, overwrought, meretricious. (*pallid, exsanguineous, bare, unadorned, nude, sober, chaste*)

flounder—roll, blunder, bungle, boggle, wallow, tumble. (*emerge, flow, course, career, speed, rise, flourish, skim*)

flourish—prosper, thrive, speed, triumph, brandish, wave. (*fail, fade, decline, miscarry, founder, arrest, sheathe, ground*)

flow—stream, issue, progress, glide, course, career, run. (*halt, stick, stickle, stop, hesitate, fail, stint, beat, recoil, regurgitate, ebb*)

flurry—agitate, excite, worry, ruffle, fluster. (*soothe, compose, quiet, calm, mesmerize*)

foible—peccadillo, failing, fault, weakness, infirmity. (*crime, atrocity, enormity, sin*)

follow—pursue, chase, accompany, obey, imitate, succeed, result, ensue, attend, shadow, observe, copy. (*avoid, elude, quit, disobey, precede, cause, produce, abandon, shun*)

folly—madness, nonsense, misconduct, imprudence, silliness, foolishness, weakness, absurdity, imbecility. (*sense, wisdom, sanity, judgment, prudence, sobriety*)

foment—excite, cherish, fan, propagate, encourage. (*allay, extinguish, discourage, extirpate, quench*)

fond—loving, attached, affectionate, foolish, silly, weak, doting, empty, enamored, devoted. (*unloving, averse, unaffectionate, strong-minded, austere, rational, well-grounded, sensible, undemonstrative*)

foolish—senseless, idiotic, crazed, shallow, weak, silly, injudicious, irrational, absurd, contemptible, objectionable, witless, brainless, imbecile, preposterous, ridiculous, nonsensical, simple. (*sensible, sane, deep, clearsighted, sound, sagacious, strongminded, wise, prudent, judicious, calculating, advisable, eligible*)

forbidding—repulsive, deterrent, prohibitory, offensive. (*attractive, encouraging, alluring, seductive, permissive*)

force—power, strength, agency, instrumentality, compulsion, cogency, vigor, might, dint, vehemence, pressure, host, army, coercion, validity, violent, (*feebleness, weakness, counteraction, neutralization. inefficiency, inconclusiveness, debility, pointlessness*)

foreign—strange, exotic, outlandish, alien, irrelevant, extraneous. (*domestic, native, congenial, pertinent, germane*)

forfeit—fine, penalty, mulct, amercement, damages, loss. (*premium, bribe, douceur, remuneration, compensation, reward, gratuity*)

forge—work, frame, produce, elaborate, fabricate, counterfeit, feign, falsify, form, shape, make falsely. (*shatter, batter, shiver, blast, fuse, detect, expose, verify, misconstrue, misfabricate, misshape*)

forget—lose, pretermit, unlearn, obliviate, overlook. (*acquire, learn, remember, recollect, mind, retain, treasure*)

form—shape, mould, fashion, constitute, arrange, frame, construct, contrive, make, produce, create, devise. (*deform, dislocate, distort, dissipate, derange, dismember, disintegrate, analyze, disorganize*)

formal—regular, complete, shapely, sufficient, correct, stately, dignified, ceremonious, pompous, stiff, precise, explicit, exact, affected, methodical. (*irregular, incomplete, informal, inadequate, incorrect, easy, unassuming, unceremonious*)

formality—ceremony, parade, affectation, stateliness, punctiliousness, etiquette.

former—preceding, antecedent, previous, prior, earlier, ancient, bygone, anterior, first-mentioned, foregoing. (*succeeding, subsequent, posterior, latter, modern, coming, future*)

fortunate—lucky, propitious, happy, felicitous, prosperous, auspicious, providential, successful. (*unlucky, unfortunate, unhappy, infelicitous*)

forward—advanced, ready, eager, anxious, obtrusive, self-assertive, impertinent, progressive, onward, confident, bold, presumptuous. (*tardy, backward, reluctant, indifferent, slow, retiring, modest*)

found—establish, institute, fix, set, build, set up, base, endow, rest, ground, plant, root. (*disestablish, subvert, supplant, uproot*)

foundation—institution, establishment, footing, base, basis, origin, ground, groundwork, rudiments, substratum, underlying principle. (*disestablishment, superstructure*)

fragrant—odorous, scented, perfumed, balmy, sweet-smelling, aromatic, sweet-scented, odoriferous, spicy. (*inodorous, scentless, fetid*)

frail—irresolute, erring, mutable. (*resolute, virtuous, lasting*)

frank—ingenuous, candid, open, unreserved, artless, free, familiar, honest, easy, sincere, outspoken, plain. (*disingenuous, close, reserved*)

freakish—sportful, frisky, whimsical, fanciful, capricious, erratic. (*steady, sober, demure, unwhimsical, unfanciful, reliable, consistent, uniform, equable*)

free—detached, playing, operating, open, unoccupied, unobstructed, unimpeded, permitted, unhindered, exempt, gratuitous, unconditional, at liberty, clear, liberal, untrammelled, unconfined, careless, loose, easy, munificent, unreserved, frank, bountiful, generous, bounteous. (*subservient, bound, shackled, restricted, clogged, occupied, obstructed, impeded, compulsory, unlawful, biased, subject, liable, amenable, conditional, qualified, niggardly, stingy*)

frequent—many, repeated, numerous, recurrent, general, continual, usual, common. (*few, solitary, rare, scanty, casual*)

fresh—new, young, vigorous, cool, recent, renewed, unimpaired, untarnished, unfaded, blooming, ruddy, novel, untried, modern, unskilled. (*old, stale, jaded, weary, former, stagnant, ordinary, original, impaired, tarnished, faded, decayed, pallid, sickly, putrid, mouldy, musty, fusty*)

fretful—irritable, fractious, peevish, impatient, petulant, waspish. (*patient, forbearing, contented, meek, resigned, unmurmuring*)

friction—rubbing, grating, attrition, abrasion, contact. (*lubrication, detachment, isolation, noncontact*)

friend—associate, companion, acquaintance, familiar, ally, chum, messmate, coadjutor, confidant, adherent. (*opponent, foe, adversary, antagonist, enemy*)

friendly—well-inclined, well-disposed, amicable, kindly, social, neighborly, sociable, affectionate, favorable, cordial. (*ill-inclined, ill-disposed, hostile, inimical, adverse, antagonistic*)

frightful—terrible, horrible, alarming, ugly, hideous, monstrous, dreadful, direful, awful, shocking, horrid, terrific. (*pleasing, attractive, beautiful, fair, encouraging, lovely*)

frivolous—trifling, silly, trivial, petty, worthless. (*serious, earnest, important, grave*)

frolic—play, game, sport, festivity, entertainment, gambol, gayety, lark, spree, merry-making, prank. (*study, undertaking, purpose, engagement, occupation*)

frugal—sparing, economical, parsimonious, abstinent, abstemious, temperate, saving, thrifty, provident. (*profuse, luxurious, extravagant, prodigal, self-indulgent, intemperate*)

fruitful—productive, prolific, pregnant, fraught, causative, effectual, useful, successful, fertile, abundant, plenteous, fecund, plentiful. (*unproductive, sterile, barren, fruitless, ineffectual, useless, abortive*)

fulfil—fill, complete, discharge, verify, accomplish, achieve, execute, effect. (*neglect, ignore, disappoint, falsify.*

fulsome—excessive, gross, loathsome, nauseous, sickening, fawning, offensive. (*chaste, sober, nice, delicate*)

function—office, part, character, capacity, business, administration, discharge, operation, exercise, power, duty, employment. (*usurpation, maladministration, misconduct, misdemeanor*)

fundamental—primary, important, indispensable, essential. (*secondàry, unimportant, adventitious, ascititious, non-essential*)

funny—sportive, droll, comical, laughable, humorous, jocose, ridiculous, ludicrous, diverting. (*dull, tedious, mournful, lugubrious, dismal, grave, serious, sad, lamentable*)

furnish—supply, provide, equip, afford, yield, bestow, purvey, give. (*withhold, withdraw, dismantle*)

fuss—stir, excitement, tumult, worry, ado, bustle, flurry, fidget. (*quiet, peace, sedateness, tranquility, composure, calm*)

future—forthcoming, coming, advenient. (*gone, bygone, past*)

G

gabble—prate, jabber, jargon, stuff, babble, rattle, twaddle, gibber, chatter, gibberish. (*conversation, speech, eloquence, reticence, taciturnity, mincing, mouthiness, euphuism, grandiloquence*)

gain—acquire, get, win, procure, obtain, profit, benefit, earn, attain, realize, achieve, reap, reach. (*lose, forfeit, suffer*)

gallant—brave, chivalrous, intrepid, courteous, heroic, fearless, courageous, valiant, bold, splendid, showy, gay. (*cowardly, churlish, discourteous*)

game—sport, recreation, pastime, amusement, frolic, diversion, play. (*study, toil, labor, business, duty, weariness, flagging*)

garble—misrepresent, misquote, mutilate, cook, dress, color, falsify, pervert, distort. (*quote, cite, extract, recite*)

gaudy—tawdry, fine, meretricious, bespangled, glittering, showy, gay, garish. (*rich, simple, handsome, chaste*)

gauge—measure, fathom, probe. (*survey, conjecture, view, scan, guess, observe, mismeasure*)

gawky—awkward, ungainly, uncouth, clumsy, clownish. (*neat, handy, graceful, handsome*)

gay—merry, blithe, lively, jolly, sportive, sprightly, smart, festive, gladsome, pleasuresome, cheerful. (*heavy, melancholy, grave, sad, sombre, dull, dowdy*)

generous—noble, chivalrous, liberal, disinterested, bountiful, magnanimous, open-hearted, munificent, honorable. (*mean, ignoble, illiberal, selfish, churlish*)

genial—warm, cordial, balmy, cheering, merry, festive, joyous, hearty, revivifying, restorative. (*cold, cutting, harsh, deleterious, noxious, deadly, blighting, destructive, ungenial, lethal*)

genteel—polite, well-bred, refined, courteous, fashionable, elegant, aristocratic, polished, graceful. (*rude, boorish, ill-bred, clownish, unfashionable, unpolished, inelegant, plebeian*)

gentle—courteous, polite, high-bred, mild, bland, tame, docile, amiable, meek, soft, placid, tender. (*rough, rude, coarse, fierce, savage*)

genuine—authentic, true, real, pure, unalloyed, natural, unaffected, sincere, unadulterated, veritable, sound. (*spurious, fictitious, adulterated, apocryphal*)

get—gain, procure, acquire, earn, obtain, attain, secure, achieve. (*lose, forfeit, surrender, forego*)

ghastly—deathlike, wan, grim, cadaverous, spectral, pallid, hideous, shocking. (*blooming, fresh, comely, seemly, buxom, ruddy*)

giddy—whirling, vertiginous, thoughtless, inconstant, unsteady, lofty, beetling, dizzy, hare-brained, flighty. (*stationary, slow, ponderous, thoughtful, earnest, steady, low, unelevated, wary, circumspect*)

gift—donation, present, grant, boon, gratuity, benefaction, endowment, talent, faculty, alms, douceur. (*reservation, refusal, wages, purchase,* *earnings, compensation, remuneration, inanity, stupidity, forfeit, penalty, fine, surrender)*

gist—essence, pith, marrow, substance, kernel, force, main point. *(surplusage, redundancy, additament, environment, accessories, garb, clothing)*

give—bestow, grant, confer, impart, yield, produce, surrender, concede, present, afford, communicate, furnish. *(withhold, withdraw, refuse, retain, grasp, fail, restrain, deny)*

glad—happy, joyous, pleased, gratified, blithesome, gleeful, gladsome, delighted, cheerful, elated, joyful. *(unhappy, sorrowful, disastrous, sorry, disappointed, dismal)*

glare—beam, shine, gleam, ray, radiate, glow. *(shimmer, scintillate, glitter, smoulder, glimmer, glisten, glister, sparkle, flash, flicker)*

glassy—vitreous, smooth, polished, glacial, glabrous, brittle, transparent, crystalline, pellucid, limpid, glossy, silken. *(rough, uneven, rugged, pliant, tough, opaque, luteous, muddy, turbid, scabrous)*

glory—brightness, radiance, effulgence, honor, fame, celebrity, pomp, luster, magnificence, splendor, renown. *(obscurity, ignominy, cloud, dishonor, degradation)*

glut—*v.* gorge, fill, stuff, cram, satiate, cloy, surfeit. *(disgorge, empty, void)*

glut—*n.* surplus, redundancy, superfluity, overstock. *(scarcity, drainage, exhaustion, dearth, failure, scantiness)*

go—move, depart, pass, travel, vanish, reach, extend, proceed, stir, set out, budge. *(stand, stay, come, remain, persist, abide, rest, endure, lack, fail)*

good—*a.* right, complete, virtuous, sound, pious, benevolent, propitious, serviceable, suitable, efficient, sufficient, competent, valid, real, actual, considerable, honorable, reputable, righteous, proper, true, upright, just, excellent. (*wrong, imperfect, unsound, vicious, profane, niggardly, unpropitious, unserviceable, unsuitable, inefficient, inadequate, incompetent, invalid, fictitious, supposititious, inconsiderable, mean, disgraceful, disreputable, bad, evil*)

good—*n.* boon, benefit, advantage, gain, blessing, mercy, virtue, prosperity, weal, profit, interest, welfare. (*hurt, injury, loss, detriment, evil, disadvantage, ill, calamity, infliction, curse*)

goodly—pleasant, desirable, excellent, fair, comely, considerable, graceful, fine. (*unpleasant, undesirable, uncomely, inconsiderable*)

gorgeous—magnificent, splendid, costly, rich, superb, grand, strong. (*poor, naked, bare, cheap, dingy, threadbare*)

govern—rule, direct, control, moderate, guide, sway, supervise, manage, command, conduct. (*misrule, misdirect, miscontrol*)

grace—favor, beauty, condescension, kindness, elegance, charm, excellence, pardon, mercy. (*disfavor, deformity, unkindness, pride, inelegance, awkwardness, gawkiness*)

gracious—affable, courteous, benignant, kind, civil, condescending, merciful, friendly, tender, gentle, beneficent. (*haughty, discourteous, ill-disposed, ungracious, churlish*)

gradual—slow, continuous, unintermittent, gradational, regular, step by step, progressive. (*sudden, momentary, instantaneous, periodic, recurrent, intermittent, discontinuous, broken, disconnected*)

grand—large, dignified, imposing, important, eventful, magnificent, grandly, majestic, august, exalted, stately, splendid, lofty, elevated, pompous, gorgeous, sublime, superb. (*little, undignified, unimposing, secondary, inferior, unimportant,* *petty, paltry, beggarly, mean, common, insignificant)*

graphic—picturesque, illustrative, descriptive, pictorial, forcible, vivid, feeling, described, picturesquely. (*unpicturesque, unillustrative, undescriptive*)

grateful—pleasant, acceptable, agreeable, thankful, obliged, welcome. (*unpleasant, disagreeable, ungrateful, disobliged*)

gratify—please, satisfy, indulge, humor. (*displease, dissatisfy, disappoint, stint, discipline, inure, harden, deprive, deny*)

gratitude—thankfulness, gratefulness. (*unthankfulness, ingratitude, thanklessness, resentment, indignation*)

grave—sad, serious, momentous, weighty, pressing, sedate, demure, thoughtful, sober, sombre, solemn, important, aggravated, heavy, cogent. (*joyous, merry, facetious, unimportant, ridiculous, trivial, light, frivolous, futile.*)

great—big, wide, huge, numerous, protracted, excellent, large, immense, bulky, majestic, gigantic, vast, grand, sublime, august, eminent, magnanimous, noble, powerful, exalted, noticeable. (*little, narrow, puny, scanty, few, short, mean, ignoble, weak, unimportant*)

greedy—gluttonous, voracious, hungry, desirous, avaricious. (*abstemious, abstinent, indifferent, contented*)

grief—trouble, tribulation, woe, mourning, regret, affliction, sorrow, sadness. (*joy, exultation, delight, elation, hilarity*)

grieve—trouble, burden, annoy, distress, bewail, wound, pain, sorrow, hurt, afflict, mourn, lament, complain, deplore. (*ease, console, soothe, please, rejoice, exult, gratify, alleviate*)

grim—fierce, ferocious, terrible, hideous, ugly, ghastly, sullen, stern. (*mild, docile, attractive, placid, benign*)

groan—moan, whine, growl, grumble. (*giggle, cackle, chuckle, titter, laugh*)

groundless—vain, suppositious, unfounded, baseless, fanciful, gratuitous, chimerical, false. (*well-founded, substantial, authoritative, actual, authentic*)

group—cluster, bunch, knot, assemblage, collocation, class, collection, clump, order, assembly. (*isolation, individual, crowd, confusion, medley*)

grudge—*v.* spare, retain, covet, envy, withhold. (*spend, impart, welcome, satisfy, gratify*)

grudge—*n.* spite, grievance, aversion, rancor, hatred, pique, dissatisfaction, discontent, refusal. (*welcome, satisfaction, approval, contentment, complacency, bestowal, benefaction*)

gruff—rough, surly, bearish, harsh, rude, blunt. (*smooth, mild, affable, courteous*)

guess—conjecture, surmise, divine, suppose, suspect, fancy, imagine. (*examine, prove, investigate, establish, demonstrate, elaborate, deduce*)

guide—lead, direct, conduct, pilot, regulate, superintend, influence, train, manage. (*mislead, misconduct, misdirect, mismanage, misregulate, misguide, miseducate, betray, deceive*)

gush—burst, stream, flow, gush, spout, rush, pour out, flow out. (*drip, drop, dribble, trickle, strain, drain, ooze, filter, percolate*)

H

habit—habituation, custom, familiarity, association, inurement, usage, practice, way, manner. (*dishabituation, inexperience, inconversance, desuetude*)

habitual—regular, ordinary, perpetual, customary, usual, familiar, accustomed, wonted. (*irreg-*

ular, extraordinary, occasional, unusual, exceptional, rare)

half—moiety, bisection, dimidiation. (*integrity, entirety, totality, whole*)

halt—stop, rest, limp, falter, hammer, stammer, demur, dubitate, pause, hold, stand still, hesitate. (*advance, decide, determine, speed, flow, career*)

handsome—comely, good-looking, generous, liberal, beautiful, ample, pretty, graceful, lovely, elegant. (*uncomely, ill-looking, ungenerous, illiberal, unhandsome*)

handy—near, convenient, useful, helpful, manageable, dexterous, ready, expert. (*remote, inconvenient, awkward, useless, cumbrous, unwieldy, unhandy*)

happy—lucky, fortunate, felicitous, successful, delighted, joyous, merry, blithesome, prosperous, glad, blissful. (*unlucky, unfortunate, infelicitous, unsuccessful, sorrowful, sorry, disappointed, dull, lugubrious, desponding, unhappy*)

hard—firm, dense, solid, compact, unyielding, impenetrable, arduous, difficult, grievous, distressing, rigorous, oppressive, exacting, unfeeling, stubborn, harsh, forced, constrained, inexplicable, flinty, severe, cruel, obdurate, hardened, callous. (*soft, fluid, liquid, elastic, brittle, penetrable, easy, mild, lenient, tender, ductile, uninvolved, simple, intelligible, perspicuous*)

hardship—trouble, burden, annoyance, grievance, calamity, infliction, endurance, affliction. (*pleasure, amusement, alleviation, recreation, gratification, relief, assuagement, facilitation, boon, treat*)

hardy—inured, robust, strong, resolute, stouthearted, vigorous, intrepid, brave, manly, valiant. (*weak, uninured, delicate, irresolute, enervated, debilitated, tender, fragile*)

harm—hurt, mischief, injury, detriment, damage, evil, wrong, misfortune, ill, mishap. (*benefit, boon, amelioration, improvement, reparation, compensation, healing, remedy*)

harmonious—congruous, accordant, proportioned, uniform, melodious, musical, dulcet, tuneful, consistent, peaceful, agreeable, amicable, friendly, concordant. (*incongruous, discordant, disproportioned, unshapely, harsh, unmelodious, sharp, grating, unfriendly, riotous, unpeaceful, quarrelsome*)

hasty—speedy, rapid, superficial, hurried, irascible, impetuous, reckless, head-long, crude, incomplete, undeveloped, immature, swift, precipitate, fiery, passionate, slight, quick, excitable, rash, cursory. (*slow, leisurely, careful, close, reflective, developed, matured, complete, elaborate, thoughtful, deliberate*)

hateful—abominable, detestable, vile, odious, heinous, execrable, loathsome, repulsive. (*lovable, lovely, desirable, delightful, attractive, enticing, enjoyable, tempting, pleasant*)

have—own, possess, feel, entertain, accept, bear, enjoy, keep. (*want, need, lose, forego, discard, reject, miss, desiderate, covet, desire*)

hazard—peril, risk, jeopardy, danger, chance, imperil, dare. (*safety, security, protection, warrant, certainty, calculation, law*)

hazy—foggy, nebulous, misty, filmy, gauzy, cloudy, murky, caliginous. (*diaphanous, clear, crystalline, transparent*)

head—top, crown, chief, leader, ruler, mind, source, section, division, topic, gathering, culmination, crisis, leadership, guide, commander, acme, summit. (*tail, bottom, follower, servant, retainer, subordinate, subordination, inferiority, body, bulk, subject, continuation*)

heart—core, nucleus, kernel, interior, center, character, disposition, courage, hardihood, nature, life, feeling, benevolence. (*exterior, hand, action, aspect, manifestation, conduct, deed, timidity*)

hearty—healthy, robust, cordial, sound, warm, honest, earnest, genuine, well, sincere, heartfelt, hale. (*unhealthy, delicate, infirm, cold, insincere*)

heat—warmth, ardor, passion, excitement, fever, ebullition, intensity. (*coolness, indifference, subsidence, calmness, composure, reflection*)

heavy—weighty, ponderous, inert, slow, stupid, dull, impenetrable, stolid, cumbrous, grievous, afflictive, oppressive, burdensome, sluggish, laborious, depressed. (*light, trifling, trivial, agile, active, quick, joyous, alleviative, consolatory, inspiriting, animating, buoyant*)

heighten—exalt, increase, enhance, intensify, color, vivify, aggravate, raise, exaggerate, lift up, amplify. (*lower, depress, diminish, deteriorate, abase, temper, tone, extenuate, modify, qualify*)

heinous—hateful, flagrant, detestable, flagitious, atrocious, odious, abominable, execrable, enormous. (*excellent, laudable, meritorious, praiseworthy, distinguished, justifiable, excusable, palliable*)

help—aid, succor, remedy, prevent, avoid, assist, promote, co-operate, relieve, second. (*oppose, obstruct, aggravate, incur*)

hereditary—inherited, ancestral, lineal. (*conferred, acquired, won*)

hesitate—dubitate, waver, demur, scruple, falter, stammer, pause, doubt. (*decide, determine, run, flow, career*)

hide—conceal, secrete, mask, dissemble, store, protect, disguise, ensconce, screen, cover, burrow. (*expose, discover, exhibit, manifest, betray, strip*)

hideous—frightful, unshapely, monstrous, horrid, horrible, ugly, grisly, grim, ghastly. (*graceful, beautiful, captivating attractive*)

high—elevated, lofty, tall, eminent, excellent, noble, haughty,· violent, proud, exalted. (*depressed, low, stunted, ignoble, mean, base, affable*)

hinder—prevent, interrupt, obstruct, retard, debar, embarrass, impede, thwart, block, stop. (*accelerate, expedite, enable, promote, facilitate*)

hoarse—harsh, grating, husky, raucous, rough, gruff. (*mellifluous, mellow, rich, sweet, melodious*)

hold—keep, grasp, retain, support, restrain, defend, maintain, occupy, possess, sustain, regard, consider, cohere, continue, have. (*drop, abandon, surrender, fail, release, desert, forego, vacate, concede, break, cease*)

hollow—*a.* empty, concave, foolish, weak, faithless, insincere, artificial, unsubstantial, void, flimsy, transparent, senseless vacant, unsound, false. (*full, solid, well-stored, strong, firm, sincere, true, genuine, substantial, sound*)

homely—plain, coarse, uncomely. (*handsome, beautiful, refined, courtly*)

honest—honorable, upright, virtuous, proper, right, sincere, conscientious. (*dishonest, dishonorable, vicious, improper, wrong, insincere*)

honor—respect, reverence, nobility, dignity, eminence, reputation, fame, high-mindedness, spirit, self-respect, renown, grandeur, esteem. (*disrespect, contempt, irreverence, slight, obscurity, degradation, disgrace, abasement, demoralization, cowardice, dishonor, infamy*)

honorary—gratuitous, unofficial, unremunerative, nominal, titular. (*official, remunerative, professional, jurisdictional*)

hope—anticipation, prospect, vision, longing, confidence, desire, expectation, trust. (*despair, despondency, distrust, disbelief, abandonment, abjuration*)

horrible—abominable, detestable, dreadful, fearful, hideous, ghastly, terrific, hateful, direful, horrid, awful, frightful. (*lovely, desirable, enjoyable, attractive, beautiful, fair, pleasant, amiable*)

huge—enormous, monstrous, colossal, vast, bulky, large, great, prodigious, immense, stupendous, gigantic. (*petty, undersized, pigmy, puny*)

humane—benign, kind, tender, merciful, benevolent, compassionate. (*unkind, cruel, unmerciful, inhuman*)

humble—low, lowly, obscure, meek, modest, unassuming, unpretending, submissive. (*high, lofty, eminent, proud, boastful, arrogant, assuming, pretentious*)

humor—disposition, temper, mood, caprice, jocoseness, pleasantry, frame, drollery, fun. (*nature, personality, mind, will, purpose, seriousness*)

hurt—*v.* wound, bruise, harm, injure, damage, pain, grieve. (*heal, soothe, console, repair, reinstate, compensate, benefit*)

hurt—*n.* harm, injury, damage, wound, detriment, mischief. (*benefit, pleasure*)

hurtful—mischievous, injurious, pernicious, baleful, deleterious, baneful, noxious, detrimental, prejudicial. (*helpful, remedial*)

hypocritical—pharisaical, sanctimonious, smug, smooth, mealy, unctuous, mincing. (*plain-spoken, candid, truthful, sincere, genuine, transparent*)

I

idea—image, notion, conception, belief, doctrine, supposition, understanding, fiction, fancy, thought, opinion, impression, sentiment. (*object, form, subject, thing, reality*)

ideal—mental, notional, conception, intellectual, creative, spiritual, poetical, supposititious, fictitious, unreal, imaginary, chimerical, fanciful, imaginative. (*physical, visible, material, tangible, historical, real, actual, palpable, substantial*)

idle—void, unoccupied, waste, vain, empty, unemployed, useless, inactive, lazy, indolent. (*tilled, occupied, populated, filled, employed, assiduous, industrious*)

ignoble—mean, base, dishonorable, humble, plebeian, lowly. (*honorable, noble, eminent, exalted, lordly, grand, notable, illustrious*)

ignominious—shameful, scandalous, dishonorable, infamous. (*honorable, reputable, creditable*)

ignorant—untaught, uneducated, uninformed, unlearned, illiterate, unlettered. (*wise, learned, cultured, cultivated, well-informed*)

illusion—dream, mockery, deception, delusion, hallucination, phantasm, vision, myth, false show, error, fallacy. (*form, reality, body, substance*)

illustrious—renowned, glorious, brilliant, deathless, eminent, distinguished, celebrated, conspicuous, noble, famous. (*ignominious, disgraceful, disreputable, inglorious, infamous*)

ill-will—antipathy, hatred, malevolence, dislike, aversion. (*good-will, beneficence*)

imaginative—creative, conceptive, ideal, poetical, romantic, inventive, original. (*unimaginative, unpoetical, unromantic, prosaic, matter-of-fact, literal, uninventive*)

imagine—conceive, suppose, surmise, understand, fancy, fabricate, deem, presume, think, apprehend. (*represent, exhibit, demonstrate, prove, substantiate, verify, depict*)

imitate—represent, copy, resemble, follow, portray, depict, repeat, pattern after, mock, ape, counterfeit, mimic. (*misrepresent, caricature, alter, vary, dissimilate, differentiate, modify, remodel, distort*)

immediate—proximate, contiguous, present, direct, instant, next. (*distant, remote, future, mediate*)

impair—deteriorate, injure, reduce, damage, enfeeble, vitiate, diminish, lessen. (*enhance, improve, augment, repair*)

impassible—immaterial, immortal. (*passible, mortal*)

impediment—hindrance, obstacle, obstruction, stumbling block. (*aid, aidance, help, assistance, succor, support, furtherance, coadjuvancy*)

imperative—urgent, irresistible, dictatorial, inexorable, peremptorily, compulsory, obligatory. (*indulgent, lenient, mild, entreative, supplicatory, optional, discretional*)

imperious—arrogant, exacting, dictatorial, authoritative, domineering, haughty, lordly. (*yielding, submissive, compliant, docile, ductile, lenient, gentle, mild*)

implement—instrument, utensil, tool, appliance. (*labor, work, science, art, manufacture, agriculture*)

implicate—connect, associate, charge, criminate, involve, entangle, infold, compromise. (*disconnect, dissociate, acquit, extricate*)

imply—involve, mean, indicate, suggest, hint, import, denote, include. (*express, declare, state, pronounce*)

importance—weight, moment, consequence, significance, signification, avail, concern. (*unimportance, insignificance, nothingness, immateriality*)

important—significant, expressive, relevant, main, leading, considerable, great, dignified, influential, weighty, momentous, material, grave, essential. (*insignificant, trivial, inexpressive, ir-*

relevant, inconsiderable, petty, mean, uninfluential, secondary, unimportant, minor)

impotent—weak, powerless, useless, feeble, helpless, nerveless, enfeebled. (*strong, vigorous, powerful, virile*)

impressive—forcible, solemn, affecting, imposing, important. (*weak, unimpressive, feeble, tame, jejune, dry, vapid, unimportant, insignificant*)

improvement—advancement, amendment, progress, increase, correction, proficiency. (*degeneracy, degeneration, deterioration, debasement, retrogradation, retrogression*)

impudent—impertinent, insolent, saucy, shameless, brazen-faced, rude, bold, immodest. (*servile, obsequious, sycophantic, bashful, retiring, diffident, deferential, modest*)

impulse—incentive, push, incitement, force, influence, instigation, feeling, sudden thought, motive. (*rebuff, repulse, premeditation, deliberation*)

inadvertence—inadvertency, oversight, negligence, inattention, carelessness [see **blunder**] (*correction, attention*)

inaudible—low, inarticulate, suppressed, muttering, mumbling, stifled, muffled. (*audible, outspoken, sonorous, articulate, clear, ringing, loud*)

incapable—unqualified, unable, unfitted, weak, incompetent, feeble, disqualified, insufficient. (*qualified, able, fitted, strong, clever*)

incidental—casual, occasional, appertinent, concomitant, concurrent, accidental, fortuitous. (*systematic, regular, independent, disconnected, irrelative, essential, immanent, inherent, uniform, invariable*)

incivility—discourtesy, ill-breeding, ill-manners, uncourteousness. (*civility, urbanity, good manners, politeness*)

inclement—harsh, tyrannical, cruel, unmerciful, severe, stormy, rough, rigorous. (*mild, benign, clement, genial, merciful*)

inclination—leaning, slope, tendency, disposition, proneness, aptness, predilection, bias, bent, attachment, affection, liking, wish. (*inaptitude, inaptness, dislike, disinclination*)

incoherent—unconnected, incongruous, inconsequential, loose. (*coherent, connected*)

incomparable—matchless, unique, consummate, transcendent. (*common, ordinary, average*)

inconsolable—cheerless, joyless, spiritless, melancholy, gloomy, disconsolate, comfortless, forlorn, heartsick, in despair. (*cheerful, hopeful, consolable*)

inconstant—fickle, mutable, variable, fitful, unstable, unsteadfast, changeable. [*see* **capricious** *and* **changeless**]

incontestable—indisputable, unquestionable, unassailable, impregnable. (*dubious, questionable, problematical, supposititious, arbitrary, assumptive, hypothetical*)

inconvenience—incommode, discommode, distrust, molest. (*suit, aid, benefit, subserve, assist, help*)

increase—advance, heighten, dilate, enhance, aggregate, pile up, raise, magnify, spread. (*lessen*)

incredible—surpassing belief, fabulous, marvelous. (*credible, believable*)

inculcate—impress, urge, enforce, infuse, instill, implant, press, teach. (*insinuate, suggest, disavow, abjure, denounce*)

incumbent—pressing, binding, coercive, indispensable, urgent, devolvent, obligatory. (*optional, discretional*)

incurable—irremediable, irredeemable, terminal. (*tractable, removable, remediable*)

indecent—indelicate, immodest, improper.

indelible—indestructible, indefeasible, ineffaceable, persistent, irreversible. (*mutable, evanescent, transient, effaceable*)

indescribable—unaccountable, inexpressible, ineffable, unutterable. (*familiar, ordinary*)

indestructible—imperishable, indiscerptible. (*perishable, destructible, dissoluble*)

indicate—show, evidence, betray, evince, manifest, declare, specify, denote, point out, betoken, designate, mark. (*conceal, contradict, negative, misindicate, misdirect, falsify*)

indifference—triviality, unimportance, insignificance, coolness, carelessness, apathy, insensibility, composure. (*importance, significance, weight, gravity, eagerness, interest, affection, ardor*)

indiscriminate—mixed, confused, medley, promiscuous, ill-assorted, undiscerning, undistinguishing, undiscriminating. (*careful, sorted, select, discerning*)

indispensable—necessary, essential, requisite, needful, expedient. (*unnecessary, unessential, inexpedient, dispensable*)

individual—personal, specific, peculiar, indivisible, identical, singular, idiosyncratic, special, single, separate, particular. (*general, common, collective, plural*)

indivisible—minute, atomic, ultimate. (*divisible, discerptible, separable*)

indorse—sanction, approve, subscribe, accept. (*protest, repudiate, cancel, abjure, renounce*).

induce—produce, cause, prompt, persuade, instigate, impel, actuate, urge, influence, move, prevail on. (*slave, prevent, disincline, dissuade*)

indulge—spoil, pamper, humor, gratify, cherish, bask, revel, grovel, foster, favor, allow. (*thwart, *deny, contradict, disappoint, discard, abjure, counteract, renounce, mortify, discipline)*

indulgent—compliant, tender, tolerant. (*harsh, severe, rough*) [see **submissive**]

industrious—diligent, laborious, busy, assiduous, active, hardworking. (*lazy, shiftless, idle*)

ineffable—inexpressible, inconceivable, insurpassable, indeclarable, indescribable, exquisite, perfect. (*common, trivial, superficial, vulgar, conversational, colloquial, obvious, commonplace*)

ineffectual—fruitless, useless, vain, idle, unavailing, abortive, inoperative, ineffective. (*effective, effectual, successful*)

inexcusable—unmitigated, unpardonable, indefensible, unjustifiable. (*mitigable, pliable, justifiable, vindicable, defensible, pardonable*)

inexhaustible—incessant, unwearied, indefatigable, perennial, illimitable. (*limited, scant, poor*)

inexpedient—undesirable, inadvisable, disadvantageous. (*advisable, profitable, expedient*)

infamy—despair, degradation, disgrace, ignominy, obloquy, extreme vileness, dishonor. (*honor, reputation, celebrity, glory, renown*)

infatuation—fatuity, hallucination, madness, self-deception. (*clear-sightedness, sagacity, wisdom, sanity, soundness*)

inference—deduction, corollary, conclusion, consequence. (*statement, proposition, enunciation*)

inferiority—subordination, minority, poverty, mediocrity, subjection, servitude, depression. (*superiority, majority, excellence, eminence, independence, mastery, exaltation, elevation*)

infidel—skeptic, unbeliever, heretic, freethinker. (*believer, Christian, devotee, pietist*)

inflame—fire, kindle, excite, rouse, fan, incense, madden, infuriate, exasperate, irritate, imbitter, anger, enrage. (*quench, extinguish, allay, cool, pacify, quiet*)

influence—effect, control, causation, affection, impulse, power, credit, character, sway, weight, ascendancy, prestige, authority. (*inefficiency, ineffectiveness, inoperativeness, nullity, neutrality, inefficacy*)

influential—potent, powerful, efficacious, forcible, persuasive, controlling, guiding, considerable. (*weak, ineffective, inoperative, unpersuasive, inconsiderable*)

information—instruction, advice, counsel, notice, notification, knowledge. (*concealment, hiding, occultation, mystification, ignorance*)

infringe—break, violate, transgress, contravene. (*observe, conserve, preserve, keep within bounds*)

ingenious—skillful, adept, clever, inventive, ready, frank, sincere. (*unskillful, slow, uninventive, unready*)

ingenuous—noble, candid, generous, frank, sincere, straightforward, honorable, open, artless, honest. (*mean, reserved, sly, disingenuous, insincere*)

ingredient—element, component, constituent. (*non-ingredient, refuse, residuum, counter-agent, incongruity*)

inherent—innate, congenial, immanent, ingrained, inborn, intrinsic, natural, inbred. (*foreign, ascititious, temporary, separable, extraneous*)

initiative—start, leadership, commencement, example. (*wake, rear, prosecution, termination*)

injunction—mandate, order, command, exhortation, precept. (*disobedience, insubordination, non-compliance, non-observance*)

injurious—hurtful, deleterious, prejudicial, noxious, detrimental, baleful, pernicious, wrongful, mischievous, damaging, baneful. (*helpful, beneficial, advantageous*)

innocence—innocuousness, inoffensiveness, guilelessness, guiltlessness, simplicity, purity, sinlessness. (*hurtfulness, offensiveness, guile, guilt, contamination, corruption, impurity, sinfulness*)

innocuous—inoffensive, harmless, wholesome. (*obnoxious, hurtful, deleterious, insidious*)

inquiry—interrogation, question, asking, investigation, search, examination, research, scrutiny, exploration. (*conjecture, guess, intuition, hypothesis, assumption, supposition*)

insatiable—voracious, unappeasable, omnivorous, ravenous, rapacious, greedy. (*moderate, delicate, fastidious, dainty, squeamish*)

insidious—wily, treacherous, designing, dangerous, deceitful, sly, crafty, artful. (*straightforward, sincere, undesigning, innocuous*)

insinuate—introduce, insert, worm, ingratiate, intimate, suggest, infuse, hint. (*withdraw, retract, alienate, extract*)

insipid—tasteless, vapid, uninteresting, characterless, flavorless, flat, insulse, lifeless, prosy, stupid. (*tasty, sapid, relishing, racy, interesting, engaging*)

insist—stand, demand, maintain, contend, persist, persevere, urge. (*abandon, waive, concede, surrender, yield, forego*)

insolent—haughty, overbearing, contemptuous, abusive, saucy, impertinent, opprobrious, offensive, pert, outrageous, scurrilous, rude.

insolvent—bankrupt, ruined, penniless, beggared. (*flush, flourishing, monied, thriving*)

inspire—animate, inspirit, inflame, imbue, impel, encourage, inhale, enliven, cheer, breathe in, infuse, exhilarate. (*depress, dispirit, discourage, deter*)

instance—entreaty, request, prompting, persuasion, example, solicitation, case, illustration, exemplification, occurrence, point, precedence. (*dissuasion, depreciation, warning, rule, statement, principle, misexemplification*)

instill—pour, infuse, introduce, import, implant, insinuate, inculcate. (*drain, strain, extract, eradicate, eliminate, remove, extirpation*)

instinctive—natural, voluntary, spontaneous, intuitive, impulsive. (*cultivated, forced, reasoning, rationalistic*)

instruction—teaching, education, information, counsel, advice, direction, order, command. (*misteaching, misinformation, misguidance, misdirection, misinstruction, obedience, pupilage*)

insufferable—intolerable, unpermissible, unallowable, unendurable, unbearable. (*tolerable, allowable, endurable, supportable*)

insupportable—unbearable, intolerable, insufferable, unendurable. (*endurable, comfortable, to be borne*)

integrity—uprightness, honor, honesty, probity, truthfulness, candor, single-mindedness, conscientiousness, entireness, rectitude, completeness, parity. (*unfairness, sleight, underhandedness, meanness, chicanery, duplicity, fraud, roguery, rascality*)

intellectual—mental, metaphysical, psychological, inventive, learned, cultured. (*unintellectual, unmetaphysical, unlearned*)

intelligence—understanding, apprehension, comprehension, conception, announcement, report, rumor, tidings, news, information, publication, intellectual capacity, mind, knowledge, advice, notice, instruction, intellect. (*misunderstanding, misinformation, misconception, stupidity, dullness, suppression, ignorance, darkness, concealment, si-*

lence, non-publication, misguidance, misintelligence, misreport, misapprehension)

intensity—tension, force, concentration, strain, attention, eagerness, ardor, energy. (*laxity, debility, relaxation, languor, indifference, coolness, hebetude, diminution*)

intentional—purposed, designed, deliberate, intended, done on purpose, contemplated, premeditated, studied. (*undesigned, casual, unintentional, accidental, fortuitous*)

intercourse—correspondence, dealing, intercommunication, intimacy, connection, commerce. (*reticence, suspension, cessation, disconnection, interception, interpellation*)

interest—concern, business advantage, profit, attention, curiosity, behalf, cause, share. (*unconcern, disconnection, repudiation, disadvantage, loss, inattention, incuriosity, indifference*)

intermediate—intervening, included, interposed, comprised, middle, moderate, interjacent. (*circumjacent, surrounding, enclosing, embracing, outside, extreme, excluded, exclusive*)

interpret—translate, render, construe, explain, expound, expone, represent, declare, understand, elucidate, decipher, solve. (*misinterpret, misunderstand, mistake, misconceive, falsify, distort, misdeclare, misrepresent*)

interrupt—break, disconnect, discontinue, intersect, disturb, stop, hinder. (*continue, prosecute, expedite*)

interval—interim, meantime, period, gap, intermission, interspace, cessation, space between, season. (*continuity, simultaneousness, uninterruptedness*)

intimate—impart, communicate, announce, declare, tell, suggest, hint, insinuate, mention briefly. (*reserve, repress, withhold, conceal*)

intoxication—venom, poison, obfuscation, bewilderment, delirium, hallucination, ravishment, ecstasy, inebriation, drunkenness, inebriety. (*antidote, clarification, sobriety, sanity, ebriety, melancholy, depression*)

intricate—complicated, involved, mazy, labyrinthine, entangled, tortuous. (*simple, uninvolved, plain, direct, obvious*)

introduction—induction, importation, leading, taking, presentation, insertion, commencement, preliminary, preface, initiative, portico, vestibule, entrance, gate, preamble, prelude. (*eduction, extraction, exportation, elimination, ejection, estrangement, conclusion, completion, end, egress*)

introductory—prefatory, initiatory, commendatory, precursory, preliminary, preparatory. (*completive, final, conclusive, alienative, supplemental, terminal, valedictory*)

intuition—instinct, apprehension, recognition, insight. (*information, learning, instruction, elaboration, acquirement, induction, experience*)

invalid—infirm, sick, weakly, frail, feeble. (*strong, vigorous, healthy, well*)

invent—discover, contrive, concoct, imagine, elaborate, conceive, design, devise, fabricate, originate, find out, frame, forge, feign. (*imitate, copy, execute, reproduce*)

invincible—impregnable, immovable, inexpugnable, unsubduable, irresistible, indomitable, unconquerable, insuperable, insurmountable. (*weak, spiritless, powerless, puny, effortless*)

involve—implicate, confound, mingle, envelop, compromise, include, complicate, entangle. (*separate, extricate, disconnect*)

irreligious—undevout, ungodly, godless, profane, impious. (*religious, godly, reverent, reverential, pious, devout*)

irrepressible—unrepressible, ungovernable, uncontrollable, insuppressible, free, unconfined, excitable. (*repressible, governable, controllable, calm, bound down*)

irresponsible—unbound, unencumbered, unaccountable, not answerable, excusable, lawless, arbitrary, despotic. (*responsible, obligatory, binding, imperative, chargeable on, under obligation, lawful, legal, legitimate*)

J

jealous—envious, self-anxious, covetous, invidious, suspicious. (*unenvious, liberal, genial, self-denying, indifferent, unjealous*)

jingle—rhyme, chime, tinkle, tingle. (*euphony, consonance, melody, harmony*)

join—unite, adhere, adjoin, add, couple, connect, associate, annex, append, combine, link, accompany, confederate. (*separate, disjoin, subtract, disconnect*)

jollification—revelry, festivity, conviviality, fun, carnival, merry-making. (*weariness, tediousness, soberness, tedium, monotony*)

jolly—gay, joyful, gladsome, mirthful, genial, jovial, jubilant, robust, lively, plump, merry. (*sad, mournful, joyless, cheerless, unmirthful, lugubrious, morose, gloomy, lean*)

jostle—hustle, push, thrust, jog, jolt, incommode. (*clear, lead, extricate, convoy, escort, precede, pilot, attend*)

joy—gladness, pleasure, delight, happiness, exultation, transport, felicity, ecstasy, rapture, bliss, gaiety, mirth, merriment, festivity, hilarity, charm, blessedness. (*sorrow, pain, trouble, misery, melancholy, grief, affliction, tears, depression, despondency, despair*)

jubilant—joyous, triumphant, festive, congratulatory, exultant. (*doleful, mournful, sorrowful, wailing, penitent, penitential, lugubrious, remorseful*)

judgment—decision, determination, adjudication, sagacity, penetration, judiciousness, sense, intellect, belief, estimation, opinion, verdict, sentence, discernment, discrimination, intelligence, prudence, award, condemnation. (*argument, consideration, inquiry speculation, proposition, investigation, pleading, insagacity, injudiciousness, evidence, pronunciation*)

judicious—wise, sagacious, expedient, sensible, prudent, discreet, well-judged, well-advised, polite, discerning, thoughtful. (*foolish, unwise, silly, imprudent, indiscreet, ill-judged, ill-advised, impolitic, inexpedient, rash, blind, injurious*)

juggle—conjure, cheat, bamboozle, shuffle, trick, beguile, circumvent, swindle, overreach, mystify, mislead. (*expose, correct, enlighten, guide, lead, undeceive, disillusionize, detect*)

just—exact, fitting, true, fair, proportioned, harmonious, honest, reasonable, sound, honorable, normal, impartial, equitable, upright, regular, orderly, lawful, right, righteous, proper. (*inexact, misfitted, disproportioned, ill-proportioned, untrue, inharmonious, unfair, unreasonable, unsound, dishonorable, partial, unequitable, unjust, irregular, abnormal, disorderly*)

justice—equity, impartiality, fairness, right, reasonableness, propriety, uprightness, desert, integrity. (*injustice, wrong, partiality, unfairness, unreasonableness, unlawfulness, inadequateness*)

juvenile—youthful, young, infantine, boyish, girlish, early, immature, adolescent, pubescent, childish, puerile. (*mature, later, manly, womanly, elderly, aged, senile, anile, superannuated, adult*)

K

keen—eager, vehement, sharp, piercing, penetrating, acute, cutting, biting, severe, sarcastic, satirical, ardent, prompt, shrewd. (*indifferent, languid, blunt, dull, blind*)

keep—hold, restrain, retain, detain, guard, preserve, suppress, repress, conceal, tend, support, maintain, conduct, continue, obey, haunt, observe, frequent, celebrate, protect, adhere to, practice, hinder, sustain. (*release, acquit, liberate, send, dismiss, betray, neglect, divulge, discard, abandon, intermit, disobey, disregard, transgress, forsake, desert, obviate*)

kind—*n.* style, character, description, designation, denomination, genus, species, sort, class, nature, set, breed. (*dissimilarity*)

kind—*a.* benevolent, benign, tender, indulgent, humane, clement, lenient, compassionate, gentle, good, gracious, forbearing, kind-hearted. (*unkind, harsh, severe, cruel, hard, illiberal*)

knot—tie, bond, intricacy, difficulty, perplexity, cluster, collection, band, group, protuberance, joint. (*loosening, unfastening, dissolution, solution, explication, unraveling, dispersion, multitude, crowd, indentation, evenness, smoothness, cavity*)

knowing—shrewd, astute, discerning, sharp, acute, sagacious, penetrating, proficient, skillful, intelligent, experienced, well-informed, accomplished. (*simple, dull, innocent, gullible, undiscerning, stolid, silly*)

knowledge—apprehension, comprehension, recognition, understanding, conversance, experience, acquaintance, familiarity, cognizance, notice, information, instruction, learning, enlightenment, scholarship, attainments, acquirements. (*misapprehension, inobservance, incomprehension, misunderstanding, misconception, inconversance, inexperience, ignorance, unfamiliarity, incognizance, misinformation, deception, misinstruction, uneducatedness, untutoredness, rudeness, illiterateness*)

L

laborious—assiduous, diligent, painstaking, indefatigable, arduous, burdensome, toilsome, wearisome, industrious, hard-working, active, difficult, tedious. (*idle, indiligent, lazy, indolent, easy, facile, light, feasible, simple*)

laconic—terse, curt, epigrammatic. (*prolix, wordy, tedious, prosy, garrulous, circumlocutory, loquacious*)

lame—weak, faltering, hobbling, hesitating, ineffective, impotent, crippled, halt, defective, imperfect. (*robust, agile, potent, efficient, satisfactory, cogent, convincing, telling, effective*)

language—speech, talk, conversation, dialect, discourse, tongue, diction, phraseology, articulation, accents, vernacular, expression. (*jargon, jabber, gibberish, babel, gabble, cry, whine, bark, howl, roar, obmutescence, dumbness, muteness, inarticulateness, speechlessness*)

languid—faint, weary, feeble, unnerved, unbraced, pining, drooping, enervated, exhausted, flagging, spiritless. (*strong, healthy, robust, vigorous, active, braced*)

large—big, bulky, extensive, abundant, capacious, ample, liberal, comprehensive, enlightened, catholic, great, vast, wide. (*small, mean, narrow, circumscribed, contracted, scanty, illiberal, niggardly, bigoted, petty, sordid*)

last—*v.* continue, remain, hold, endure, abide, live. (*cease, fail, fade, fly, wane, depart, disappear, terminate*)

last—*a.* latest, ending, final, concluding, hindmost, past, extreme, lowest, remotest, ultimate. (*first, introductory, initiatory, opening, foremost, ensuing, highest, minor, next, nearest*)

laughter—merriment, glee, derision, ridicule, cachinnation, contempt. (*weeping, tears, mourning, sorrow, admiration, veneration, respect, whimper, whine*)

law—rule, edict, regulation, decree, command, order, statute, enactment, mode, method, sequence, principle, code, legislation, adjudication, jurisdiction, jurisprudence. (*misrule, disorder, anarchy, rebellion, insubordination, hazard, chance, irregularity, caprice, casualty, accident*)

lawful—legal, permissible, orderly, right, allowable, fair, constitutional, rightful, legitimate. (*illegal, impermissible, unlawful, wrong, lawless, unfair*)

lay—place, establish, deposit, allay, prostrate, arrange, dispose, put, spread, set down. (*erect, raise, lift, excite, disarrange, disorder, scrape, abrade*)

lead—*v.* conduct, guide, precede, induce, spend, pass, commence, inaugurate, convoy, persuade, direct, influence. (*misconduct, mislead, follow, dissuade, abandon, leave, misguide*)

lead—*n.* priority, pre-eminence, initiative, guidance, control. (*subordination, inferiority, submission*)

lean—*v.* incline, rest, support, tend, bend, depend, hang, repose, confide, slope. (*stabilitate, erect, re-erect, raise, rise, straighten*)

lean—*a.* meagre, lank, tabid, emaciated, shrivelled, bony, thin, scraggy, skinny, slender, scanty. (*fat, brawny, plump, well-conditioned*)

learned—conversant, erudite, read, skilled, scholarly, literary, knowing, well-informed, versed. (*inconversant, illiterate, ignorant, unlearned, unscholarly*)

learning—knowledge, erudition, literature, lore, letters, acquirements, attainments, scholarship, education, tuition, culture. (*ignorance, boorishness, illiterateness, emptiness, sciolism, intuition, revelation, inspiration*)

leave—liberty, permission, license, concession. (*restriction, prohibition, prevention, inhibition, refusal*)

legend—myth, fable, marvelous story, fiction. (*history, fact, actual occurrence*)

lengthy—diffuse, prolix, tedious, long-drawn, verbose. (*concise, compendious, curt, short, brief, laconic, compact, condensed, succinct*)

lesson—precept, warning, instruction, lecture, homily, information. (*misinstruction, misguidance, misinformaticn*)

level—*n.* plane, surface, floor, equality, aim, platform, ground, co-ordinateness, horizontalness. (*unevenness, acclivity, declivity, inequality, inco-ordinateness, verticality*)

level—*v.* plane, smooth, roll, flatten, equalize, raze. (*roughen, furrow, disequalize, graduate*)

level—*a.* horizontal, plain, flat, even, smooth. (*rough, uneven, broken, rolling*)

libel—defamation, detraction, traducement, calumny, slander, defamatory publication, lampoon. (*retraction, vindication, apology, eulogy, panegyric, puff, advocacy, encomium*)

liberal—free, gentle, refined, polished, generous, bountiful, catholic, enlarged, copious, ample, profuse, large, handsome, munificent, abundant, noble-minded, bounteous, tolerant, plentiful. (*churlish, low, mean, boorish, ungenerous, illiberal grasping, niggardly, avaricious, greedy, gainful, narrow-minded, bigoted, prejudiced, contracted, scanty, inadequate*)

liberty—freedom, leave, independence, permission, privilege, license, franchise, immunity, insult, impropriety, volition, voluntariness, exemption. (*slavery, servitude, restraint, constraint, submission, dependence, obligation, compulsion, deference, respect, considerateness, necessity, fatality, predestination*)

licentious—voluptuous, dissolute, rakish, debauched, self-indulgent, lax, profligate, loose, unbridled. (*temperate, strict, sober, self-controlled, ascetic, self-denying, rigid.*)

lie—*n.* falsehood, untruth, fabrication, subterfuge, evasion, fib, fiction, falsity. (*truth, fact, veracity*).

lie—*v.* rest, repose, be, remain. (*rise, move, stir*)

life—vitality, duration, existence, condition, conduct, animation, vivacity, personality, state, society, morals, spirit, activity, history, career. (*mortality, decease, death, non-existence, dullness, torpor, portraiture, lethargy, lifelessness*)

lift—raise, elevate, upraise, upheave, exalt, hoist, elate, erect. (*lower, sink, depress, crush, overwhelm, degrade, dash, cast, hurl*)

light—*n.* luminosity, radiance, beam, gleam, phosphorescence, scintillation, coruscation, flash, brightness, brilliancy, effulgence, splendor, blaze, candle, lamp, lantern, explanation, instruction, illumination, understanding, interpretation, day, life. (*darkness, dimness, obscurity, shade, duskiness, gloom, extinction, misinterpretation, ignorance, misunderstanding, night, death, confusion, mystification, tenebrosity*)

light—*a.* imponderous, portable, unweighty, buoyant, volatile, easy, digestible, scanty, active, unencumbered, empty, slight, gentle, unsteady, capricious, vain, frivolous, characterless, thoughtless, unthoughtful, unconsidered, inadequate, incompact, unsubstantial, inconsiderable, not difficult, bright, whitish, trifling. (*heavy, ponderous, weighty, immovable, leaden, solid, hard, indigestible, full, lazy, encumbered, burdened, oppressed, weighed, loaded, laden, ballasted, grave, serious, important, violent, steady, firm, principled, cautious, reflective, reliable, liable, sensible, earnest, thoughtful, well-considered, adequate, stiff, compact, dark, dark-colored*)

likeness—similarity, resemblance, correspondence, similitude, parity, copy, imitation, portrait, representation, image, effigy, carte de visite, picture. (*dissimilarity, dissimilitude, disparity, inequality, unlikeness, original*)

line—cord, thread, length, outline, row, direction, verse, course, method, succession, sequence, continuity. (*breadth, contents, space, divergency, deviation, fluctuation, variation, interruption, discontinuance, solution*)

liquid—fluid, liquescent, melting, running, watery, fluent, soft, mellifluous, limpid, flowing, clear, smooth. (*solid, solidified, concrete, congealed, hard, dry, indissolvable, insoluble, harsh, discordant*)

listen—hear, attend, hearken, incline, give ear, heed. (*disregard, ignore, refuse, repudiate*)

literal—exact, grammatical, verbal, close, real, positive, actual, plain. (*general, substantial, metaphorical, free, spiritual*)

literary—erudite, scholarly, studious. (*illiterate, unscholarly, unstudious*)

literature—lore, erudition, reading, study, learning, attainment, scholarship, literary works. (*genius, intuition, inspiration*)

little—small, tiny, pigmy, diminutive, short, brief, scanty, unimportant, insignificant, slight, weak, inconsiderable, trivial, illiberal, mean, petty, paltry, dirty, shabby, dwarf. (*big, bulky, large, enormous, huge, monstrous, full-sized, long, full, developed, much, important, grave, serious, momentous, liberal, generous, noble, high-minded, handsome*)

live—*v.* vegetate, grow, survive, continue, abide, dwell, last, subsist, behave, act, breathe, exist. (*die, perish, wither, demise, migrate, vanish, fade, fail, languish, depart, drop, decrease*)

live—*a.* animate. (*inanimate, defunct*)

load—*n.* weight, lading, cargo, oppression, incubus, drag, burden. (*refreshment, support, solace, alleviation, emptiness, lightness*)

load—*v.* burden, charge, lade, cargo, cumber, oppress. (*disburden, unload, disencumber, lighten, alleviate, believe*)

loan—advance, mortgage, hypothecation. (*recall, resumption, foreclosure*)

locate—place, establish, settle, fix, dispose, lodge. (*displace, disestablish, dislodge, remove*)

lofty—elevated, towering, high, dignified, eminent, stately, haughty, majestic, airy, tall. (*depressed, low, stunted, undignified, ordinary, unstately, mean, unimposing, unassuming, affable*)

logical—close, argumentative, sound. (*inconclusive, illogical, fallacious*)

lonesome—forlorn, dreary, forsaken, wild, solitary, desolate, lonely. (*cheerful, befriended, festive, frequented, populous, gay, animated, bustling*)

long—protracted, produced, dilatory, lengthy, tedious, prolix, extensive, diffuse, far-reaching. (*short, curt, curtailed, brief, speedy, quick, concise, condensed*)

loose—*v.* untie, unfasten, let go. (*tie, fasten, hold, retain*)

loose—*a.* unbound, detached, flowing, scattered, sparse, incompact, vague, inexact, rambling, dissoluted, licentious. (*bound, tied, fastened, tight, moored, lashed, secured, thick, close, dense, compact, pointed, accurate, exact, consecutive, strict, logical, scientific, conscientious*)

lose—miss, drop, mislay, forfeit. (*keep, retain, find, recover, locate, earn, guard, treasure, economize, utilize, preserve, abandon, discard, reject*)

loss—mislaying, dropping, forfeiture, missing, privation, waste, detriment, damage. (*preservation, recovery, earning, satisfaction, restoration, economy, augmentation, advantage, gain*)

lot—chance, fortune, fate, hazard, ballot, doom. (*law, provision, arrangement, disposal, design, purpose, plan, portion, allotment*)

loud—sounding, sonorous, resonant, noisy, audible, vociferous, clamorous, obstreperous. (*soft, gentle, subdued, whispering, rustling, murmuring, babbling, pattering, tinkling, dulcet, inaudible, quiet*)

love—affection, attachment, passion, devotion, benevolence, charity, kindness. (*hatred, dislike, disaffection, alienation, estrangement, bitterness,* *coldness, indifference, repugnance, infidelity, desertion, unkindness, malice, uncharitableness)*

lovely—amiable, lovable, enchanting, beautiful, pleasing, delightful, charming. (*unamiable, unlovable, hateful, hideous, plain, homely, unattractive, unlovely)*

lover—suitor, wooer, sweetheart, swain, beau. (*husband, wife, mate)*

low—abated, sunk, depressed, stunted, declining, deep, subsided, inaudible, cheap, gentle, dejected, degraded, mean, abject, base, unworthy, lowly, feeble, moderate, frugal, repressed, subdued, reduced, poor, humble. (*elevated, lofty, tall, ascending, rising, high, exorbitant, violent, loud, excited, elated, eminent, considerable, influential, highminded, honorable, proud, strong, aggravated, intensified, raised, wealthy, rich)*

lower—*v.* depress, decrease, reduce, bate, abate, drop, humiliate, sink, debase, humble, diminish. (*hoist, raise, heighten, exalt, increase, aggrandize, elevate)*

lower—*a.* inferior. (*higher, superior)*

loyal—submissive, obedient, faithful, allegiant, true, constant. (*insubmissive, insurgent, malcontent, rebellious, disobedient, unfaithful, unallegiant, untrue, inconstant, disaffected)*

lucky—fortunate, auspicious, prosperous, successful, favorable. (*unlucky, unfortunate, inauspicious, unprosperous, adverse, ill-fated, disastrous, luckless)*

ludicrous—ridiculous, farcical, laughable, comic, droll, funny, comical. (*serious, momentous, grave, sad, sorrowful, mournful, tragic, lugubrious, melancholy, sombre, doleful)*

lunatic—madman, maniac, monomaniac. (*solon, philosopher, luminary, genius)*

lurid—murky, lowering, wan, dismal, gloomy. (*bright, luminous)*

luscious—sweet, delicious, sugary, honied, delightful, toothsome, delightsome. (*sour, sharp, tart, bitter)*

luxurious—voluptuous, self-indulgent, pleasurable, sensual, pampered. (*hard, painful, self-denying, ascetic, hardy*)

luxury—effeminacy, epicurism, voluptuousness, wantonness, self-indulgence, softness, animalism, delicacy, dainty, profuseness. (*hardness, asceticism, stoicism, self-denial, hardship*)

lying—mendacious, false, untrue, untruthful. (*true, veracious*)

M

mad—insane, demented, furious, lunatic, infuriated, crazy, maniacal, frantic, rabid, wild, distracted. (*sane, sound, sensible, quiet, composed, unexcited, sober*)

madden—infuriate, enrage, exasperate, inflame. (*calm, pacify, assuage, mesmerize, lay*)

magnanimous—noble, high-minded, exalted, high-souled, great-souled, lofty, honorable. (*mean, little-souled*)

magnificent—grand, magnanimous, noble, splendid, superb, august, imposing, gorgeous, stately, majestic, dignified, sublime, pompous. (*petty, mean, little, paltry, flat, beggarly, small minded, ordinary, tawdry, unimposing, tame*)

maid—maiden, girl, damsel, lass, virgin. (*matron, married woman*)

main—bulk, majority, body, principal, trunk, chief, leading, most important, first. (*portion, section, minority, branch, limb, tributary, member, subordinate, inferior*)

majority—superiority, elder-ship, priority, bulk, preponderance, seniority. (*inferiority, juniority, minority*)

make—create, produce, fashion, frame, fabricate, construct, effect, do, perform, execute, find, gain, compel, establish, constitute, reach, mould, shape, form, bring about. (*annihilate, unmake, undo, dismember, disintegrate, destroy, defeat, miss, lose, mar, disestablish*)

manage—handle, manipulate, control, conduct, administer, mould, regulate, contrive, train, husband, direct, wield. (*mismanage, misconduct, upset, derange, misuse*)

manageable—easy, feasible, possible, docile, tractable, practicable. (*difficult, impracticable, impossible, unmanageable, intractable, refractory, untamable*)

management—treatment, conduct, administration, government, address, skill, superintendence, skillful treatment. (*maltreatment, misconduct, maladministration, misgovernment, maladroitness*)

manifest—visible, obvious, distinct, conspicuous, indubitable, clear, evident, plain, patent, apparent, open. (*invisible, dubious, inconspicuous, indistinct*)

manly—bold, courageous, generous, open, chivalrous, frank, firm, noble, stately, fine, mature, masculine, brave, fearless, hardy, vigorous, manlike, manful, dignified. (*womanish, childish, timid, unmanly, dastardly, weak, puny, ungrown, boyish*)

manner—mode, method, style, form, fashion, carriage, behavior, deportment, habit, sort, kind. (*work, project, design, performance, life, action, proceeding, appearance, being*)

manners—deportment, behavior, carriage, courtesy, politeness, intercourse, demeanor. (*misdemeanor, misbehavior, unmannerliness*)

manufacture—make, production, fabrication, composition, construction, manipulation, molding. (*use, employment, consumption, wear*)

many—numerous, abundant, frequent, manifold, divers, sundry, multifarious. (*few, scarce, rare, infrequent*)

mark—*n.* trace, token, sign, symptom, impression, vestige, indication, note. (*erasure, obliteration, effacement, unindicativeness, plainness*)

mark—*v.* stamp, label, sign, indicate, decorate, brand, stigmatize, signalize, note, observe, regard, heed, specify, specialize. (*ignore, overlook, omit,*

*mislabel, mismark, misindicate, misobserve, mis-
specify*)

martial—military, brave, warlike. (*unmartial,
unmilitary, peaceful*)

marvel—wonder, prodigy, admiration, portent,
miracle, astonishment, amazement, phenomenon.
(*incuriosity, unconcern, joke, trifle, farce, bagatelle,
moonshine, cipher, drug, imposture, juggle*)

masculine—male, manly, manful, hardy, courageous, virile. (*female, feminine, womanish, womanly, effeminate*)

mask—*n.* pretext, screen, pretense, ruse, cover,
hypocrisy. (*truth, nakedness, detection, exposure,
unmasking, verity, openness, candor*)

mask—*v.* hide, screen, blink, cloak, disguise.
(*expose, unmask, detect*)

master—*n.* lord, ruler, governor, owner, pos-
sessor, proprietor, teacher, professor, adept, chief.
(*servant, slave, subject, property, learner, pupil, tyro*)

master—*v.* conquer, overcome, subdue, overpower. (*yield, fail, surrender, succumb*)

masterly—finished, artistic, consummate, skillful, clear, dexterous, expert. (*clumsy, rude, bungling, unskilled, botchy, maladroit*)

match—*n.* equal, mate, companion, contest, competition, tally, equality, pair. (*superior, inferior,
mismatched, oddity, disparity, inequality*)

match—*v.* equal, compare, oppose, pit, adapt,
sort, suit, mate. (*fail, exceed, predominate, surpass, mismatch, dissociate, separate, misfit, misadapt, missort*)

matchless—consummate, incomparable, peer-
less, surpassing, inimitable. (*common, ordinary,
every-day, commonplace*)

matter—substance, stuff, subject, body, importance, (or, prefixing the definite article) the visible,
tangible, substantial, corporal, physical, ponder-
able. (*immateriality, spirituality, mind, intellect,*

spirit, *the invisible, unseen, spiritual, moral, mental, intellectual*)

meager—thin, lean, lank, scanty, barren, dry, tame. (*stout, fat, brawny, abundant, fertile, copious*)

mean—*a.* common, low, base, spiritless, dishonorable, contemptible, despicable, beggarly, sordid, vulgar, niggardly, vile, middle, intermediate, average. (*high, exalted, eminent, spirited, honorable, lordly, princely, munificent, liberal, generous, extreme, excessive, exorbitant*)

mean—*n.* medium, moderation, balance, average. (*extreme, excess, preponderance, disproportion, deficiency, shortcoming, inadequacy*)

mean—*v.* intend, purpose, design, signify, denote, indicate, hint, suggest. (*say, state, enunciate, do, execute, perform*)

meanness—penuriousness, littleness, selfishness, baseness, smallness, illiberality, ungenerousness, sordidness. (*nobleness, unselfishness, liberality, generousness, large-heartedness*)

means—resources, instrument, media. (*end, purpose, object*)

mechanical—habitual, automatic, unreflective, spontaneous, effortless, unimpassioned. (*labored, self-conscious, feeling, forced, spirited, appreciative, lifelike, lively, animated, impassioned*)

meddlesome—officious, obtrusive, intrusive, interfering. (*unofficious, inobtrusive, unmeddlesome*)

mediocrity—mean, commonplace, medium, average, sufficiency. (*excellence, superiority, rarity, brilliance, distinction*)

meek—mild, gentle, submissive, modest, yielding, unassuming. (*bold, arrogant, self-asserting, irritable, proud, high-spirited*)

melancholy—gloomy, sad, dejected, disconsolate, dismal, moody, hypochondriacal, cast down. (*lively, sprightly, gladsome, gleesome, blithesome, happy, cheerful, gamesome, mirthful, merry*)

mellow—ripe, rich, full-flavored, jovial, mature, soft. (*unripe, harsh, sour, acid, acrid, crabbed, sober, dry*)

memorable—great, striking, remarkable, conspicuous, prominent, noticeable, illustrious, extraordinary, famous, distinguished. (*petty, trifling, ordinary, insignificant, unnoticeable, trivial, mediocre, slight*)

memory—remembrance, reminiscence, perpetuation, recollection, retention, retrospect, fame. (*forgetfulness, oblivion*)

mend—repair, restore, correct, promote, improve, rectify, reform, amend, ameliorate, better. (*damage, impair, pervert, retard, deteriorate, falsify, spoil, corrupt*)

menial—domestic, attendant, dependent, servile, drudge. (*paramount, sovereign, supreme, lordly, independent, uncontrolled, autocratic*)

mental—intellectual, subjective, metaphysical, psychical, psychological. (*corporal, objective, physical, bodily*)

mention—declaration, notice, announcement, observation, remark, hint, communication. (*silence, suppression, forgetfulness, omission*)

mercantile—commercial, interchangeable, wholesale, retail, marketable. (*stagnant, unmarketable, unmercantile*)

merchant—trader, dealer, importer, tradesman, trafficker. (*shopman, salesman, hawker, huckster, peddler, chandler, costermonger*)

merciful—compassionate, kind-hearted, clement, gracious, kind. (*pitiless, unrelenting, remorseless, inexorable*)

mere—pure, unmixed, absolute, uninfluenced, unadulterated, unaffected, simple. (*mixed, compound, impure, biased*)

merit—goodness, worth, worthiness, desert, excellence. (*badness, demerit, unworthiness, worth-*

lessness, weakness, imperfection, error, defect, fault, failing)

meteoric—momentary, flashing, displosive, phosphorescent, pyrotechnic, coruscant, volcanic. (*Permanent, beaming, burning, steady, persistent, enduring*)

method—order, system, rule, way, manner, mode, course, process, regularity, arrangement. (*disorder, conjecture, quackery, empiricism, experimentation, assumption, guess-work*)

methodical—methodic, orderly, systematical, systematic, regular. (*disorderly, unmethodical, unsystematical, irregular*)

middling—ordinary, average, pretty well, not bad, well enough.

midst—middle, centre, thick, throng, heart. (*outskirt, confine, edge, limit, extreme, purlieu, margin*)

might—strength, force, power, ability. (*weakness, infirmity, feebleness*)

mild—moderate, lenient, calm, gentle, genial, tempered, soft, meek, tender, placid. (*violent, wild, fierce, savage, strong, severe, merciless, harsh, bitter*)

mind—soul, spirit, intellect, understanding, opinion, sentiment, judgment, belief, choice, inclination, desire, will, liking, purpose, spirit, impetus, memory, remembrance, recollection. (*body, limbs, organization, action, proceeding, conduct, object, indifference, coolness, aversion, forgetfulness, obviousness*)

mindful—regardful, attentive, thoughtful, careful, recollective. (*regardless, inattentive, mindless, oblivious*)

mingle—mix, compound, blend, confound, confuse, intermingle, associate, amalgamate. (*separate, segregate, sift, sort, analyze, discompound, eliminate, classify, unravel, avoid*)

minister—servant, officer, delegate, official, ambassador, subordinate, ecclesiastic, clergyman, priest, parson, divine, preacher, pastor, shepherd, reverend, curate, vicar. (*monarch, government, master, superior, principal, head, layman, fold, flock, congregation*)

minute—diminutive, microscopic, tiny, exact, searching, specific, detailed. (*monstrous, enormous, huge, inexact, superficial, general, broad, comprehensive*)

mischief—damage, hurt, detriment, disservice, annoyance, injury, ill-turn, damage, harm. (*compensation, good-turn, benefit, favor, gratification*)

mischievous—detrimental, injurious, spiteful, wanton. (*beneficial, advantageous, reparatory, conservative, careful, protective*)

miser—niggard, churl, skinflint, curmudgeon, screw, scrimp, hunks. (*prodigal, spendthrift, rake*)

miserable—abject, forlorn, pitiable, wretched, worthless, despicable, disconsolate. (*respectable, worthy, happy, contented, comfortable*)

misery—wretchedness, heartache, woe, unhappiness. (*happiness, glee*)

mock—jeer, ridicule, flout, mimic, insult, ape, deride, deceive, imitate. (*salute, welcome, respect, admire, compliment*)

model—standard, pattern, example, type, mold, design, kind. (*imitation, copy, production, execution, work*)

moderate—*v.* control, soften, allay, regulate, repress, govern, temper. (*disturb, disorganize, excite, misconduct*)

moderate—*a.* limited, temperate, calm, dispassionate, sober, abstinent, sparing, steady, ordinary. (*extravagant, intemperate, rigorous, excessive, violent, extraordinary*)

modern—present, existent, new, new-fangled, new-fashioned, recent, late, novel, later. (*past, bygone, former, olden, ancient, old-fashioned, antiquated, obsolete*)

modesty—sobriety, diffidence, bashfulness, humility, pure-mindedness. (*vanity, conceit, self-*

sufficiency, self-admiration, foppery, coxcombry, wantonness, shamelessness, effrontery)

moment—instant, second, importance, twinkling, trice, weight, force, gravity, consequence, avail. *(age, period, century, generation, triviality, insignificance, worthlessness, unimportance, inefficacy)*

monopoly—privilege, engrossment, appropriation, exclusiveness, preoccupancy, impropriation. *(participation, partnership, community, competition, free-trade)*

monotonous—uniform, unvaried, dull, humdrum, undiversified, tedious. *(varying, changing)*

monstrous—prodigious, portentous, marvelous, deformed, abnormal, hideous, preposterous, intolerable. *(ordinary, familiar, unnoticeable, fair, comely, shapely, regular, natural, reasonable, just)*

moral—mental, ideal, intellectual, spiritual, ethical, probable, inferential, presumptive, analogous, virtuous, well-conducted. *(physical, material, practical, demonstrative, mathematical, immoral, vicious)*

mortal—human, ephemeral, sublunary, short-lived, deadly, fatal, perishable, destructive. *(divine, immortal, celestial, life-giving, venial, salutiferous superficial)*

motive—inducement, purpose, design, prompting, stimulus, reason, impulse, incitement. *(execution, action, effort, deed, attempt, project, preventive, deterrent, dissuasive)*

move—change, go, progress, stir, affect, agitate, actuate, impel, propose, advance, propel, instigate, provoke. *(stand, stop, lie, rest, stay, allay, deter, prevent, arrest, withdraw)*

movement—motion, move, change of place. *(stop, rest, pause, stillness, quietness)*

much—abundant, plenteous, greatly, abundantly, far, considerable, ample. *(little, scant, slightly, shortly, short, near.)*

muddle—fail, waste, fritter away, confuse, derange, misarrange. *(clarify, manage, economize, classify, arrange)*

muggy—foggy, misty, dank, damp, murky, dim, vaporous, cloudy. (*clear, bright, vaporless*)

multitude—crowd, swarm, accumulation, throng concourse, number, host, mob, rabble. (*paucity, scantiness, sprinkling*)

munificent—liberal, princely, bounteous, generous. (*niggardly, beggarly*)

murmur—undertone, whisper, mutter, grumble, complaint, repining. (*clamor, vociferation, bawling, outcry, defiance, execration, salutation, acclamation*)

muscular—powerful, brawny, robust, sinewy, strong, stalwart, athletic, lusty, sturdy. (*debile, flabby, feeble, lanky*)

musical—melodious, harmonious, dulcet, concordant, rythmical, tuneful, mellifluous. (*unmelodious, inharmonious, harsh, discordant.*)

musty—fusty, rank, mouldy, frowzy, stale, sour, fetid, mildewed. (*fragrant, fresh, balmy, aromatic, odorous*)

mutter—murmur, mumble. (*enunciate, exclaim, pronounce, vociferate*)

mysterious—dim, obscure, unrevealed, unexplained, unaccountable, reserved, veiled, hidden, secret, incomprehensible, mystic, inexplicable. (*clear, plain, obvious, explained, understood, easy, explainable, simple, frank, communicative*)

mystery—enigma, puzzle, obscurity, secrecy, veil, shroud, arcanum. (*publication, solution, commonplace, truism, matter-of-fact*)

mystify—confuse, bamboozle, hoodwink, puzzle, confound, mislead, obfuscate. (*illumine, enlighten, inform, guide*)

N

naked—nude, bare, unclothed, denuded, undraped, defenseless, destitute, unqualified, uncolored, unvarnished, mere, simple. (*dressed, robed, draped, muffled, protected, qualified, veiled, shrouded, colored, varnished*)

name—*n.* designation, cognomenation, appelation, title, fame, reputation, authority, appointment, stead, representation. (*namelessness, anonymousness, misnomer, pseudonym, obscurity, ingloriousness, disrepute, individuality, person*)

name—*v.* specify, designate, call, indicate. (*misname, miscall, misdesignate, misindicate, hint, suggest, shadow, adumbrate*)

narrow—straight, straightened, slender, thin, spare, contracted, limited, cramped, pinched, scant, close, scrutinizing, near, bigoted, niggardly, tight. (*wide, broad, ample, thick, expanded, easy, liberal*)

nasty—foul, offensive, odious, disagreeable, indelicate, impure, gross, unclean, obscene. (*nice, pleasant, sweet, savory, agreeable, pure*)

natural—intrinsic, essential, regular, normal, cosmical, true, probable, consistent, spontaneous, artless, original. (*ascititious, adventitious, abnormal, monstrous, unnatural, fictitious, improbable, unsupposable, forced, artful, affected*)

nature—essence, creation, constitution, structure, disposition, truth, regularity, kind, sort, character, species, affection, naturalness. (*thing, object, subject, man, being, creature, monstrosity, unnaturalness, art, fiction, romance, invention*)

near—nigh, close, adjacent, neighboring. (*sometimes used in the sense of parsimonious*) (*far, distant, remote*)

necessary—certain, inevitable, indispensable, requisite, essential, compulsory, needful, expedient. (*contingent, casual, optional, discretional, unnecessary, unessential, free*)

necessity—indispensableness, inevitableness, need, indigence, requirement, want, fate, destiny. (*dispensableness, uncertainty, superfluity, uselessness, competence, affluence, casualty, contingency, freedom, choice*)

neglect—slight, overlook, omit, disregard, disesteem, despise, contemn. (*consider, respect, notice, observe, regard, esteem, tend, attend, foster, study*)

neglect—negligence, disregard, omission, failure, default, slight, carelessness, remissness. (*attention, consideration, respect, notice, regard, esteem*)

nerve—strength, firmness, resolution. (*nerveless, forceless, feeble, weak, enfeebled, impotent, palsied*)

new—novel, recent, fresh, modern. (*old, ancient, antique, antiquated, obsolete*)

nice—fastidious, scrupulous, accurate, neat, discerning, dainty, pleasant, agreeable, exact, fine, finished, particular. (*coarse, unscrupulous, inaccurate, rude, rough, undiscriminating, nasty, nauseous, disagreeable*)

nobility—distinction, dignity, rank, peerage, lordship, loftiness, generosity, rank, aristocracy. (*obscurity, meanness, commonalty, serfdom, paltriness, contemptibleness, plebeianism*)

noble—grand, aristocratic, generous, illustrious, exalted, worthy, magnanimous, dignified, excellent, lofty-minded, honorable, fine. (*mean, plebeian, ignoble, paltry*)

noisome—hurtful, harmful, nocuous, pestilential. (*wholesome, salutary, salubrious, beneficial*)

noisy—loud, clamorous, stunning. (*still, soft, inaudible, whispering, soothing, musical, melodious, harmonious, tuneful, subdued, gentle, noiseless*)

nominal—trifling, supposititious, ostensible, professed, pretended, formal. (*real, deep, serious, important, grave, substantial, actual, intrinsic, veritable, essential*)

nonsense—absurdity, trash, folly, pretense, jest, balderdash. (*sense, wisdom, truth, fact, gravity, philosophy, science, reason*)

notice—observation, cognizance, heed, advice, news, consideration, visitation, mark, note. (*oversight, disregard, misinformation, mistidings, neglect,*

slight, connivance, ignorance, incognizance, heedless-
ness, amnesty, omission)

notion—apprehension, idea, conception, judgment, opinion, belief, expectation, sentiment.
(*misapprehension, falsification, misbelief, misjudg-*
ment, frustration, misconception)

notorious—known, undisputed, recognized, allowed. (*suspected, reported, reputed*)

nuisance—offense, annoyance, plague, pest,
trouble. (*gratification, blessing, pleasure, delight,*
benefit)

O

obedience—submission, compliance, subservience. (*resistance, rebellion, violation, transgression,*
antagonism, disobedience)

obesity—fatness, fleshiness, corpulence, plump-
ness, corpulency, *embonpoint*. (*leanness, thinness*)

obey—submit, comply, yield. (*resist, disobey,*
refuse)

object—appearance, sight, design, end, aim,
motive, intent, view, goal. (*idea, notion, concep-*
tion, fancy, subject, proposal, purpose, effect)

object to—oppose, contravene, obstruct, demur
to, except to, gainsay, disapprove. (*approve, ap-*
prove of)

oblige—compel, coerce, necessitate, force, benefit,
favor, accommodate, gratify, bind, constrain. (*re-*
lease, acquit, induce, persuade, annoy, disoblige)

obliging—kind, considerate, compliant, complaisant, accommodating. (*discourteous, rude, cross-*
grained, perverse, unaccommodating, disobliging)

obscene—impure, immodest, indecent, lewd,
foul, indelicate, filthy, disgusting, foul-mouthed.
(*pure, modest, decent*)

obscure—dark, dim, lowering, indistinct, enigmatical, uncertain, doubtful, unascertained, humble, unintelligible, mean. (*bright, luminous, dis-*
tinct, lucid, plain, plain spoken, intelligible, unam-
biguous, ascertained, eminent, prominent)

observance—attention, fulfilment, respect, celebration, performance, ceremony, custom, form, rule, practice. (*inobservance, inattention, breach, disrespect, disregard, desuetude, disuse, non-performance, informality, unceremoniousness, omission*)

observant—regardful, attentive, mindful, obedient, watchful, heedful. (*disregardful, neglectful, unmindful, disobedient, heedless*)

observation—contemplation, study, remark, attention, notice, comment. (*disregard, oversight, inadvertence, inattention, silence, ignorance*)

obstacle—impediment, obstruction, hindrance, objection, bar, difficulty, check. (*course, proceeding, career, advancement*)

obstinate—headstrong, stubborn, refractory, self-willed, pertinacious, obdurate, perverse, intractable. (*amenable, complaisant, yielding, docile, ductile, characterless, irresolute, wavering*)

obvious—plain, self-evident, manifest, explicit, apparent, open, patent. (*remote, obscure, far-fetched, involved, latent*)

occasion—conjuncture, opportunity, occurrence, cause, need, event, reason, necessity, opening, ground. (*untimeliness, unseasonableness, frustration*)

occult—latent, hidden, unrevealed, mysterious, secret, dark, unknown. (*developed, plain, patent, clear, familiar, exposed, open*)

occupation—employment, avocation, possession, usurpation, encroachment, tenure, calling, pursuit, trade, business, holding. (*idleness, vacancy, leisure, abandonment, vacation, resignation*)

odd—alone, sole, unmatched, remaining, over, fragmentary, uneven, singular, peculiar, queer, quaint, fantastical, uncommon, nondescript. (*aggregate, consociate, matched, balanced, squared, integrant, even, common, usual, regular, normal*)

odious—hateful, offensive, detestable, abominable, hated. (*delectable, grateful, acceptable, pleasant*)

offense—attack, sin, crime, umbrage, transgression, misdeed, injury, wrong, affront, outrage, insult, trespass, indignity, misdemeanor. (*defense, innocence, guiltlessness*)

offensive—aggressive, obnoxious, distasteful, displeasing, foul, fetid, unsavory. (*defensive, grateful, pleasant, savory*)

offer—propose, exhibit, proffer, present, tender, extend, adduce, volunteer. (*withhold, withdraw, retract, retain, alienate, divert*)

office—service, duty, appointment, function, employment, station, business, post. (*leisure, vacancy, resignation, sinecure*)

officious—meddling, interfering, pushing, forward, intrusive, intermeddling. (*backward, negligent, remiss, unofficious, retiring, modest, backward*)

often—frequently, repeatedly. (*infrequently, seldom*)

old—aged, pristine, long-standing, ancient, preceding, antiquated, obsolete, senile, antique. (*youthful, young, recent, fresh, modern, subsequent, new-fashioned, current*)

ominous—portentous, suggestive, threatening, foreboding, premonitory, unpropitious. (*auspicious, propitious, encouraging*)

open—*v.* unclose, lay open, lay bare, expose, explain, disclose, initiate, begin, commence. (*close, shut up, conceal, inclose, mystify, misinterpret, conclude, cover*)

open—*a.* accessible, free, available, unshut, unfolded, public, free, unrestricted, unreserved, unaffected, genuine, barefaced, undisguised, aboveboard, liberal, unclosed, candid, frank, ingenuous, unsettled, undetermined. (*inaccessible, closed, barred, unavailable, shut, close, secretive, reserved, settled, determined*)

opening—aperture, gap, opportunity, space, commencement, initiation, start, inauguration, hole, fissure, chink, beginning. (*occlusion, obstruction,*

stop-gap, unreasonableness, contretemps, inopportuneness, enclosure, termination, close, end, conclusion)

operation—agency, action, exercise, production,
influence, performance. (*cessation, inaction, rest,
inoperativeness, inefficacy, inefficiency, misoperation*)

opinion—conviction, view, judgment, notion,
idea, impression, estimation, theory.

opportunity—occasion, turn, opening, convenience. (*inopportuneness, unseasonableness, lapse,
omission, contretemps*)

opposition—resistance, hostility, obstacle, obstruction

opposite—facing, adverse, repugnant, inconsistent, irreconcilable, contrary, antagonistic,
counter, contradictory. (*agreeing, coincident, consentaneous*)

oppressive—heavy, overpowering, unjust, gall-
ing, extortionate, grinding. (*light, just, compassionate*)

order—*n.* arrangement, condition, sequence,
direction, rank, grade, class, decree, succession,
series, method, injunction, precept, command.

order—*v.* arrange, dispose, regulate, adjust, direct, command, classify, ordain, enjoin, prescribe,
appoint, manage. (*disarrangement, confusion, un-
settlement, inversion, execution, disorder*)

ordinary—settled, wonted, conventional, plain,
inferior, commonplace, humdrum, matter of fact.
(*extraordinary, unusual, uncommon, superior*)

organization—structure, form, construction.
(*disorganization*)

origin—source, commencement, spring, cause,
derivation, rise, beginning. (*termination, conclusion, extinction*)

original—primary, initiatory, primordial, peculiar, pristine, ancient, former, first. (*subsequent, terminal, modern, later, derivative*)

oust—eject, dispossess, deprive, evict, eject, dislodge, remove. (*install, reinstate, readmit, restore*)

outcast—castaway, reprobate, vagrant, vagabond, exile

outlandish—strange, queer, grotesque, foreign, rustic, barbarous, rude. (*fashionable, modish, native*)

outline—delineation, sketch, contour, draft, plan. (*form, substance, figure, object, subject, field, ground, bulk, space*)

outrage—outbreak, offense, wantonness, mischief, abuse, ebullition, violence, indignity, affront, insult. (*moderation, self-control, self-restraint, subsidence, coolness, calmness*)

outrageous—excessive, unwarrantable, unjustifiable, wanton, flagrant, nefarious, atrocious, violent. (*moderate, justifiable, reasonable*)

outset—opening, start, commencement, exordium, beginning, inauguration, preface. (*close, termination, conclusion, peroration*)

outward—external, apparent, visible, sensible, superficial, ostensible, forthcoming, extrinsic, extraneous. (*internal, intrinsic, withdrawn, inapparent, inward*)

overcome—vanquish, conquer, surmount, exhaust, defeat.

overflow—redundancy, exuberance, superabundance, deluge, inundation. (*deficiency, exhaustion, subsidence*)

overlook—condone, connive, disregard, oversee, supervise, inspect, survey, review, excuse, pardon, forgive, neglect. (*visit, scrutinize, investigate, mark*)

oversight—error, omission, mistake, neglect, slip, inadvertence, inspection, superintendence. (*scrutiny, correction, emendation, attention, mark, notice*)

overthrow—destroy, subvert, upset, overturn, ruin, demolish, defeat, rout, overcome, discomfit, invert, overset, reverse. (*restore, reinstate, construct, regenerate, redintegrate, revive, re-edify*)

overwhelm—crush, quell, extinguish, drown, subdue, swamp. (*raise, reinvigorate, reinstate, reestablish, rescue, extricate*)

owing—due, imputable, ascribable, attributable. (*casually, perchance, by chance, by accident*)

own—possess, hold, have, acknowledge, avow, admit, confess. (*alienate, forfeit, lose, disclaim, disavow, disinherit, disown, abjure, abandon*)

P

pacify—appease, conciliate, calm, still, soothe, quiet, tranquilize. (*exasperate, agitate, excite, irritate, rouse, provoke*)

pack—*n.* burden, bundle, package, lot, parcel, load.

pack—*v.* stow, compact, compress, cook. (*unpack, unsettle, jumble, displace, misarrange, dissipate, neutralize*)

pain—*n.* penalty, suffering, distress, uneasiness, grief, labor, effort, anguish, torture, agony. (*reward, remuneration, ease, gratification, joy, pleasure, felicity, relief, alleviation, enjoyment, delight*)

pain—*v.* hurt, grieve, afflict, torment, rack, agonize, trouble, torture, aggrieve, annoy, distress. (*gratify, please, delight, rejoice, charm, relieve, ease, refresh*)

painful—afflicting, distressful, grieving, grievous, excruciating, hurting.

painstaking—careful, attentive, diligent, laborious. (*careless, negligent*)

palatable—tasteful, savory, appetizing, delicious, toothsome.

pale—pallid, wan, faint, dim, undefined, etiolated, sallow, cadaverous. (*ruddy, high-colored, conspicuous, deep*)

palmy—prosperous, glorious, distinguished, victorious, flourishing. (*depressed, inglorious, undistinguished, unflourishing*)

paltry—mean, shabby, shuffling, trifling, prevaricating, shifty, contemptible, pitiable, vile, worthless, beggarly, trashy. (*noble, honorable, candid, conscientious, determined, straightforward, estimable, admirable, worthy, magnificent*)

pang—paroxysm, throe, agony, convulsion, smart, anguish, pain, twinge. (*pleasure, enjoyment, gratification, delight, delectation, fascination, refreshment*)

paradox—contradiction, enigma, mystery, absurdity, ambiguity. (*precept, proposition, axiom, truism, postulate*)

parallel—correspondent, congruous, correlative, analogous, concurrent, equidistant. (*different, opposed, incongruous, irrelative, unanalogous, divergent, contrariant*)

paralyze—deaden, benumb, prostrate, enervate, debilitate, enfeeble. (*give life, strengthen, nerve, lift up, restore*)

pardon—forgive, condone, absolve, acquit, remit, excuse, overlook. (*condemn, punish, visit*)

pardonable—venial, excusable. (*inexcusable, unpardonable*)

parsimonious—sparing, close, penurious, frugal, niggardly, illiberal, stingy. (*liberal, unsparing, profuse, extravagant*)

part—portion, piece, fragment, fraction, division, member, constituent, element, ingredient, share, lot, concern, interest, participation, side, party, interest, faction, behalf, duty. (*whole, completeness, entirety, integrity, totality, mass, bulk, body, compound, transaction, affair*)

partake—share, participate, accept, derive. (*forfeit, relinquish, forego, cede, yield, afford*)

partial—restricted, local, peculiar, specific, favoring, inequitable, unfair, biased, particular. (*unrestricted, total, universal, general, impartial, equitable, just, fair, unbiased*)

particular—local, specific, subordinate, detailed, partial, special, fastidious, minute, scrupulous, careful, accurate, exact, circumstantial, precise, delicate, nice. (*universal, general, unspecial, comprehensive, unscrupulous, uncareful, inaccurate, inexact, rough, coarse, indiscriminate, undiscriminating*)

partisan—adherent, follower, party man, henchman, clansman, supporter, disciple

partition—barrier, division, enclosure, compartment, interspace, separation, distribution, allotment, screen. (*non-partition, non-distinction, non-separation, inclusion, comprehension, combination, amalgamation, incorporation, coalition, union, concatenation, generalization, collection*)

partner—associate, sharer, participator, colleague, coadjutor, confederate, accomplice, partaker, companion, spouse. (*rival, alien, competitor, opponent, counter-agent*)

passable—traversable, navigable, penetrable, admissible, tolerable, ordinary. (*impassable, impervious, impenetrable, inadmissible, excellent*)

passage—journey, thoroughfare, road, course, avenue, route, channel, clause, phrase, sentence, paragraph. (*chapter, book*)

passive—inactive, inert, quiescent, unresisting, unquestioning, negative, enduring, patient. (*active, alert, resistant, positive, insubmissive, malcontent, vehement, impatient*)

pastime—recreation, entertainment, amusement, diversion, play, sport. (*business, study, labor, task, occupation, work*)

patent—obvious, evident, indisputable, plain. (*dubious, ambiguous, questionable*)

pathetic—affecting, moving, emotional, tender, melting. (*ludicrous, unimpassioned, farcical, unaffecting*)

patience—endurance, resignation, submission, perseverance. (*resistance, insubmissiveness, repining, rebellion, inconsistency, impatience*)

pattern—model, sample, archetype, exemplar, specimen, shape, precedent, mold, design, shape. (*monstrosity, caricature, perversion, misrepresentation*)

pause—*n.* stop, cessation, suspension, halt, intermission, rest. (*continuance, advancement, perseverance*)

pause—*v.* cease, suspend, intermit, forbear, stay, wait, hesitate, demur, stop, desist. (*continue, proceed, advance, persist, persevere*)

peace—quiet, tranquility, calm, repose, pacification, order, calmness, reconciliation, harmony, concord. (*noise, disturbance, tumult, agitation, hostility, disorder, embroilment, war, discord, variance, strife*)

peaceable—unwarlike, inoffensive, quiet, peaceful, innocuous, mild, unquarrelsome, serene, placid. (*pugnacious, warlike, litigious, quarrelsome, savage, fierce, hostile, violent, bellicose, restless*)

peculiar—private, personal, characteristic, exceptional, exclusive, special, specific, particular, unusual, singular, uncommon, strange, rare, odd. (*public, common, general, universal, unspecial, ordinary*)

peculiarity—speciality, individuality, distinctiveness, idiosyncrasy. (*generality, universality, community, uniformity, homology, homogeneity, connaturality*)

people—nation, community, populace, mob, crowd, vulgar, herd, mass, persons, inhabitants, commonalty, fellow-creatures, tribe, race, group. (*aristocracy, nobility, government, ruler, oligarchy*)

perceive—discern, distinguish, descry, observe, feel, touch, see, recognize, understand, know. (*miss, misobserve, overlook, misunderstand, misconceive, misperceive*)

perception—cognizance, apprehension, sight, understanding, discernment. (*incognizance, ignorance, imperception, misapprehension, misunderstanding*)

peremptory—decisive, express, absolute, authoritative, dictatorial, dogmatic, imperious, despotic, positive. (*suggestive, entreative, mild, postulatory, hortatory*)

perfect—consummate, complete, full, indeficient, immaculate, absolute, faultless, impeccable, infallible, unblemished, blameless, unexceptionable, mature, ripe, pure. (*incomplete, meagre, faulty, scant, short, deficient, defective, imperfect, peccable, fallible, blemished, marred, spoilt*)

perfectly—fully, wholly, entirely, completely, totally, exactly, accurately. (*imperfectly, incompletely, partially, inaccurately*)

perform—accomplish, do, act, transact, achieve, execute, discharge, fulfil, effect, complete, consummate, enact. (*miss, mar, misperform, misexecute, botch, misenact, misconduct, spoil*)

perhaps—possibly, peradventure, perchance, maybe. (*certainly, inevitably*)

perilous—hazardous, dangerous. (*safe, secure, certain*)

period—time, date, epoch, era, age, duration, continuance, limit, bound, end, conclusion, determination. (*eternity, datelessness, immemoriality, infinity, perpetuity, illimitability, endlessness, indefiniteness, indeterminateness*)

periodic—stated, recurrent, regular, systematic, calculable. (*indeterminate, eccentric, irregular, incalculable, spasmodic, fitful*)

permeable—penetrable, pervadable, percolable. (*impenetrable, impermeable*)

perpetual—constant, unceasing, endless, eternal, everlasting, unfailing, perennial, continual, enduring, incessant, uninterrupted. (*inconstant, periodic, recurrent, temporary, transient, falling, exhaustible, occasional, momentary, casual*)

perplex—embarrass, puzzle, entangle, involve, encumber, complicate, confuse, bewilder, mystify, harass, entangle. (*clear, enlighten, explicate, disentangle, simplify, elucidate, disencumber*)

perseverance—persistence, steadfastness, constancy, indefatigability, resolution, tenacity. (*inconstancy, unsteadfastness, fitfulness, caprice, ir-*

resoluteness, vacillation, wavering, indecision, variableness, levity, volatility)

persuade—induce, influence, incline, convince, dispose, urge, allure, incite. (*deter, disincline, indispose, mispersuade, misinduce, coerce, compel*)

perverse—forward, untoward, stubborn, fractious, wayward, unmanageable, intractable, crochety. (*docile, ductile, amenable, governable, complacent, accommodating, pleasant, obliging*)

pet—darling, fondling, favorite, cosset, jewel, minion, idol. (*horrow, bugbear, aversion, scarcecrow*)

petition—supplication, entreaty, craving, application, appeal, salutation, prayer, request, instance. (*deprecation, expostulation, protest, command, injunction, claim, demand, requirement, exaction, dictation*)

petty—small, mean, paltry, ignoble, trifling, narrow, trivial, contemptible. (*large, large-hearted, noble, generous, chivalrous, magnificent, liberal, broad*)

philanthropy—humanity, love of mankind, generosity, charity, benevolence. (*misanthropy, hatred of men, selfishness, stinginess*)

philosopher—doctor, savant, teacher, master, schoolman. (*ignoramus, sciolist, freshman, tyro, greenhorn, fool, booby, dunce*)

philosophical—wise, sound, conclusive, scientific, accurate, enlightened, rational, calm, unprejudiced. (*unsound, crude, vague, loose, inaccurate, popular, unscientific, sciolistic, unphilosophical*)

physical—natural, material, visible, tangible, substantial, corporeal. (*mental, moral, intellectual, spiritual, immaterial, invisible, intangible, unsubstantial, supernatural, hyperphysical*)

picture—likeness, resemblance, drawing, painting, representation, image, engraving. (*original*)

picturesque—comely, seemly, graceful, scenic, artistic, pictorial, graphic. (*unseemly, uncouth, rude, unpicturesque, ugly, flat, tame, monotonous, dead*)

pinch—squeeze, grip, press, compress, nip, distress.

piquant—pungent, sharp, lively, racy, severe, biting, cutting, smart, stimulating, keen, stinging, tart. (*tame, dull, flat, characterless, insipid*)

pithy—terse, forceful, laconic, expressive, concise, spongy. (*weak, characterless, diluted, pointless, flat, vapid*)

pity—mercy, compassion, tenderness, commiseration, ruth, sympathy, condolence. (*cruelty, hardheartedness, relentlessness, pitilessness, ruthlessness*)

place—locate, assign, fix, establish, settle, attribute, situate, put, set. (*disturb, remove, unsettle, disarrange, disestablish, misplace, misattribute, misassign, uproot, transplant, extirpate, eradicate, transport*)

plain—level, even, flat, smooth, open, clear, unencumbered, unobstructed, uninterrupted, manifest, evident, obvious, unmistakable, simple, easy, natural, unaffected, homely, unsophisticated, open, unvarnished, unembellished, unreserved, artless. (*uneven, undulating, rugged, rough, abrupt, broken, confused, encumbered, obstructed, interrupted, questionable, uncertain, dubious, ambiguous, enigmatical, hard, abstruse, affected, fair, beautiful, sophisticated, artful, varnished, embellished*)

plan—*n.* design, drawing, sketch, draft, scheme, ground-plot, project, contrivance, stratagem, device.

plan—*v.* contrive, devise, sketch out, design, hatch.

platonic—cold, intellectual, unsensual, mental, philosophical. (*ardent, animal, sensual, passionate, sexual*)

plausible—specious, superficial, passable, unctuous, fair-spoken, pretentious, ostensible, right, apparent, colorable, feasible, probable. (*genuine, sterling, unmistakable, profound*)

playful—lively, sportive, jocund, frolicsome, gay, vivacious, sprightly. (*somber, dull*)

plea—excuse, vindication, justification, ground, defense, apology, entreaty, request. (*charge, accusation, impeachment, action*)

pleasant—grateful, agreeable, acceptable, pleasurable, desirable, gratifying, cheerful, enlivening, sportive, delicious, delectable, jocular, satisfactory, exquisite, merry. (*unpleasant, ungrateful, disagreeable, obnoxious, unacceptable, offensive, unlively, lugubrious, dull, ill-humored*)

pleasure—enjoyment, gratification, sensuality, self-indulgence, voluptuousness, choice, preference, will, inclination, purpose, determination, favor, satisfaction, indulgence. (*pain, suffering, affliction, trouble, asceticism, self-denial, abstinence, disinclination, aversion, indisposition, denial, refusal*)

plebeian—low, vulgar, low-born, low-bred, coarse, ignoble. (*patrician, noble, aristocratic, refined, high-born, high-bred*)

plodding—painstaking, industrious, persevering, laborious, studious. (*indiligent, unindustrious, distracted, inattentive, impatient, unpersevering, flighty, fitful*)

plot—*n.* scheme, plan, stratagem, combination, conspiracy, machination.

plot—*v.* devise, concoct, conspire, contrive, frame, hatch, plan, scheme.

plump—well-conditioned, well-rounded, chubby, strapping, bouncing, fleshy, brawny, full, fat, round, massive, portly. (*ill-conditioned, lean, emaciated, scraggy, weazen, macilent, lank, raw-boned, shriveled, flaccid, tabid*)

plunge—dip, dive, douse, duck, submerge, immerse, precipitate, sink, overwhelm, thrust under, pitch headlong. (*emerge, issue, soar, raise, extricate, rescue*)

poetical—metrical, rhythmic, versified, lyric, rhyming, imaginative, creative, romantic, fictitious, dreamy, flighty. (*unmetrical, unrhythmical, prosaic, unpoetical, unversified, unimaginative, commonplace, historical, mathematical, logical, matter-of-fact, veracious, sober*)

poisonous—venomous, infectant, vicious, corruptive, vitiative, noxious, baneful, malignant, morbific, peccant, virulent, pestiferous, mephitic, deleterious. (*wholesome, genial, beneficial, sanative, invigorative, healthful, innoxious, restorative, remedial, hygeian*)

polite—elegant, refined, well-bred, courteous, obliging, complaisant, civil, courtly, polished, genteel, accomplished. (*awkward, rude, uncouth, ill-bred, discourteous, boorish, clownish, disobliging*)

politic—prudent, wise, sagacious, provident, diplomatic, judicious, cunning, wary, well devised, discreet. (*imprudent, unwise, improvident, undiplomatic, impolitic*)

pompous—magnificent, gorgeous, splendid, showy, sumptuous, ostentatious, stately, lofty, grand, bombastic, turgid, stiff, inflated, pretentious, coxcombical, assuming. (*unpretending, unobtrusive, modest, unassuming, plain-mannered, humbleminded*)

ponder—think over, meditate on, weigh, consider, cogitate, deliberate, ruminate, reflect, amuse, study, resolve

poor—indigent, moneyless, impecunious, penniless, weak, meager, insufficient, deficient, faulty, unsatisfactory, inconsiderable, thin, scanty, bald. (*rich, wealthy, copious, affluent, abundant, liberal, large, ample, moneyed, sufficient, satisfactory, considerable*)

popular—common, current, vulgar, public, general, received, favorite, beloved, prevailing, approved, wide-spread, liked. (*exclusive, restricted, scientific, esoteric, unpopular, odious, detested*)

positive—real, actual, substantial, absolute, independent, unconditional, unequivocal, explicit, fixed, settled, definitive, indisputable, decisive, express, enacted, assured, confident, direct, dogmatic, over-bearing, dogmatical. (*negative, insubstantial, unreal, fictitious, imaginary, relative, contingent, dependent, conditional, implied, dubious, questionable, moral, uncertain, doubtful, indirect, occasional suspicious*)

possess—occupy, enjoy, have, hold, entertain, own. (*abandon, renounce, abjure, surrender, lose, forfeit, resign*)

possible—practicable, feasible, likely, potential. (*impracticable, impossible*)

postpone—defer, delay, prorogue, procrastinate. (*expedite, dispatch, accelerate*)

poverty—want, need, indigence, destitution.

power—faculty, capacity, capability, potentiality, ability, strength, force, might, energy, susceptibility, influence, dominion, sway, command, government, agency, authority, rule, jurisdiction, effectiveness. (*incapacity, incapability, impotence, inability, weakness, imbecility, inertness, insusceptibility, subjection, powerlessness, obedience, subservience, ineffectiveness*)

powerful—strong, potent, puissant, masterful, mighty. (*weak, poor*)

practice—usage, habit, exercise, experience, exercitation, action, custom, manner, performance. (*disuse, dishabituation, inexperience, theory, speculation, nonperformance*)

practice—perform, exercise, deal in, carry on.

praise—eulogize, laud, commend, honor, glorify, compliment, celebrate, puff, extol, applaud, panegyrize. (*blame, censure, discommend, reprove*)

pray—beg, beseech, entreat, implore, solicit, supplicate, adjure, invoke, crave.

prayer—petition, supplication, entreaty, orison, benediction, suit, request.

precaution—forethought, provision, premunition, anticipation, pre-arrangement, care, providence. (*carelessness, thoughtlessness, improvidence*)

preceding—precedent, former, foregoing, prior, previous, antecedent, anterior.

precious—dear, valuable, costly, cherished, treasured, beloved, estimable, of great value. (*cheap, valueless, worthless, unvalued, disesteemed, unappreciated, vile*)

precise—definite, exact, nice, pointed, accurate, correct, particular, formal, explicit, scrupulous, terse, punctilious, ceremonious, formal. (*indefinite, vague, inexact, rough, inaccurate, loose, circumlocutory, ambagious, tortuous, informal, unceremonious*)

predict—prophesy, foretell, forecast, prognosticate, forebode, foreshadow.

prediction—prophecy, prognostication, vaticination, fore-announcement, premonstration, foretelling, forebodement, presage, augury, foreshowing. (*narration, relation, history, account, report*)

preface—introduction, proem, prelude, prologue, preamble, premiss. (*peroration, sequel, appendix, epilogue, postscript*)

prefer—choose, elect, select, fancy, promote, advance, further. (*reject, postpone, defer, withhold, degrade, depress*)

prejudice—prepossession, prejudgment, predisposition, bias, unfairness, injury, harm, impairment, detriment, partiality, disadvantage, damage. (*judgment, fairness, impartiality, advantage*)

premature—hasty, crude, unauthenticated, untimely, precocious, precipitate, too early, rash, unseasonable. (*ripe, timely, seasonable, opportune*)

premium—reward, guerdon, encouragement, douceur, enhancement, bribe, recompense, bonus, prize, bounty. (*penalty, fine, amercement, mulct, forfeit, depreciation*)

preparation—provision, readiness. (*unpreparedness, without provision*)

prepare—fit, adapt, qualify, adjust, provide, arrange, order, lay, plan, equip, furnish, ready. (*misfit, misadapt, misprovide, derange, disarrange, demolish, subvert, disconcert*)

prepossessing—attractive, alluring, charming, winning, taking, engaging. (*repulsive, unattractive, sinister*)

preposterous—monstrous, exorbitant, unreasonable, absurd, irrational, foolish, ridiculous. (*just,* *due, fair, reasonable, moderate, right, judicious, orderly, sound*)

presence—nearness, influence, intercourse, closeness. (*remoteness, absence, separation, distance*)

preserve—defend, guard, save, keep safe, uphold, protect, maintain, rescue, spare. (*ruin, destroy*)

president—chairman, moderator, principal, superintendent. (*member, subordinate, constituent, corporation, society, ward, institution*)

press—urge, crowd, compel, force, squeeze, crush, compress, express, constrain, hurry, instigate, inculcate, impress, throng, encroach, lean, weigh, harass. (*relax, inhibit, persuade, entice, allure, solicit, touch, skim, graze, free, liberate, ease, avoid, relieve*)

presume—suppose, anticipate, apprehend, venture, take for granted, conjecture, believe, deem, assume. (*infer, deduce, prove, argue, retire, withdraw, hesitate, distrust*)

pretend—feign, simulate, offer, allege, exhibit, propound, affect, profess. (*verify, unmask, detect, test, substantiate, refute*)

pretense—excuse, pretext, fabrication, simulation, cloak, mask, color, show, garb, plea, assumption, make believe, outside show, pretension. (*verity, reality, truth, simplicity, candor, guilelessness, openness, veritableness, actuality, fact*)

pretty—handsome, attractive, neat, trim, tasteful, pleasing, beautiful, fine, comely. (*ugly, grotesque*)

prevailing—controlling, ruling, influential, operative, predominant, prevalent, rife, ascendant, most general, most common. (*mitigated, diminishing, subordinate, powerless*)

prevent—hinder, obstruct, bar, neutralize, nullify, thwart, intercept, anticipate, forefend, frustrate, obviate, checkmate. (*promote, aid, facilitate, expedite, encourage, advance, accelerate, induce, cause, produce*)

price—cost, figure, charge, expense, compensation, value, appraisement, worth. (*donation, discount, allowance, remittance, abatement*)

pride—loftiness, haughtiness, lordliness, self-exaltation, arrogance, conceit, vain-glory. (*lowliness, meekness, modesty, self-distrust*)

priggish—coxcombical, dandified, foppish, affected, prim, conceited. (*plain, sensible, unaffected, simple-minded, simple-mannered*)

prim—formal, precise, demure, starched, stiff, self-conscious, unbending, priggish. (*unformal, easy, genial, unaffected, natural, free, naive*)

primary—first, original, earliest, elementary, main, chief, principal, important, leading, primitive, pristine. (*secondary, subordinate, posterior, unimportant, inferior, subsequent, later*)

primitive—old-fashioned, primeval, quaint, simple, unsophisticated, archaic, pristine. (*modern, new-fangled, sophisticated, modish*)

princely—imperial, munificent, magnificent, superb, august, regal, royal, supreme. (*beggarly, mean, niggardly, poverty-struck*)

principal—highest, first, main, leading, chief, primary, foremost, pre-eminent, prominent. (*inferior, subordinate, secondary, supplemental, subject, auxiliary, minor*)

principle—source, origin, motive, cause, energy, substance, element, power, faculty, truth, tenet, law, doctrine, axiom, maxim, postulate, rule. (*exhibition, manifestation, application, development, issue, exercise, operation, formation, action*)

private—special, peculiar, individual, secret, not public, retired, privy. (*general, public, open, unconcealed*)

privilege—prerogative, immunity, franchise, right, liberty, advantage, claim, exemption. (*disfranchisement, disqualification, exclusion, prohibition, inhibition*)

prize—booty, spoil, plunder, prey, forage, trophy, laurels, guerdon, premium, honors, ovation, palm. (*loss, forfeiture, fine, penalty, amercement, sacrifice, disappointment, failure, brand, stigma, infamy, mulct*)

probability—likelihood, presumption, verisimilitude, chance, appearance. (*unlikelihood, improbability, impossibility, inconceivableness*)

probable—likely, presumable, credible, reasonable. (*unlikely, unreasonable, incredible*)

proceed—move, pass, advance, progress, continue, issue, emanate, flow, arise. (*recede, deviate, retreat, stand, stop, stay, desist, discontinue, ebb, retire*)

procession—train, march, caravan, file, cortege, cavalcade, retinue. (*rabble, herd, rush, disorder, mob, confusion, rout*)

prodigal—lavish, profuse, extravagant, reckless, wasteful, squandering, improvident. (*frugal, saving, hoarding, economical, niggardly, miserly, close, close-fisted*)

prodigious—marvelous, portentous, wonderful, astounding, enormous, monstrous, amazing, surprising, remarkable, extraordinary, huge, vast. (*ordinary, common-place, every-day, usual, familiar, moderate*)

produce—*v.* exhibit, bear, furbish, afford, cause, create, originate, yield, extend, prolong, lengthen. (*withdraw, retain, stifle, withhold, neutralize, destroy, annihilate, curtail, shorten, contract, reduce*)

produce—*n.* product, yield, fruit, profit, effect, consequence, result, amount.

product—fruit, result, issue, consequence, effect, emanation, work. (*cause, principle, power, motive, energy, operation, action, tendency, law*)

production—origination, evolution, formation, genesis, product, manufacture, growth.

profane—unconsecrated, secular, temporal, unsanctified, unholy, irreligious, irreverent, ungodly, wicked, godless, impious, blasphemous. (*holy, consecrated, sacred, · spiritual, sanctified, reverent, religious, godly, pious, devout*)

profess—declare, avow, acknowledge, own, confess, pretend, proclaim, lay claim to. (*conceal, suppress, disown, disavow, repudiate, renounce, abjure*)

profit—gain, emolument, advantage, avail, acquisition, benefit, service, use, improvement. (*loss, detriment, damage, disadvantage, waste*)

profitable—gainful, advantageous, desirable, beneficial, useful, productive, remunerative, lucrative. (*unprofitable, disadvantageous, undesirable, detrimental, unbeneficial, unprofitable, useless, vain, fruitless, unproductive, unremunerative*)

program—advertisement, notice, plan, catalogue, schedule, performance. (*review, rehearsal, repetition, resume, analysis, precis*)

progress—advancement, advance, movement, proceeding, way, journey, proficiency, speed, growth. (*delay, stoppage, retreat, stay, retrogression, failure, relapse*)

project—plan, purpose, design, scheme, contrivance, device, venture. (*hazard, chance*)

prominent—jutting, protuberant, relieved, embossed, extended, manifest, conspicuous, eminent, distinguished, main, important, leading, characteristic, distinctive. (*receding, concave, rebated, indented, hollowed, engraved, intailed, withdrawn, inconspicuous, minor, secondary, unimportant, indistinctive, undistinguishable, subordinate*)

promiscuous—mingled, confused, undistinguished, unselected, unarranged, undistributed, unassorted, common, unreserved, casual, disorderly, unordered. (*sorted, select, orderly, arranged, distributed, reserved, assorted, exclusive, nice*)

promise—*v.* pledge, engage, assure, covenant, pledge, stipulate.

promise—*n.* engagement, assurance, word, pledge, oath, covenant.

promote—aid, further, advance, excite, exalt, raise, elevate, prefer. (*discourage, repress, hinder, check, allay, depress, degrade, dishonor*)

prompt—ready, alert, responsive, active, quick, brisk, apt, unhesitating. (*unready, sluggish, irresponsive, inactive*)

pronounce—articulate, utter, declare, propound, deliver, assert, affirm, enunciate, express. (*mispronounce, mispropound, misaffirm, suppress, stifle, silence, choke, swallow, gabble, mumble*)

proof—test, trial, examination, criterion, essay, establishment, comprobation, demonstration, evidence, testimony, scrutiny. (*disproof, failure, invalidity, short-coming, fallacy, undemonstrativeness, reprobation*)

proper—peculiar, appertinent, personal, own, constitutional, special, befitting, adapted, suited, suitable, appropriate, just, fair, equitable, right, decent, becoming, fit. (*common, inappertinent, alien, universal, non-special, unbefitting, unadapted, unsuited, unsuitable, inappropriate, wrong, indecent, unbecoming, improper*)

property—quality, attribute, peculiarity, nature, characteristic, possessions, goods, wealth, estate, gear, resources, ownership.

proportion—adaptation, relation, rate, distribution, adjustment, symmetry, interrelationship, uniformity, correlation. (*misproportion, misadjustment, incongruity, disparity, disharmony, disorder, irrelation, disproportion*)

propose—offer, tender, proffer, bring forward, purpose, intend, mean, propound, move, design.

prosaic—dull, matter-of-fact, tedious, prolix. (*poetic, animated, interesting, lively, fervid, eloquent, graphic*)

prospect—view, vision, field, landscape, hope, anticipation, probability. (*viewlessness, dimness, obscurity, darkness, cloud, veiling, occultation, hopelessness, improbability*)

prospectus—program, plan, catalogue, announcement, bill, scheme, compendium, brochure. (*subject, transaction, proceeding*)

prosperity—success, weal, welfare, good fortune, well-being, good luck. (*unsuccess, woe, adversity, failure, reverse*)

protect—defend, fortify, guard, shield, preserve, cover, secure, save, vindicate. (*betray, endanger, imperil, abandon, expose*)

proud—arrogant, haughty, imperious, supercilious, presumptuous, boastful, vainglorious, vain, ostentatious, elated, self-satisfied, lofty, imposing, magnificent, self-conscious. (*deferential, humble, affable, unpresuming, meek, lowly, ashamed, unimposing, mean*)

prove—try, assay, test, establish, demonstrate, ascertain, argue, show, confirm, examine, substantiate, make trial of, verify, ascertain. (*pass, pretermit, misdemonstrate, misindicate, refute, disprove, contradict, disestablish, neutralize*)

proverbial—notorious, current, acknowledged, unquestioned. (*dubious, unfounded, suspicious, suspected, questionable*)

provide—prepare, arrange, procure, afford, supply, contribute, yield, cater, furnish, get, agree, produce, collect, stipulate. (*misprovide, neglect, overlook, withhold, retain, appropriate, refuse, deny, alienate, divert, misemploy, mismanage*)

province—tract, region, department, section, sphere, domain, territory. (*metropolis, center, capital*)

provision, provisions—preparation, arrangement, produce, supply, anticipation, food, supplies, victuals, edibles, eatables. (*neglect, misprovision, forgetfulness, thoughtlessness, oversight, destitution, want, dearth, starvation, dole, pittance*)

provoke—educe, summon, rouse, irritate, excite, challenge, vex, impel, offend, exasperate, anger, tantalize. (*allay, relegate, pacify, soothe, conciliate*)

proxy—agency, substitution, representation, agent, substitute, representative, deputy, commissioner, lieutenant, delegate. (*principalship, personality, principal, person, authority, deputer*)

prudent—wise, wary, cautious, circumspect, discreet, careful, judicious. (*foolish, unwary, incautious, uncircumspect, indiscreet, rash, imprudent, silly, reckless, audacious*)

prudish—coy, over-modest, over-nice, squeamish, reserved, demure. (*promiscuous*)

public—open, notorious, common, social, national, exoteric, general, generally known. (*close, secret, private, domestic, secluded, solitary, personal, individual*)

pull—draw, drag, adduce, extract, tug, haul, pluck. (*push, eject, extrude, propel*)

punch—perforate, poke, pierce, puncture, terebrate, bore. (*stop, plug, seal, bung*)

punish—chastise, castigate, chasten, correct, whip, scourge, discipline. (*reward, recompense, remunerate, indemnify*)

pupil—scholar, learner, student, tyro, novice, ward. (*teacher, master, proficient, adept, guardian*)

puppy—youth, fop, coxcomb, prig. (*boor, clown, lout*)

pure—clear, unmixed, simple, genuine, sheer, mere, absolute, unadulterated, uncorrupted, unsullied, unblemished, chaste, real, clean, spotless, immaculate, undefiled, unspotted, guileless, innocent, guiltless. (*foul, turbid, impure, adulterated, corrupt, sullied, stained, tarnished, defiled, mixed, guilty*)

purpose—*v.* intend, determine, design, resolve, mean, propose. (*chance, risk, hazard, revoke, miscalculate, venture, stake*)

purpose—*n.* intention, design, mind, meaning, view, object, aim, end, scope, point, resolve. (*chance, fortune, fate, accident, hazard, lot, casualty, lottery, hit*)

push—press, drive, impel, shove, press against propel, butt, thrust, urge, expedite, accelerate, reduce. (*pull, draw, drag, adduce*)

put—place, lay, set, propose. (*remove, raise, displace, transfer, withdraw*)

puzzle—*v.* pose, perplex, embarrass, bewilder, confound, mystify, confuse. (*enlighten, instruct, illumine*)

puzzle—*n.* embarrassment, bewilderment, enigma, confusion, conundrum, intricacy, labyrinth. (*disentanglement, solution, explanation, extrication, clue*)

Q

quack—empiric, mountebank, charlatan, impostor, pretender, humbug. (*dupe, gull, victim*)

quaint—curious, recondite, abstruse, elegant, nice, affected, whimsical, odd, antique, archaic, fanciful, singular, old-fashioned. (*commonplace, ordinary, usual, coarse, common, modern, modish, fashionable, dowdy*)

qualified—fitted, adapted, competent, suitable.

quality—condition, character, property, attribute, peculiarity, disposition, temper, sort, kind, description, capacity, power, virtue, nature, tendency. (*anomalousness, heterogeneousness, nondescript, incapacity, weakness, indistinctiveness, ineffectiveness, disqualification, negation, disability*)

quantity—measure, amount, bulk, size, sum, portion, aggregate, muchness, part, share, division. (*margin, deficiency, deduction, want, inadequacy, scantiness, insufficiency, loss, deterioration, diminution, waste, wear, leakage*)

quarrel—brawl, altercation, affray, squabble, feud, tumult, dispute, wrangle, variance, disagreement, misunderstanding, hostility, quarreling, embroilment, bickering, broil. (*confabulation, conversation, chat, pleasantry, conciliation, friendliness, peace, amity, good-will*) quarrelsome—choleric, irascible, petulant, litigious, pugnacious, brawling, fiery, hot-tempered, contentious, irritable. (*peaceable, amenable, genial, unquarrelsome, inoffensive, mild, meek, conciliatory, bland, suave*)

quarter—region, district, locality, territory, mercy, forbearance, pity. (*extermination, mercilessness, unsparingness, pitilessness, ruthlessness*)

queer—odd, whimsical, quaint, cross, strange, crochety, singular, eccentric. (*ordinary, common, usual, familiar, customary*)

question—*v.* ask, inquire, interrogate, doubt, investigate, dubitate, controvert, dispute. (*dictate, state, assert, pronounce, enunciate, concede, endorse, affirm, grant, allow*)

question—*n.* inquiry, interrogation, doubt, scrutiny, investigation, topic. (*reply, response, solution, answer, explanation, admission, concession*)

questionable—doubtful, dubious, problematical, disputable, debatable, uncertain, suspicious. (*certain, evident, self-evident, obvious, indisputable*)

quick—fast, rapid, speedy, expeditious, swift, hasty, prompt, ready, clever, sharp, shrewd, adroit, keen, fleet, active, brisk, nimble, lively, agile, alert, sprightly, transient, intelligent, irascible. (*slow, tardy, sluggish, inert, inactive, dull, insensitive*)

quiet—*n.* rest, repose, stillness, calm, appeasement, pacification, silence, peace. (*unrest, motion, noise, agitation, excitement, disturbance, turmoil, tumult*)

quiet—*v.* allay, appease, still, pacify, hush, lull, tranquilize, soothe, calm. (*rouse, excite, disturb, agitate, stir, urge, goad*)

quit—leave, resign, abandon, relinquish, discharge, release, surrender, give up, depart from, forsake. (*seek, occupy, invade, bind, enforce, haunt, enter*)

quite—perfectly, entirely, completely, wholly, truly, altogether, totally. (*partially, imperfectly, barely, insufficiently, hardly*)

quote—cite, name, **adduce, plead, allege,** note, repeat. (*disprove, refute, retort, oppose, contradict, traverse, misquote, misadduce, rebut*)

R

racy—fine-flavored, fresh, rich, pungent, piquant, spirited, smart, lively, vivacious, spicy. (*flavorless, dull, stupid*)

radical—original, fundamental, thorough-going, unsparing, extreme, entire, innate, natural, essential, immanent, ingrained, underived, deep-seated. (*derived, ascititious, adventitious, superficial, extraneous, partial, moderate, conservative, acquired*)

rage—*n.* fury, rabidity, choler, indignation, frenzy, anger, ire, dudgeon, mania, passion, madness, ferocity. (*reason, moderation, gentleness, temperateness, calmness, quiescence, mitigation, assuagement, tranquillity, mildness, softness*)

rage—*v.* rave, storm, fume, be furious, be violent. (*be calm, be composed, be peaceful*)

raise—lift, heave, elevate, exalt, advance, promote, heighten, enhance, awaken, rouse, excite, call forth, cultivate, rear, produce, collect, summon, erect, originate, propagate. (*lay, cast, depress, degrade, retard, dishonor, lower, depreciate, lull, compose, quiet, calm, blight, destroy, disperse, disband, stifle, hush, silence, neutralize, confute*)

range—rank, dispose, class, place, order, collocate, file, concatenate, ramble, stroll, rove. (*disturb, disconnect, disorder, derange, intermit, disconnect, remain, be stationary*)

rank—*n.* row, line, tier, order, degree, grade, dignity. (*disconnection, disorder, incontinuity, solution, intermission, hiatus, plebeianism, meanness, commonalty*)

rank—*a.* luxuriant, exuberant, extreme, excessive, rampant.

rankle—fester, smoulder, burn, irritate, gall, disquiet. (*heal, cool, close, calm, quiet, compose*)

rapid—quick, swift, speedy, accelerated, flying. (*slow, tardy, retarded, cumbrous, lazy*)

rare—scarce, choice, infrequent, excellent, few, exceptional, sparse, unusual, singular, uncommon, incomparable, extraordinary, unique, dispersed, valuable, precious, thin, volatile. (*common, frequent, abundant, numerous, mean, ordinary, usual, regular, crowded, dense, vulgar, worthless, cheap, valueless*)

rash—headstrong, audacious, hasty, precipitate, reckless, foolhardy, careless, adventurous, thoughtless, indiscreet, venturesome, overventuresome, incautious, unwary, heedless. (*wary, cautious, calculating, discreet, unventuresome, dubitating, hesitating, reluctant, timid*)

rashness—hastiness, precipitancy, recklessness, venturesomeness, temerity, precipitation, indiscretion. (*slowness, carefulness, cautiousness, discretion*)

rate—*n.* tax, impost, assessment, duty, standard, allowance, ratio, quota, worth, price, value.

rate—*v.* compute, calculate, estimate, value, scold, abuse, appraise.

rational—sane, sound, intelligent, reasoning, reasonable, judicious, sober, sensible, probable, equitable, moderate, fair. (*insane, unsound, weak, silly, unintelligent, absurd, injudicious, fanciful, extravagant, preposterous, unreasoning, unreasonable, irrational, exorbitant*)

ravel—separate, undo, untwist, unwind, disentangle. (*entangle, complicate, conglomerate, confuse*)

ravish—entrance, transport, enchant, enrapture, charm, violate, outrage, debauch.

raw—uncooked, unprepared, unfinished, unripe, crude, unseasoned, inexperienced, fresh, green, unpracticed, untried, bare, bald, exposed, galled, chill, bleak, piercing. (*cooked, dressed, prepared, finished, ripe, mature, mellow, seasoned, experienced, expert,* *adept, habituated, familiar, practiced, trained, tried, covered, healed, balmy, genial)*

reach—extend, thrust, stretch, obtain, arrive at, attain, gain, grasp, penetrate, strain, aim. (*fail, stop, cease, revert, rebate, miss, drop*)

read—peruse, interpret, decipher, unravel, discover, recognize, learn. (*misread, misinterpret, overlook, misobserve*)

ready—prompt, alert, expeditious, speedy, unhesitating, dexterous, apt, skillful, handy, expert, facile, easy, opportune, fitted, prepared, disposed, willing, free, cheerful, compliant, responsive, quick. (*unready, tardy, slow, hesitating, reluctant, dubitating, awkward, unhandy, clumsy, remote, inaccessible, unavailable, inopportune, unsuited, unfitted, unprepared, indisposed, unwilling, constrained, grudging, unaccommodating, incompliant, irresponsive*)

real—actual, veritable, existent, authentic, legitimate, true, genuine, developed. (*fictitious, imaginary, unreal, non-existent, untrue, false, artificial, adulterated, assumed, pretended, potential, possible*)

really—veritably, truly, indeed, unquestionably. (*questionably, possibly, perhaps, falsely, untruly, fictitiously*)

reason—*n.* ground, account, cause, explanation, motive, proof, apology, understanding reasoning, rationality, right, propriety, justice, order, object, sake, purpose. (*pretext, pretense, misinterpretation, falsification, misconception, disproof, unreasonableness, absurdity, fallacy, irrationality, wrong, unreason, impropriety, unfairness, folly, aimlessness, unaccountableness*)

reason—*v.* debate, discuss, argue, infer, deduce, conclude.

reassure—rally, restore, encourage, inspirit, animate, countenance. (*discourage, cow, brow-beat, intimidate, discountenance*)

rebuff—*v.* rebuke, repel, repulse, check, snub, oppose.

rebuff—*n*. rebuke, discouragement, repulsion, check. (*welcome, acceptance, encouragement*)

rebuke—reprove, chide, rebuff, reprimand, censure. (*approve, encourage, eulogize, applaud, incite*)

receipt—acknowledgment, reception, voucher

receive—take, accept, admit, hold, entertain, assent to. (*give, impart, afford, reject, discharge, emit*)

reception—admission, admittance, acceptance, acceptation, entertainment. (*denial, protest, repudiation, rejection, non-acceptance, dismissal, discardment, renunciation, abjuration*)

recess—cavity, nook, withdrawal, retirement, retreat, seclusion, privacy, vacation, holiday. (*promontory, protrusion, projection, publicity, worktime*)

reckless—careless, heedless, incautious, foolhardy, thoughtless, rash, over-venturesome, regardless, inconsiderate, improvident. (*careful, heedful, cautious, timid, chary, thoughtful, calculating, provident, considerate, wary, circumspect*)

reckon—compute, calculate, count, regard, estimate, value, account, consider, argue, infer, judge. (*miscompute, miscalculate, misestimate, misreckon*)

recognize—identify, acknowledge, concede, know again, avow, own, allow. (*ignore, overlook, misobserve, repudiate, disavow, disown, disallow*)

recollect—recover, recall, remember, bethink, bring to mind, call up, think of. (*forget, lose*)

recommend—commend, confide, praise, applaud, approve, advise. (*discommend, disapprove, warn, dissuade*)

recompense—*v*. requite, remunerate, reward, indemnify, satisfy, repay, reimburse, compensate. (*damnify, injure, misrequite, dissatisfy*)

recompense—*n*. reward, indemnification, satisfaction, remuneration, amends.

reconcile—unite, conciliate, propitiate, pacify, harmonize, adjust, adapt, suit, reunite. (*separate,* *sever, dissever, estrange, disharmonize, derange, alienate*)

record—registry, entry, enrollment, list, index, catalogue, register, schedule, roll, scroll, enumeration, inventory, muniment, instrument, archive, memorandum, remembrance. (*obliteration, oblivion, nonregistration, desuetude, obsolescence, immemorality, disremembrance*)

recover—regain, repossess, resume, retrieve, recruit, heal, cure, revive, restore, reanimate, save. (*lose, forfeit, miss, sacrifice, deteriorate, impair, decay, decline, relapse*)

recovery—repossession, regaining, reinstatement, vindication, renovation, restitution, re-establishment, retrieval, rectification, replacement, reanimation, resuscitation, revival, redemption. (*loss, forfeiture, privation, deprival, sacrifice, abandonment, relapse, retrogression, decay, declension, incurableness, ruin*)

recreation—refreshment, cheer, reanimation, amusement, diversion, revival, holiday, sport, pastime, relaxation. (*weariness, toil, lassitude, labor, fatigue, employment, assiduity, work*)

redeem—repurchase, regain, retrieve, make amends for, recompense, ransom, liberate, rescue, recover, satisfy, fulfill, discharge. (*pledge, lose, forfeit, abandon, betray, surrender, sacrifice*)

reduce—lessen, diminish, curtail, attenuate, impoverish, narrow, contract, weaken, impair, subdue, subjugate, bring, refer, subject, classify, convert. (*enlarge, magnify, increase, augment, produce, extend, amplify, broaden, expand, renovate, invigorate, restore, repair, liberate, free, except, dissociate, transform*)

refer—attribute, associate, assign, advert, connect, relate, point, belong, allude, apply, appeal. (*disconnect, dissociate, misapply, misappertain, alienate, misbeseem, disresemble*)

reference—relation, regard, intimation, allusion.

refinement—clarification, purification, filtration, sublimation, polish, elegance, cultivation, civilization, subtility, finesse, sophistry. (*turbidity, grossness, foulness, coarseness, impurity, unrefinement, rudeness, inelegance, boorishness, broadness, bluntness, unsophisticatedness*)

reflect—return, image, mirror, exhibit, consider, think, cogitate, meditate, contemplate, ponder, muse, ruminate, heed, advert, animadvert. (*divert, dissipate, idle, dream, wander, rove, star-gaze, woolgather, connive, disregard, overlook*)

reform—amend, ameliorate, correct, rectify, better, reclaim, regenerate, remodel, reconstitute, reorganize, improve. (*corrupt, vitiate, worsen, deteriorate, perpetuate, stabilitate, confirm, impair, deform, stereotype*)

refresh—cool, refrigerate, invigorate, revive, reanimate, renovate, recreate, renew, restore, cheer, freshen, brace. (*heat, oppress, weary, burden, afflict, annoy, tire, fatigue, exhaust, debilitate, enervate, relax*)

refuse—*v.* deny, withhold, reject, decline, repudiate. (*grant, afford, yield, concede, acquiesce*)

refuse—*n.* offal, scum, dregs, sediment, recrement, sweepings, trash, offscourings, debris, remains, dross. (*cream, pickings, first-fruits, flower, prime*)

regard—behold, view, contemplate, esteem, consider, deem, affect, respect, reverence, revere, value, conceive, heed, notice mind. (*miss, overlook, disregard, despise, dislike, contemn, hate, loathe, misconsider, misconceive, misestimate, misjudge*)

regardless—heedless, inconsiderate, careless, unmindful, inattentive, unobservant, disregarding, indifferent, despising. (*careful, considerate, regardful, attentive, prudent, cautious, circumspect, scrupulous, mindful*)

regret—*v.* grieve, lament, repent, miss, desiderate, deplore. (*welcome, hail, approve, abandon, abjure, forget, disregard*)

regret—*n.* sorrow, grief, concern, remorse, lamentation, repentance. (*see* **grief**)

regular—customary, normal, ordinary, orderly, stated, recurrent, periodical, systematic, methodic, established, recognized, formal, symmetrical, certain. (*unusual, exceptional, abnormal, capricious, rare, irregular, disordered, fitful, unsymmetrical, variable, eccentric, erratic, uncertain*)

regulation—rule, law, adjustment, disposal, method, government, order, control, arrangement. (*misrule, disorder, anarchy, misgovernment, maladministration, disarrangement, nonregulation, caprice, license, insubjection, uncontrol*)

reject—repel, renounce, throw by, cast away, repudiate, decline, discard, refuse, exclude. (*hail, welcome, accept, appropriate, choose, select, admit*)

rejoice—delight, glory, exult, joy, triumph, gladden, delight, revel, be glad, cheer, please, enliven, gratify. (*mourn, grieve, lament, weep, sorrow, repent, trouble, afflict, oppress, weary, depress, disappoint, burden, darken, distress, pain, sadden, vex, annoy*)

relation—reference, aspect connection, narration, proportion, bearing, affinity, homogeneity, association, relevancy, pertinency, fitness, harmony ratio, relative, agreement, kinsman, kindred, appurtenancy. (*irrelation, disconnection, dissociation, irrelevancy, impertinency, disproportion, misproportion, unfitness, unsuitableness, heterogeneity, disharmony, disagreement, alien*)

release—free, loose, liberate, discharge, quit, acquit, exempt, extricate, disengage, indemnify. (*bind, constrain, confine, shackle, fetter, yoke*)

reliance—confidence, trust, dependence, assurance. (*distrust, misgiving, suspicion, diffidence*)

relief—succor, support, release, extrication, alleviation, mitigation, aid, help, assistance, remedy, redress, exemption, deliverance, refreshment, comfort. (*oppression, aggravation, intensification, burdensomeness, trouble, exhaustion, weariness, discomfort*)

religion—faith, creed, theology, belief, profession, piety, sanctity, godliness, holiness. (*unbelief, irreligion, godlessness, atheism, impiety, sacrilege, scoffing, blasphemy, skepticism, profanity, hypocrisy, sanctimoniousness, pharisaism, formalism, reprobation*)

religious—pious, godly, devout, devotional, divine, holy, sacred. (*impious, ungodly, undevout, sacrilegious, blasphemous, skeptical, profane*)

relish—zest, recommendation, enhancement, flavor, savor, gusto, taste, appetite, piquancy, sapidity. (*drawback, disflavor, disrecommendation, nauseousness, disrelish, insipidity, unsavoriness*)

remain—stay, continue, wait, stop, tarry, halt, sojourn, rest, dwell, abide, last, endure, accrue, survive. (*fly, vanish, remove, depart, speed, hasten, press, flit, disappear, pass*)

remarkable—observable, noticeable, extraordinary, unusual, rare, striking, noteworthy, notable, distinguished, famous, peculiar, prominent, singular. (*unremarkable, unnoticeable, ordinary, mean, commonplace, every-day, undistinguished*)

remedy—cure, restorative, counteraction, reparation, redress, relief, help, specific. (*evil, disease, hurt, infection, plague, ill, impairment, deterioration, aggravation, provocation*)

remember—recollect, recall, retain, bear in mind, mind. (*forget, obliviate, disregard, overlook*)

remembrance—recollection, memory, memorial, token, souvenir, memento, reminiscence. (*forgetfulness, oblivion*)

remiss—slack, careless, negligent, inattentive, wanting, slow, slothful, idle, lax, dilatory, tardy, remissful. (*energetic, careful, attentive, active, assiduous, alert, painstaking, diligent, strict*)

remit—relax, pardon, absolve, forego, discontinue, surrender, forgive, resign. (*increase, intensity, enforce, exact*)

remorse—compunction, anguish, self-condemnation, penitence, sting of conscience. (*complacency, self-approval, self-congratulation*)

remote—distant, indirect, unconnected, unrelated, foreign, alien, heterogeneous, separate, contingent. (*near, close, direct, connected, related, homogeneous, immediate, proximate, essential, present, pressing, urgent, actual*)

remove—displace, separate, abstract, transport, carry, transfer, eject, oust, dislodge, suppress, migrate, depart. (*restore, conserve, stabilitate, perpetuate, establish, reinstate, reinstall, install, fix, fasten, stay, remain, dwell, abide, stand*)

render—give, present, return, restore, give up, apportion, assign, surrender, pay, requite, deliver. (*keep, retain, withhold, appropriate, alienate, misapportion, misappropriate, misrequite*)

renew—recreate, restore, refresh, renovate, rejuvenate, furbish, recommence, repeat, reiterate, reissue, regenerate, reform, transform. (*impair, wear, deteriorate, vitiate, exhaust, discontinue, corrupt, weaken, defile, deprave*)

renounce—reject, abjure, disclaim, disown, forego, disavow, deny, quit, resign, abandon, recant, relinquish, repudiate. (*acknowledge, recognize, claim, maintain, assert, propound, own, vindicate, avow, profess, hold, retain, defend*)

renowned—famous, celebrated, wonderful, illustrious.

repay—remunerate, reimburse, recompense, reward, retaliate, requite, refund. (*defraud, misappropriate, embezzle, waste, alienate, extort, confiscate, exact*)

repeal—*v.* abolish, revoke, rescind, cancel, annul, recall, abrogate, reverse, discontinue, make void. (*continue, establish, pass, institute, sanction, enact, perpetuate, confirm*)

repeal—*n.* abrogation, rescission, revocation, annulment. (*continuance, establishment, perpetuation*)

repeat—reiterate, iterate, renew, cite, quote, relate, rehearse, recapitulate, reproduce. (*discontinue, drop, discard, abandon, ignore, suppress, misrepeat, misquote, misrecite, misrepresent, misinterpret, misconvey*)

repeatedly—frequently, again and again, often. (*seldom, rarely*)

repentance—penitence, contrition, compunction, regret, remorse, sorrow, self-reproach, self-condemnation. (*impenitence, obduracy, recusancy, hardness, reprobation, self-approval*)

repetition—iteration, reiteration, dwelling upon, diffuseness, verbosity, relation.

replace—restore, supply, substitute, reinstate, rearrange, re-establish. (*move, abstract, withdraw, remove, damage, deprive*)

reply—*v.* replicate, answer, respond, rejoin. (*ignore, drop, pretermit, pass, disregard*)

reply—*n.* answer, rejoinder, response, replication. (*pass by, ignoring*)

report—*v.* announce, relate, tell, circulate, notify, narrate, recite, describe, detail, communicate, declare. (*silence, hush, suppress, misreport, misrepresent, misrelate, falsify*)

report—*n.* tidings, announcement, relation, narration, recital, description, communication, declaration, news, rumor, fame, repute, noise, reverberation. (*silence, suppression, misannouncement, fabrication, noiselessness*)

represent—portray, delineate, reproduce, exhibit, personate, state, describe, indicate, embody, enact, illustrate, denote, play, dramatize, resemble. (*misportray, misdelineate, distort, falsify, caricature, misrepresent*)

representative—agent, commissioner, proxy, deputy, substitute, embodiment, personation, delegate, vicar, vicegerent, principal, sovereign, constituency. (*autocrat, dictator*)

reproach—blame, censure, taunt, rebuke, upbraid, reprobate, reprove. (*laud, praise, approve, commend*)

reprobate—castaway, villain, ruffian, miscreant, scapegrace, scalawag. (*example, pattern, mirror, model, paragon*)

repudiate—disavow, disown, discard, cast off, abjure, renounce, disclaim, divorce. (*avow, own, vindicate, assert, retain, vaunt, claim, profess, recognize, acknowledge, accept*)

repulsive—forbidding, deterrent, ungenial, odious, ugly, unattractive, disagreeable, revolting. (*charming, agreeable, attractive, winning, captivating, fascinating, alluring, seductive, pleasant*)

reputable—respectable, creditable, honorable, estimate. (*unrespectable, discreditable, dishonorable, disgraceful, disreputable*)

rescue—retake, recover, recapture, liberate, extricate, save, deliver, preserve. (*endanger, imperil, betray, surrender, abandon, expose*)

resemblance—likeness, similarity, similitude, semblance, representation, portrait, reflection, image. (*unlikeness, dissimilarity, disresemblance, difference, contrariety*)

resent—repel, resist, rebel, recalcitrate, take ill. (*acquiesce, submit, condone, pardon, overlook*)

reserve—reservation, retention, limitation, backwardness, coldness, shyness, coyness, modesty. (*boldness, rashness, recklessness, immodesty*)

residence—sojourn, stay, abode, home, habitation, domicile, mansion

resist—withstand, oppose, hinder, check, thwart, baffle, disappoint. (*weaken, yield, give up, surrender*)

resolute—determined, decided, fixed, steadfast, steady, constant, persevering, bold, firm, unshaken. (*weak, infirm, shy, cowardly, inconstant*)

resource—material, means, supplies, expedients, wealth, riches. (*destitution, exhaustion, lack, drain, nonplus, poverty*)

respect—regard, esteem, honor, revere, venerate.

respond—answer, reply, rejoin.

rest—remainder, overplus, remnant, residue, others.

restless—unquiet, uneasy, disturbed, disquieted, sleepless, agitated, anxious, unsettled, roving, wandering. (*steady, quiet, settled*)

restrain—check, hinder, stop, withhold, repress, curb, suppress, coerce, restrict, abridge, limit, confine. (*give full rein to, let go, release, free*)

result—effect, consequence, conclusion, inference, issue, event.

retain—keep, hold, restrain. (*yield, give up*)

retire—withdraw, leave, depart, secede, recede.

retort—repartee, answer.

retreat—retirement, departure, withdrawment, seclusion, solitude, privacy, asylum, shelter, refuge. (*advance, forward march*)

return—restore, requite, repay, recompense, render, remit, report.

reveal—communicate, disclose, divulge, unveil, uncover, open, discover, impart, show. (*keep secret, withhold, cover, conceal, hide*)

revengeful—vindictive, resentful, spiteful, malicious. (*open, ingenuous, frank, hearty, generous, kind, cordial*)

revenue—receipts, returns, income, proceeds, wealth, result. (*expense, outgo*)

reverence—awe, honor, veneration, adoration.

review—re-examination, resurvey, retrospect, survey, reconsideration, revise, revision

reward—recompense, compensation, remuneration, pay, requital, retribution.

rich—wealthy, affluent, opulent, ample, copious, abundant, fruitful, costly, sumptuous, precious, generous, luscious. (*poor, weak, straitened, cheap, scanty, sordid*)

ridicule—derision, wit, banter, raillery, burlesque, mockery, irony, satire, sarcasm, gibe, jeer, sneer.

ripe—mature, mellow, complete, finished. (*green, young, incomplete, unfinished*)

rise—arise, mount, ascend, climb, scale.

risk—danger, hazard, peril, jeopardy, exposure.

rival—competitor, emulator, antagonist.

road—way, highway, street, lane, pathway, route, passage, course.

robbery—theft, depredation, spoliation, despoliation, despoilment, plunder, pillage, freebooting, piracy.

romance—fable, novel, fiction, tale.

romantic—sentimental, fanciful, fictitious, extravagant, wild, chimerical.

room—space, compass, scope, latitude.

round—circular, spherical, globular, globose, orbicular, orbed, cylindrical, full, plump, rotund. (*square, oblong, angular, lean, thin*)

rout—defeat, smite, conquer. (*victory*)

route—roadway, path, track.

royal—kingly, regal, monarchical, imperial, kinglike, princely, august, majestic, superb, splendid, illustrious, noble, magnanimous.

ruin—destruction, downfall, perdition, fall, overthrow, subversion, defeat, bane, pest, mischief.

rule—regulation, law, precept, maxim, guide, canon, order, method, direction, control, government, sway, empire.

rustic—rural, rude, unpolished, inelegant, untaught, awkward, rough, coarse, plain, unadorned, simple, artless, honest.

S

sacred—holy, divine, hallowed, consecrated, dedicated, devoted, religious, venerable, reverend.

sad—sorrowful, mournful, gloomy, dejected, dedepressed, cheerless, downcast, sedate, serious, grave, grievous, afflictive, calamitous. (*gay, lively, happy, spirited, sprightly, jolly, fortunate, seductive*)

safe—secure, unendangered, sure. (*in danger, dangerous, exposed, risky*)

sagacity—penetration, shrewdness, judiciousness. (*stupidity, thickheadedness, dullness, foolishness*)

salutary—wholesome, healthful, salubrious, beneficial, useful, advantageous, profitable. (*unhealthy, infectious, tainted*)

sample—specimen, example, illustration.

sanction—ratify, support, endorse.

satire—lampoon, sarcasm, irony, ridicule, pasquinade, burlesque, wit, humor.

satisfaction—contentment, content, gratification, pleasure, recompense, compensation, amends, remuneration, indemnification, atonement.

satisfy—satiate, content, please, gratify, recompense, compensate, remunerate, indemnify.

saucy—impertinent, insolent, rude, impudent.

savage—ferocious, wild, uncultivated, untaught, uncivilized, unpolished, rude, brutish, brutal, heathenish, barbarous, cruel, inhuman, fierce, pitiless, merciless, unmerciful, murderous. (*cultured, refined, kind, gentle, merciful, humane, human, tame*)

save—preserve, rescue, deliver, protect, spare, reserve, prevent. (*abandon, expose, give up, throw away*)

saying—declaration, speech, adage, maxim, aphorism, apothegm, saw, proverb, by-word.

scandal—defamation, detraction, slander, calumny, opprobrium, reproach, shame, disgrace. (*honor, glory, respect*)

scanty—deficient, gaunt, meager, scarce. (*full, ample, plenty*)

scarce—rare, infrequent, deficient, uncommon. (*common, general, usual, frequent*)

scatter—disperse, dissipate, spread, strew, sprinkle. (*gather, keep together, collect, preserve*)

scheme—plan, project, design, contrivance, purpose, device, plot.

scholar—pupil, learner, disciple, learned man, sage.

science—literature, art, knowledge.

scorn—contempt, disdain, derision, contumely, despite, slight, dishonor, contempt. (*love, respect, honor, admiration, flattery*)

scrupulous—cautious, careful, conscientious, hesitating. (*unscrupulous, careless, scatterbrained, reckless, daring, dishonest*)

scurrilous—opprobrious, abusive, reproachful, insulting, insolent, offensive, gross, vile, vulgar, low, foul, foul-mouthed, indecent, scurrile, mean.

seasonable—opportune, timely, fit convenient.

secret—hidden, concealed, secluded, unseen, unknown, private, obscure, recondite, latent, covert, clandestine, privy. (*open, free, known, public*)

sectarian—heretic, partisan, schismatic.

section—part, division, portion.

security—protection, defense, guard, shelter, safety, certainty, ease, assurance, carelessness, confidence, surety, pledge. (*danger, exposure, doubt, uncertainty*)

sedate—sober, demure, serious, calm, grave, settled, serene, passive, quiet. (*flighty, frolicsome, indiscreet, ruffled, agitated, disturbed*)

seem—appear, look.

seemly—becomingly, fit, suitable, proper, appropriate, congruous, meet, decent, decorous. (*improper, immodest, unconventional, gross, rude*)

seize—catch, grasp, clutch, snatch, append, arrest, take, capture.

sense—understanding, reason, perception, sensation, feeling, meaning, import, signification, notion, opinion, judgment.

sensible—intelligent, wise, cognizant, satisfied, persuaded. (*scatterbrained, foolish, ignorant of*)

sentiment—thought, opinion, notion, sensibility, feeling.

serious—grave, solemn, important, weighty. (*gay, lively, happy, light, unimportant*)

serve—obey, minister to, subserve, promote, aid, help, assist, benefit, succor.

set—*v.* sink, settle, subside, decline, compose, consolidate, harden. (*rise, ascend, soar, mount, stir, agitate, loosen, run, soften, melt, mollify, fuse, flow*)

set—*a.* fixed, established, firm, determined, regular, formal.

settle—fix, establish, regulate, arrange, compose, adjust, determine, decide, adjudicate, quiet, allay, still, sink, fall, subside, lower, calm, acquiesce, abate, agree. (*remove, disestablish, misregulate, derange, discompose, aggravate, disorder, disturb, confuse, misdetermine, misarrange, misplace, unsettle, rise, ascend, move, disagree, increase, heighten*)

settlement—subsidence, dregs, residuum, precipitation, colonization, location, colony. (*excitement, perturbation, turbidity, fluctuation*)

several—separate, distinct, diverse, sundry, divers, various, different. (*one, same, identical, indistinguishable, inseparable, united, total, integral*)

severe—serious, austere, stern, grave, strict, harsh, rigid, rigorous, sharp, afflictive, distressing, violent, extreme, exact, critical, censorious, caustic, sarcastic, cutting, keen, better, cruel. (*gay, smiling, cheerful, relaxed, jocose, jocund, joyous, mild, genial, indulgent, light, trivial, trifling, inconsiderable, inexact, loose, uncritical, lenient, inextreme, moderate, kind, considerate, feeling, tender, gentle*)

shabby—ragged, threadbare, contemptible, beggarly, paltry.

shadowy—dim, cloudy, obscure, dark, murky, gloomy, mysterious.

shallow—shoal, slight, flimsy, trifling, simple superficial, unprofound. (*deep, profound*)

sham—phantom, ghost, delusion, illusion, mockery, shadow, pretense, counterfeit, unreality. (*substance, reality, verity, substantiality, truth*)

shame—abashment, humiliation, modesty, shamefacedness, decency, decorum, reproach, dishonor, ignominy, contempt, degradation, discredit, dispraise. (*shamelessness, barefacedness, immodesty,* *impudence, indecency, indecorum, impropriety, honor, glory, exaltation, renown, credit*)

shameful—disgraceful, degrading, scandalous, outrageous, dishonorable, indecent, unbecoming.

shape—*v.* form, mould, figure, adapt, delineate, adjust, contrive, create, execute, make. (*pervert, distort, misadapt, misdelineate, derange, discompose, miscontrive, misproduce, caricature*)

shape—*n.* figure, form, outline, mould, fashion, pattern, cast, model.

share—portion, apportionment, lot, division, participation, allowance, quota, contingent, allotment. (*whole, mass, aggregate, entirety*)

sharp—thin, fine, keen, shrewd, discerning, clever, sarcastic, acute, pointed, aculeated, penetrating, pungent, acid, shrill, piercing, afflictive, distressing, harsh, severe, cutting, eager, active, ardent, sore, hard, animated, spirited. (*thick, blunt, dull, obtuse, knobbed, rounded, bluff, mellow, bass, hollow, deep, light, trifling, trivial, mild, gentle, soft, tender, lenient, sluggish, inactive, indifferent, careless, spiritless, tame*)

shatter—split, dissipate, disrupt, derange, break in pieces, rend, demolish, shiver, dismember, disintegrate. (*construct, organize, collocate, fabricate, compose, rear, constitute*)

sheer—pure, mere, unmixed, unqualified, unmitigated, absolute, simple, unadulterated. (*mixed, qualified, adulterated, modified, partial*)

shelve—dismiss, discard, swamp, stifle, shift. (*start, prosecute, pursue, revive, agitate*)

shift—*v.* change, alter, transfer, shelve, displace, remove. (*fix, fasten, locate, insert, pitch, plant, place*)

shift—*n.* contrivance, expedient, substitute, pretext, motive, change, evasion, device, artifice, resource, transference. (*miscontrivance, fixity, steadiness, retention, location, permanence*)

shocking—sad, horrible, disgraceful, hateful, revolting, abominable, loathsome, foul. (*pleasing,* *honorable, charming, delightful, creditable, edifying, exemplary, attractive, alluring, enticing)*

short—brief, limited, scanty, inadequate, insufficient, lacking, deficient, defective, imperfect, incomplete, soon, near, narrow, weak, incomprehensive, inextensive, less, abrupt, blunt, concise, condensed. *(long, protracted, extended, unlimited, plentiful, ample, abundant, adequate, sufficient, exuberant, liberal, large, copious, complete, distant, deferred, wide, strong, comprehensive, extensive, exceeding, bland, courteous, inabrupt, expanded, diffuse)*

show—*v.* exhibit, present, demonstrate, unfold, reveal, teach, inform, conduct, manifest, evince, evidence, prove, explain. *(conceal, suppress, hide, withhold, obscure, mystify, wrap, misdemonstrate, misdeclare, contradict, refute, deny, disprove, misinterpret, falsify, misexplain)*

show—*n.* appearance, exhibition, demonstration, parade, pomp, semblance, likeness, pretext, profession, pretense, illusion. *(non-appearance, disappearance, concealment, suppression, secrecy, disguise, dissimilarity, unlikeness, ungenuineness, reality, sincerity, substance)*

showy—gay, gaudy, high-colored, gorgeous, flashy, tinsel. *(inconspicuous, unnoticeable, quiet, subdued)*

shrewd—sagacious, penetrating, astute, discriminating, intelligent, discerning, acute. *(stolid, undiscerning, unsagacious, stupid, dull)*

shrink—contract, shrivel, withdraw, retire, recoil, revolt. *(stretch, expand, dilate, venture, dare)*

shrivel—contract, dry up, wither, wrinkle, corrugate, decrease. *(expand, flatten, develop, unfold, spread, dilate)*

shuffle—confuse, interchange, shift, intershift, intermix, derange, agitate, evade, prevaricate, equivocate, quibble, cavil, sophisticate, mystify, palter, dissemble. *(deal, distribute, order, arrange, compose, confess, propound, declare, explain, elucidate, reveal)*

shy—timid, reserved, modest, bashful, suspicious, shrinking, chary. (*bold, brazen-faced, impudent, audacious, reckless*)

sick—diseased, ill, disordered, distempered, indisposed, weak, ailing, feeble, morbid, nauseated, disgusted, corrupt, impaired, valetudinarian. (*whole, well, healthy, sound, robust, strong, well-conditioned, salubrious*)

sickly—weak, diseased, disordered, ailing, feeble, pining, drooping, morbid, unhealthy, vitiated, delicate, tainted, valetudinary. (*strong, healthy, vigorous, flourishing, salubrious, sound, robust*)

side—margin, edge, verge, border, laterality, face, aspect, plane, party, interest, cause, policy, behalf. (*center, body, core, interior, essence, neutrality, disconnection, severance, secession, opposition*)

sight—seeing, perception, view, vision, visibility, spectacle, show, inspection, examination, representation, appearance. (*non-perception, invisibility, blindness, obscuration, disappearance, oversight, non-appearance, undiscernment*)

sign—token, indication, proof, memorial, expression, symbol, emblem, prefiguration, badge, type, premonition, symptom, prognostic, mark, wonder, presage, signal. (*misindication, misrepresentation, misleader*)

signal—eminent, conspicuous, remarkable, extraordinary, notable, memorable, illustrious, important, salient, distinguished. (*ordinary, common, unnoticeable, mediocre, unmemorable, unimportant*)

signify—portend, purport, prognosticate, mean, represent, indicate, communicate, denote, betoken, declare, utter, forebode, presage. (*conceal, suppress, misindicate, misdenote, nullify, refute, neutralize, preclude*)

silence—taciturnity, stillness, calm, peace, hush, muteness, secrecy, oblivion. (*garrulity, loquacity, talkativeness, chatter, noise, brawl, clamor, clatter, din, babel, tumult, agitation, restlessness, storm, un-*

rest, roar, bruit, reverberation, resonance, commotion, cackling, proclamation, publicity, fame, rumor, remembrance, repute, celebrity)

silly—simple, foolish, weak, shallow, witless, unwise, indiscreet, imprudent, absurd. (*sagacious, intelligent, astute, wise, deep, discreet, prudent, sound, rational*)

similar—correspondent, resembling, alike, common, homogeneous, concordant, harmonious, congruous. (*different, unlike, dissimilar, alien, heterogeneous, discordant, incongruous*)

simple—single, incomplex, uncompounded, unblended, isolated, pure, unmixed, mere, absolute, plain, unadorned, unartificial, artless, sincere, undesigning, single-minded, unaffected, silly, weak, unsophisticated, humble, homely, lowly, elementary, ultimate, primal, rudimentary. (*double, complex, compounded, blended, mixed, fused, multiform, multigenerous, various, compound, articulated, subdivided, organized, connected, modified, complicated, elaborate, artificial, artful, designing, insincere, double-minded, affected, self-conscious, sagacious, sophisticated, great, eminent, illustrous, complete, developed, perfect*)

simultaneous—synchronous, concomitant, concurrent. (*inconcurrent, separate, apart, intermittent, periodic*)

sin—transgression, iniquity, unrighteousness, ungodliness, wickedness, evil, impurity, crime, wrongdoing. (*sinlessness, obedience, holiness, righteousness, purity, godliness, goodness*)

sincere—pure, unmixed, genuine, unadulterated, hearty, honest, unaffected, unvarnished, candid, cordial, frank, unfeigned, true. (*impure, adulterated, dishonest, insincere, hypocritical, feigned, pretended, false*)

single—one, unique, only, individual, sole, solitary, separate, uncombined, unmarried, uncompounded. (*plural, many, collective, united, numerous, frequent, married*)

singular—single, individual, unique, eminent, extraordinary, conspicuous, consummate, unusual, uncommon, odd, whimsical quaint, peculiar, unexampled, unprecedented, solitary, sole, eccentric, fantastic, exceptional, particular, remarkable, curious, queer. (*common, frequent, numerous, ordinary, usual, unnoticeable, every-day, customary, general, regular*)

situation—locality, position, topography, state, seat, post, place, condition, residence, aspect, footing, office, birth, plight, predicament, standing. (*non-situation, non-location, absence, non-assignment, unfixedness, displacement, dislodgement*)

slender—thin, narrow, slight, slim, small, trivial, spare, inadequate, fragile, feeble, flimsy, meagre, inconsiderable, superficial. (*stout, thick, broad, robust, massive, considerable, ample, deep*)

slow—sluggish, inactive, inert, lazy, unready, tardy, late, gradual, tedious, dull, dilatory, lingering, slack. (*active, quick, fast, rapid, alert, ready, prompt, early, sudden, immediate*)

sly—cunning, subtle, crafty, artful, wily, underhanded, astute, stealthy. (*open, frank, artless, undesigning*)

small—little, deminutive, slight, minute, feeble, trivial, insignificant, paltry, narrow, mean, weak, slender, fine, inferior. (*great, large, big, considerable, bulky, extensive, ample, spacious, stout, strong, important, broad, liberal*)

smart—keen, pungent, piercing, quick, vigorous, sharp, severe, active, clever, brilliant, vivacious, witty, ready, spruce, brisk, fresh, dressy, showy. (*dull, heavy, aching, slow, inactive, stupid, sluggish, unready, slow-minded, unwitty, dowdy, shabby, clownish*)

smooth—even, plain, level, flat, polished, glossy, sleek, soft, unruffled, unobstructed, bland, oily, suave. (*uneven, rough, rugged, abrupt, precipitous, unpolished, harsh, blunt*)

smother—suffocate, stifle, repress, gag, conceal, suppress, choke, strangle, allay, swallow. (*fan, ventilate, foster, cherish, nurture, publish, promulgate, divulge, spread, excite, vent*)

sneer—scoff, gibe, jeer, taunt, disparagement, contempt, scorn, superciliousness, disdain. (*compliment, eulogy, commendation, deference*)

snub—mortify, check, rebuke, reprimand.

snug—close, housed, compressed, compact, comfortable, sheltered. (*exposed, loose, disordered, incompact, uncomfortable, bare, shivering*)

sober—temperate, unintoxicated, cool, dispassionate, reasonable, calm, self-possessed, sound, unexcited, serious, grave, sedate, steady, abstemious, moderate. (*intemperate, drunk, intoxicated, heated, excited, impassioned, unreasonable, agitated, furious, passionate, extravagant, extreme, exorbitant, immoderate, flighty, erratic, eccentric*)

society—community, polity, association, collection, companionship, fellowship, connection, participation, company, sociality, communion, intercourse, sodality. (*individuality, personality, segregation, separation, solitariness, unsociality, privacy, dissociation, disconnection*)

soft—yielding, pressible, impressible, smooth, delicate, fine, sleek, glossy, mild, gentle, balmy, kind, feeling, flexible, effeminate, luxurious, unmanly, tender, irresolute, undecided. (*hard, tough, stubborn, unyielding, rigid, unimpressible, rough, coarse, harsh, abrupt, ungentle, rigorous, cutting, severe, unkind, unfeeling, sharp, inflexible, stern, austere, ascetic, self-denying, resolute, determined*)

soften—mollify, palliate, compose, mitigate, assuage, dulcify, lenify, yield, macerate, humanize, abate, moderate. (*harden, indurate, aggravate, excite, infuriate, consolidate*)

solemn—sacred, formal, devotional, reverential, ritual, ceremonial, impressive, religious, grave, serious. (*profane, undevotional, secular, light, gay, trivial, unceremonial, informal, unsolemn*)

solid—hard, firm, compact, resistant, dense, substantial, weighty, strong, valid, just, sound, impenetrable, stable, cubic. (*soft, hollow, yielding, frail, brittle, flimsy, elastic, resilient, malleable, impressible, fluid, liquid, frivolous, light, trifling, weak, invalid, unsound, fallacious, weakly*)

solitude—loneliness, remoteness, seclusion, retirement, isolation, wildness, desertion, barrenness, wilderness, privacy. (*publicity, populousness, society, frequentedness, intercourse, resort, meeting, reunion, throng, crowd*)

solution—separation, discerption, disruption, breach, discontinuance, disconnection, disentanglement, elucidation, explanation, key, answer, resolution, disintegration. (*union, combination, amalgamation, continuity, connection, conjunction, entanglement, complication, confusion, mystification, obscurity, integration*)

sore—painful, irritated, susceptible, excoriated, raw, scarified, ulcerous, grievous, afflictive, heavy, burdensome. (*painless, sound, whole, healthful, healed, unbroken, unscarified, light, trivial, unburdensome, pleasant, untroublesome, grateful*)

sorry—grieved, pained, hurt, afflicted, woe-begone, doleful, down-hearted, mortified, vexed, dejected, poor, mean, vile, shabby, worthless. (*glad, rejoiced, delighted, pleased, gratified, fine, choice, handsome*)

sort—kind, species, nature, class, order, character, rank, manner, quality, condition, description, designation, genus. (*non-description, solitariness, uniqueness, non-classification, heterogeneity*)

sound—entire, unbroken, whole, perfect, unhurt, well-grounded, uninjured, unimpaired, healthy, firm, strong, vigorous, weighty, solid, irrefragable, irrefutable, thorough, valid, wholesome, correct, substantial. (*partial, broken, injured, impaired, unhealthy, unsound, weak, frail, fragile, light, trivial, unfounded, hollow, fallacious, imperfect, unwholesome, incorrect, unsubstantial, invalid*)

sour—tart, rancid, coagulated, turned, harsh, crabbed, austere, morose, pungent, crusty, acid, churlish, bitter, acetous, acrimonious, peevish. (*sweet, wholesome, untainted, mellow, genial, kindly*)

spacious—ample, extensive, broad, vast, capacious, large, wide, roomy, expansive. (*narrow, restricted, limited, cramped, confined, inextensive*)

spare—*v.* save, afford, grant, reserve, do without, husband, economize, retain, store, grudge, discard, omit, forbear, withhold, refrain, abstain. (*spend, squander, waste, lavish, scatter, expend, pour, indulge, vent*)

spare—*a.* scanty, unplentiful, inabundant, meagre, economical, frugal, stinted, restricted, parsimonious, niggardly, chary, superfluous, disposable, available, lean, thin, ill-conditioned. (*ample, plentiful, abundant, profuse, liberal, unrestricted, generous, bountiful, unsparing, unstinted, unbounded, available, well-conditioned*)

special—particular, specific, peculiar, appropriate, proper, distinctive, extraordinary, especial, exceptional. (*general, universal, common, generic*)

speculation—contemplation, consideration, view, weighing, thought, theory, scheme, hypothesis, conjecture. (*realization, proof, fact, verification, certainty*)

speed—dispatch, expedite, accelerate, urge, hasten, hurry, press. (*retard, delay, postpone, obstruct, drag, loiter, dawdle, linger, lag, stay*)

spend—bestow, waste, exhaust, squander, expend, lay out, consume, disburse, lavish. (*retain, save, hoard, accumulate, husband, economize*)

spirit—air, breath, life, soul, vital force, essential quality, essence, immateriality, intelligence, disembodiment, spectre, apparition, ghost, energy, ardor, enthusiasm, activity, earnestness, courage, zeal, disposition, temper, principle, motive, distillation. (*substance, body, corporeity, materiality, flesh, organization, frame, embodiment, spiritlessness, listlessness, soullessness, lifelessness, torpor, deadness,* *timidity, dejection, slowness, sluggishness)*

spirited—animated, lively, vivacious, ardent, buoyant, sprightly, courageous. (*dull, dispirited, depressed, cowardly*)

spiritual—divine, religious, holy, ghostly, ethical, immaterial, incorporeal, intellectual. (*carnal, fleshly, unspiritual, gross, material, sensuous*)

spite—malice, malevolence, grudge, pique, hatred, ill-will, vindictiveness, rancor, spleen. (*good-will, benevolence, kindliness*)

splendid—brilliant, showy, magnificent, sumptuous, gorgeous, glorious, pompous, imposing, illustrious, superb, famous, heroic, grand, signal. (*dull, obscure, tame, somber, poor, beggarly, unimposing, ordinary, ineffective, inglorious*)

split—divide, separate, rive, cleave, crack, splinter, burst, rend, sunder, disagree, secede, disunite. (*cohere, unite, amalgamate, coalesce, conform, agree, splice, consolidate, integrate*)

spoil—plunder, strip, rob, devastate, pillage, denude, corrupt, vitiate, mar, deteriorate. (*invest, enrich, endow, replenish, renovate, improve, better, ameliorate, rectify, preserve*)

spontaneous—voluntary, self-generated, self-originated, self-evolved, willing, unbidden, gratuitous. (*involuntary, imposed, compulsionary, unwilling, necessitated, coercive*)

sport—play, frolic, wantonness, joke, diversion, merriment, gaiety, fun, amusement, recreation, game, pastime. (*work, seriousness, business, earnestness*)

spread—extend, stretch, expand, open, unfurl, divulge, propagate, publish, disperse, diffuse, overlay, distribute, scatter, circulate, disseminate, ramify. (*contract, furl, gather, fold, close, shut, secrete, suppress, confine, restrict, repress, hush, conceal, recall, collect, stagnate, concentrate, localize*)

spring—leap, bound, jump, start, emerge, issue, proceed, orginate, rise, emanate, germinate, burst, flow. (*settle, alight, land, drop, arrive, issue, eventuate, end, terminate, debouch, disembogue*)

staid—grave, demure, steady, sober, sedate. (*unsteady, flighty, indiscreet, wanton, insedate, erratic, eccentric, agitated, discomposed, ruffled*)

stammer—stutter, hesitate, falter. (*speak clearly, speak unhesitatingly*)

stamp—genus, kind, description, make, mark, impression, imprint, print, brand, cast, mould, character, type. (*heterogeneity, non-description, formlessness*)

stand—rest, remain, stop, be, exist, keep one's ground, insist, depend, await, consist, hold, continue, endure, pause, halt. (*progress, move, proceed, advance, fall, fail, yield, succumb, drop, lie, vanish, fade, run, depart*)

standard—measure, gauge, criterion, test, rule, exemplar, banner, flag, type, model, scale, plummet, trutination. (*mismeasurement, misrule, misadjustment, miscomparison, inconformity, misfit, incommensurateness, non-criterion*)

state—*n.* position, condition, situation, circumstances, plight, predicament, case, province.

state—*v.* say, declare, propound, aver, set forth, narrate, specify, particularize, avow, recite. (*suppress, repress, suppose, imply, deny, contradict, retract*)

stately—dignified, imposing, lofty, elevated, lordly, proud, majestic, pompous, magnificent, grand. (*undignified, unimposing, unstately, commonplace, mean*)

stay—hold, stop, restrain, withhold, arrest, hinder, delay, obstruct, support, rest, repose, remain, continue, dwell, await, halt, abide, wait, tarry, confide, trust, lean. (*loose, liberate, send, expedite, speed, free, accelerate, hasten, oppress, depress, burden, fail, fall, proceed, move, depart, overthrow, mistrust*)

steady—firm, fixed, constant, uniform, consistent, equable, regular, undeviating, well-regulated. (*infirm, variable, unsteady, inconstant, changeable, wavering, ill-regulated*)

step—advance, pace, space, grade, remove, degree, gradation, progression, track, trace, vestige, walk, gait, proceeding, action, measure. (*retreat, recession, halting, station, standing, non-graduation, non-progression, stand-still, stop, tracklessness, untraceableness, non-impression, desinence, desistance, inaction*)

stern—severe, austere, rigid, harsh, strict, rigorous, unrelenting, unyielding, forbidding. (*lenient, genial, kindly, easy, flexible, encouraging*)

stiff—unbending, inflexible, rigid, unyielding, unpliant, strong, stubborn, obstinate, pertinacious, constrained, affected, starched, formal, ceremonious, difficult. (*pliant, flexible, flaccid, yielding, easy, unaffected, genial, affable, unceremonious*)

still—quiet, calm, noiseless, hushed, silent, pacific, serene, motionless, stagnant, peaceful, quiescent, tranquil, stationary. (*unquiet, disturbed, agitated, moved, noisy, resonant, turbulent, moving, transitional*)

stingy—close, avaricious, mean, niggardly, close-fisted, hide-bound, parsimonious, sparing, sordid, penurious. (*liberal, generous, large, handsome, lavish, bountiful, unsparing*)

stop—close, obstruct, plug, cork, bar, seal, arrest, suspend, end, rest, halt, hinder, suppress, delay, cease, terminate. (*open, expedite, clear, broach, unseal, promote, advance, farther, continue, proceed, speed, hasten*)

stout—strong, lusty, vigorous, robust, sturdy, brawny, corpulent, resolute, brave, valiant redoubtable. (*weak, debile, frail, attenuated, thin, slender, lean, irresolute, feeble, cowardly, timid*)

straight—direct, rectilinear, undeviating, unswerving, right, nearest. (*indirect, winding, incurved, tortuous, sinuous, serpentine, circuitous, waving, crooked*)

strange—foreign, alien, exotic, unfamiliar, unusual, odd, irregular, abnormal, exceptional, surprising, wonderful, marvellous, astonishing, uncommon, peculiar. (*home, domestic, familiar, usual, ordinary, common, regular, customary, commonplace, unsurprising, universal, general*)

strength—force, vigor, power, security, validity, vehemence, intensity, hardness, soundness, nerve, fibre, sinew. (*weakness, imbecility, feebleness, insolidity, insecurity, invalidity, frailty, delicacy, softness, flimsiness, hollowness*)

strenuous—strong, resolute, determined, earnest, vigorous, ardent, bold, energetic, vehement. (*weak, irresolute, undetermined, unearnest, debile, feeble, emasculate*)

strict—close, exact, accurate, rigorous, severe, stringent, nice, precise. (*loose, inexact, inaccurate, lenient, mild, indulgent, lax*)

striking—impressive, affecting, admirable, wonderful, surprising.

strong—powerful, vigorous, solid, secure, fortified, forcible, impetuous, hale, hearty, brawny, sinewy, sound, robust, cogent, influential, zealous, potent, pungent, muscular, hardy, stanch, tenacious. (*powerless, weak, frail, insecure, defenseless, feeble, mild, calm, gentle, delicate, sickly, inefficacious, unsatisfactory, unconvincing, unimpressive, vapid, impotent, unavailing, lukewarm, debile, flaccid, nerveless, tender, moderate, indifferent*)

stubborn—tough, unbending, unyielding, hard, obstinate, intractable, obdurate, stiff, harsh, inflexible, headstrong, refractory, heady, contumacious, pig-headed. (*docile, tractable, manageable, pliant, pliable, malleable, flexible*)

studious—literary, diligent, desirous, attentive, careful, thoughtful, assiduous, reflective. (*unliterary, illiterate, idle, indulgent, careless, regardless, indifferent, inattentive, negligent, thoughtless*)

stupid—dull, senseless, stolid, doltish, besotted, insensate, obtuse, prosy, addle-pated, dull-witted.

(quick, sharp, bright, sensible, sagacious, penetrating, clever)

subdue—conquer, reduce, overpower, break, tame, quell, vanquish, subdue, master, subjugate. *(aggrandize, exalt, fortify, strengthen, empower, liberate, enfranchise)*

subject—subordinate, subservient, exposed, liable, prone, disposed, obnoxious, amenable. *(superior, independent, exempt, indisposed, unliable, unamenable)*

submissive—obedient, compliant, yielding, obsequious, humble, docile, modest, passive, acquiescent, subservient. *(disobedient, incompliant, unyielding, inobsequious, recalcitrant, refractory, proud, resistant, renitent, malcontent, recusant)*

substantial—existing, real, solid, true, corporeal, material, strong, stout, massive, bulky, tangible. *(imaginary, unreal, insubstantial, fictitious, suppositious, incorporeal, chimerical, visionary, immaterial, weak, frail, airy, disembodied, spiritual, ghostly)*

subtle—sly, artful, cunning, insinuating, wily, astute, nice, discriminating, crafty, fine, shrewd, sophistical, jesuitical. *(open, frank, honest, artless, undiscriminating, rough, blunt, undiscerning, unsophisticated, simple)*

success—achievement, luck, consummation, prosperity, victory, good-fortune. *(failure, defeat, disaster, ruin)*

succession—following, supervention, consecutive, sequence, order, series, rotation, continuity, supply, suite. *(precedence, anticipation, prevention, antecedence, irregularity, disorder, non-sequence, solution, failure, intermission, break, gap, inconsecutiveness)*

suffer—bear, endure, sustain, undergo, let, permit, allow, admit, tolerate, experience, support. *(resist, repel, expel, reject, disallow, repudiate, forbid, ignore)*

sufficient—adequate, equal, competent, satisfactory, fit, qualified, adapted, suited, enough, ample. (*inadequate, unequal, incompetent, unqualified, unadapted, insufficient, unsuited, meagre, bare, scanty, short, deficient*)

suit—fit, adapt, match, adjust, harmonize, apportion, befit, beseem, tally, correspond, answer, comport, please, serve, agree, become, accord. (*misfit, misadapt, mismatch, misapportion, unbeseem, vary, differ, disagree, miscomport*)

summary—analysis, tabulation, abridgment, resumé, compendium, digest, epitome, abstract. (*dilatation, expansion, dilution*)

superb—grand, magnificent, elegant, princely, splendid, showy, proud, august, stately, gorgeous. (*mean, common, common-place, unimposing, shabby*)

supercilious—haughty, contemptuous, disdainful, arrogant, insolent. (*affable, courteous, respectful, modest, bashful*)

superficial—light, slight, imperfect, showy, external, flimsy, surface, shallow, smattering, skindeep. (*deep, profound, abstruse, recondite, accurate, exact, deep-seated*)

superior—higher, upper, better, preferable, surpassing, loftier, excellent, remarkable, eminent, conspicuous. (*inferior, lower, worse, subordinate, ordinary, common, unremarkable, average, mean, mediocre*)

supple—pliant, bending, yielding, flexible, elastic, servile, fawning, cringing, adulatory, sycophantic, lithe, limber, compliant. (*firm, unbending, unyielding, stiff, stubborn, inflexible, inelastic, independent, self-assertive, supercilious*)

supply—furnish, afford, provide, accoutre, give, minister, yield, contribute. (*expend, use, consume, waste, exhaust, absorb, demand, withhold, withdraw, retain*)

support—v. bear, uphold, sustain, underlie, befriend, assist, second, promote, further, suffer, defend, foster, nurture, nourish, cherish, endorse, maintain, continue, countenance, patronize, subsidize, help, back, stay, favor, prop. (*drop, betray, surrender, abandon, discontinue, oppose, discourage, weaken, exhaust, thwart, discountenance, disfavor, subvert, suppress*)

support—*n.* prop, stay, foundation, buttress, help, aid, assistance, influence, maintenance, living, patronage, subsistence, livelihood, food.

suppose—assume, presume, believe, divine, deem, fancy, think, regard, conceive, imagine, imply, presuppose, conjecture, guess, conclude, judge, consider. (*prove, demonstrate, substantiate, realize, disbelieve, negative, deny*)

sure—certain, secure, safe, assured, unmistakable, stable, firm, knowing, believing, confident, trusting, unquestioning, positive, unfailing, strong, permanent, abiding, enduring, infallible, indisputable, fast. (*uncertain, ignorant, dubious, doubtful, hesitating, distrustful, questioning, vacillating, weak, untrustworthy, precarious, insecure, impermanent, transient, evanescent, fallible, disputable, loose*)

susceptible—capable, impressible, tender, sensitive. (*incapable, unimpressible, insensitive, insusceptible, impassible*)

suspense—protraction, uncertainty, doubt, solicitude, cessation, pause, waiting, intermission, discontinuance, abeyance, stoppage, indetermination, indecision. (*determination, settlement, execution, continuance, uninterruption, revival, decision, finality*)

sway—*n.* wield, influence, rule, authority, government, superiority, bias, dominion, control, preponderance, domination, supremacy, mastery, ascendancy, weight, force, power. (*weakness, inferiority, subordination, irresistance, obedience, subservience, subjection*)

sway—*v.* influence, govern, rule, bias, wave, swing, wield.

sweet—saccharine, luscious, fragrant, dulcet, melodious, harmonious, musical, beautiful, lovely, wholesome, pleasing, pure, mild, winning, agreeable, fresh, gentle, amiable. (*sour, bitter, unsweet, fetid, offensive, nauseous, olid, stinking, nasty, inharmonious, discordant, unlovely, repulsive, unwholesome, putrid, tainted, ungentle, unamiable*)

swell—dilate, extend, enlarge, heighten, heave, enhance, rise, expand, increase, augment, protuberate, aggravate, amplify, distend. (*contract, curtail, shrivel, diminish, lessen, retrench, reduce, collapse, fold, narrow, condense, concentrate*)

sympathy—fellow-feeling, congeniality, commiseration, compassion, pity, concert, tenderness, agreement, condolence. (*antipathy, antagonism, incongeniality, pitilessness, mercilessness, compassionlessness, unkindness, harshness, unkindliness*)

system—method, scheme, order, regularity, classification, arrangement, rule, plan. (*disorder, derangement, confusion, fortuity, chance, medley, haphazard, incongruity, non-arrangement, non-classification*)

T

take—seize, grasp, catch, capture, siege, use, obtain, pursue, employ, follow, assume, procure, captivate, engage, interest, charm, choose, select, admit, accept, receive, conduct, transfer. (*drop, reject, abandon, surrender, lose, miss, repel*)

tall—high, lofty, towering, elevated. (*low*)

tame—domesticated, reclaimed, tamed, subjugated, broken, gentle, mild, docile, meek, spiritless, tedious, dull, flat. (*undomesticgted, unreclaimed, untamed, unbroken, savage, wild, fierce, spirited, animated, ferine, interesting, exciting, stirring, lively*)

task—work, function, labor, job, operation, business, undertaking, drudgery, toil, lesson. (*relaxation, leisure, amusement, hobby*)

taste—gustation, savor, flavor, sapidity, relish, perception, judgment, discernment, nicety, critique, sensibility, choice, zest, predilection, delicacy, elegancy, refinement. (*non-gustation, ill-savor, insipidity, disrelish, non-preception, indiscrimination, indiscernment, indelicacy, coarseness, inelegancy*)

tasteful—sapid, relishing, savory, agreeable, tasty, toothsome, palatable, elegant, refined. (*insipid, unrelishing, unsavory, unpalatable, nauseous, inelegant, tasteless, unrefined, vapid*)

teach—impart, tell, direct, instruct, inform, counsel, admonish, educate, inculcate, enlighten, advise, indoctrinate, train. (*withhold, misteach, misdirect, misinstruct, misinform, misguide, mislead*)

teacher—instructor, school-master, preceptor, tutor, professor, pedagogue, educationist, educator, school-mistress. (*pupil, scholar, disciple, learner*)

tedious—wearisome, tiresome, monotonous, dilatory, dreary, sluggish, irksome, dull, flat, prolix. (*interesting, exciting, stirring, charming, fascinating, delightful, amusing*)

tell—mention, number, enumerate, count, recount, utter, recite, state, narrate, disclose, publish, betray, divulge, promulgate, acquaint, teach, inform, explain, communicate, report, rehearse, discern, judge, discriminate, ascertain, decide, describe. (*repress, suppress, misrecount, misnarrate, miscommunicate, misdeclare, misrecite, misjudge, misdescribe*)

temporary—present, immediate, partial, limited, transient, impermanent. (*perpetual, lasting, confirmed, complete, final, perfect, permanent, entire*)

tendency—vergency, proneness, bias, gravitation, drift, scope, aim, disposition, predisposition, proclivity, leaning, inclination, attraction, conduciveness, course. (*disinclination, aversion, repulsion, contravention, deviation, divergency, tangency, divarication, opposition, renitency, reluctance, prevention, neutralization, termination*)

tender—*v.* offer, proffer, propose, bid, produce, present. (*withhold, withdraw, retain, appropriate*)

tender—*a.* delicate, frail, impressible, susceptible, yielding, soft, effeminate, weak, feeble, compassionate, affectionate, careful, jealous, gentle, mild, meek, pitiful, merciful, pathetic. (*strong, sturdy, hardy, robust, tough, iron, pitiless, unmerciful, cruel, hard-hearted, careless, liberal, lavish, unchary, ungentle, rough, rude, coarse, unsentimental, unmoving, unfeeling, unimpressive, unimpassioned, unimpressed*)

term—limit, boundary, condition, time, season, period, expression, designation, word, name, article, proviso, stipulation.

terrible—awful, fearful, dreadful, formidable, terrific, frightful, tremendous, horrible, shocking. (*informidable, unastounding, unstartling, unastonishing*)

terror—fear, dread, alarm, fright, consternation, horror, dismay. (*confidence, fearlessness, boldness, reassurance*)

test—cupel, trial, examination, proof, criterion, standard, experiment, touchstone, experience, ordeal. (*misindication, misjudgment, misproof*)

testimony—witness, evidence, attestation, affirmation, corroboration, confirmation, proof. (*refutation, contradiction, disproof, confutation, contravention, invalidation*)

theatrical—dramatic, scenic, melodramatic, showy, ceremonious, gesticulatory, pompous, meretricious, tinsel. (*chaste, genuine, simple, unaffected, quiet; subdued, mannerless, plain*)

thick—dense, condensed, inspissated, close, compact, turbid, luteous, coagulated, muddy, dull, misty, foggy, vaporous, crowded, numerous, solid, bulky, deep, confused, inarticulate. (*race, fine, thin, sparse, strained, pure, percolated, limpid, crystalline, scanty, incompact, slight, shallow, laminated, clear, articulate, distinct*)

thicken—condense, inspissate, incrassate, compact, solidify, befoul, obscure, bemire, becloud, increase, coagulate, amalgamate, commingle, intermix, crowd, multiply, enlarge, expand, extend, broaden, deepen, obstruct, confuse. (*rarify, dissipate, refine, attenuate, clear, purify, strain, percolate, clarify, defecate, depurate, brighten, lighten, open, filtrate, diminish, separate, reduce, narrow, contract, liberate, free, extricate, unravel, disentangle, loosen*)

thin—slim, slender, flimsy, attenuated, diluted, watery, meager, unsubstantial, lean.

think—ponder, meditate, consider, reflect, contemplate, conceive, imagine, apprehend, fancy, hold, regard, believe, deem, opine, purpose, judge, reckon.

thought—reflection, reasoning, cogitation, supposition, view, sentiment, meditation, conception, idea, opinion, judgment, conceit, fancy, design, purpose, intention, deliberation, care, provision. (*vacuity, incogitation, thoughtlessness, dream, hallucination, aberration, misconception, incogitancy, carelessness, improvidence, unreflectiveness*)

threatening—menacing, intimidating, minatory, comminatory, minacious, foreboding, unpromising, imminent, impending. (*encouraging, promising, reassuring, enticing, passed, overpast, withdrawn*)

tide—flow, course, current, rush, inundation, influx, stream, movement, flood. (*stagnation, arrestation, stoppage, cessation, motionlessness, subsidence*)

tight—firm, compact, fast, close, tidy, neat, smart, natty, tense, stretched. (*loose, incompact, open, flowing, loose-fitting, large, untidy, lax, relaxed*)

time—period, duration, season, interval, date, opportunity, age, era, occasion, term, space, span, spell. (*neverness, eternity, non-duration, indetermination, indeterminableness*)

timid—fearful, pusillanimous, shy, diffident, coy, timorous, afraid, cowardly, faint-hearted, inadventurous. (*bold, confident, venturesome, courageous, overventuresome, rash, audacious*)

tint—color, hue, tinge, dye, complexion. (*achromatism, decoloration, paleness, pallor, bleaching,* etiolation, colorlessness, sallowness, wanness, cadaverousness, exsanguineousness)

title—inscription, heading, denomination, style, designation, appellation, distinction, address, epithet, name. (*non-designation, indistinction, nondescript, namelessness, indenomination*)

together—unitedly, conjointly, contemporaneously, concertedly, simultaneously, coincidently, concomitantly, concurrently. (*separately, disconnectedly, independently, variously, incoincidently, inconcurrently*)

tolerable—endurable, bearable, supportable, sufferable, allowable, permissible, sufficient, passable. (*unendurable, unbearable, insupportable, insufferable, unallowable, impermissible, insufficient, intolerable*)

tongue—discourse, speech, language, dialect, idiom.

tool—utensil, implement, machine, instrument, dupe, cat's-paw, hireling.

topic—question, theme, subject, subject-matter.

tough—resistant, stubborn, lentous, fibrous, difficult, refractory, hard, unmanageable, tenacious, firm, strong. (*yielding, tender, soft, brittle, fragile, frangible, friable*)

tragedy—disaster, calamity, affliction, adversity, catastrophe, grief. (*joy, delight, boon, prosperity, comedy*)

train—*v.* lead, rear, accustom, habituate, inure, drill, exercise, practice, discipline, instruct, bend, educate. (*force, break, trail, disaccustom, dishabituate, miseducate, disqualify*)

train—*n.* suite, procession, retinue, cortege, course, series.

transfer—convey, transport, remove, sell, assign, remand, make over, transplant, give, alienate, translate, transmit, forward, exchange. (*retain, withhold, fix, appropriate, keep*)

transient—fleeting, fugitive, transitory, temporary, passing, evanescent, ephemeral, momentary, brief. (*abiding, permanent, perpetual, persistent, lasting, enduring*)

transparent—pellucid, crystalline, translucent, limpid, diaphanous, obvious, clear, indisputable, self-evident. (*thick, turbid, opaque, intransparent, mysterious, dubious, questionable*)

travel—journey, wandering, migration, rustication, pilgrimage, excursion, tramp, expedition, trip, ramble, voyage, tour, peregrination. (*rest, settlement, domestication*)

treatise—tract, essay, paper, pamphlet, disquisition, brochure, dissertation, tractate, monograph, article. (*jottings, notes, adversaria, memoranda, effusion, ephemera*)

treaty—contract, agreement, league, covenant, alliance, negotiation, convention. (*neutrality, non-interference, non-alliance, non-agreement, non-convention*)

tremble—shake, quake, quiver, totter, shiver, shudder, vibrate, jar. (*stand, steady, settle, still, calm*)

tremendous—terrible, dreadful, awful, fearful, appalling. (*unimposing, unappalling, inconsiderable*)

trial—test, gauge, experiment, temptation, trouble, affliction, grief, burden, suffering, attempt, endeavor, proof, essay, criterion, ordeal, tribulation, verification. (*non-trial, non-probation, mismeasurement, miscalculation, misestimate, trifle, triviality, alleviation, relief, disburdenment, refreshment, nonattempt, pretermission, oversight, disregard, nonverification*)

trick—artifice, contrivance, machination, guile, stratagem, wile, fraud, cheat, juggle, antic, vagary, finesse, sleight, deception, imposition, delusion, legerdemain. (*blunder, exposure, bungling, mishap, botch, fumbling, inexpertness, maladroitness, genuineness, openhandedness, artlessness*)

trifle—bauble, bagatelle, toy, straw, nothing, triviality, levity, joke, cipher, bubble, gewgaw, kickshaw, rush. (*treasure, portent, phenomenon, crisis, conjuncture, importance, urgency, weight, necessity, seriousness*)

triumph—victory, success, ovation, achievement, conquest, exultation, trophy. (*defeat, discomfiture, failure, unsuccess, abortion, baffling, disappointment*)

trivial—trifling, trite, common, unimportant, useless, nugatory, paltry, inconsiderable. (*important, weighty, critical, original, novel*)

trouble—*v.* disturb, vex, agitate, confuse, perplex, distress, annoy, harass, tease, molest, grieve, mortify, oppress. (*compose, calm, allay, appease, please, soothe, delight, gratify, recreate, entertain, relieve, refresh*)

trouble—*n.* affliction, disturbance, annoyance, perplexity, molestation, vexation, inconvenience, calamity, distress, uneasiness, tribulation, disaster, torment, misfortune, adversity, anxiety, embarrassment, sorrow, misery, grief, depression, difficulty, labor, toil, effort. (*alleviation, composure, pleasure, appeasement, delight, assuagement, happiness, gratification, boon, blessing, exultation, joy, gladness, ease, facility, luck, recreation, amusement, carelessness, indifference, indolence, inertia, indiligence*)

troublesome—tiresome, irksome, difficult, tedious, arduous, laborious, grievous, importunate, vexatious. (*easy, pleasant, amusing, facile, light, unlaborious, untroublesome*)

true—veritable, veracious, exact, precise, accurate, faithful, actual, loyal, genuine, pure, real. (*fictitious, unreliable, unhistorical, untrustworthy, inveracious, false, inaccurate, unfaithful, faithless, fickle, treacherous, erroneous, spurious, perfidious, counterfeit, adulterated*)

trust—*v.* confide, rely, credit, believe, charge, deposit, entrust, repose, hope. (*distrust, suspect, discredit, doubt, disbelieve, resume, withdraw, despair*)

trust—*n.* faith, confidence, reliance, belief, hope, expectation, credit, duty, commission, charge.

try—attempt, endeavor, strive, aim, examine, test, sound, gauge, probe, fathom. (*ignore, pretermit, reject, abandon, discard, misexamine, misinvestigate*)

turn—*v.* round, shape, mold, adapt, spin, reverse, deflect, alter, transform, convert, metamorphose, revolve, rotate, hinge, depend, deviate, incline, diverge, decline, change. (*misshape, misadapt, perpetuate, stabilitate, stereotype, fix, arrest, continue, proceed*)

turn—*n.* revolution, rotation, recurrence, change, alteration, vicissitude, winding, bend, deflection, curve, alternation, opportunity, occasion, time, deed, office, act, treatment, purpose, requirement, convenience, talent, gift, tendency, character, exigence, crisis, form, cast, shape, manner, mold, fashion, cut. (*stability, fixity, immobility, stationariness, unchangeableness, uniformity, rectilinearity, indeflection, continuity, untimeliness, incognizance, oversight, independence, non-requirement, malformation, shapelessness*)

turncoat—trimmer, deserter, renegade.

tutor—guardian, governor, instructor, teacher, preceptor, professor, master, savant. (*ward, pupil, scholar, student, disciple, learner, tyro*)

twine—twist, wind, embrace, entwine, wreath, bind, unite, braid, bend, meander. (*untwist, unwind, separate, disunite, detach, unwreath, unravel, disentwine, continue, straighten*)

twist—contort, convolve, complicate, pervert, distort, wrest, wreath, wind, encircle, form, weave, insinuate, unite, interpenetrate. (*straighten, untwist, rectify, verify, represent, reflect, render, preserve, express, substantiate, unwreath, unwind, detach, disengage, separate, disunite, disentangle, disincorporate, unravel*)

type—mark, stamp, emblem, kind, character, sign, symbol, pattern, archetype, form, model, idea, image, likeness, expression, cast, mold, fashion.

(*non-description, non-classification, inexpression, misrepresentation, misindication, falsification, abnormity, deviation, caricature, monstrosity*)

U

ugly—loathsome, hideous, hateful, frightful, uncouth, ill-favored, unsightly, ill-looking, plain, homely, deformed, monstrous, ungainly. (*attractive, fair, seemly, shapely, beautiful, handsome*)

ultimate—last, final, extreme, conclusive, remotest, farthest. (*prior, intermediate, proximate, preliminary*)

unanimous—of one mind, agreeing, like-minded. (*discordant, disagreeing*)

unanswerable—unquestionable, indisputable, undeniable, incontrovertible.

uncertain—doubtful, dubious, questionable, fitful, equivocal, ambiguous, indistinct, variable, fluctuating.

undeniable—incontestable, indisputable, unquestionable, incontrovertible.

undergo—bear, suffer, endure, sustain, experience.

underhand—clandestine, furtive, dishonest, unfair, fraudulent, surreptitious. (*openhanded, straightforward, fair, honest, undisguised*)

understand—apprehend, comprehend, know, perceive, discern, conceive, learn, recognize, interpret, imply. (*misapprehend, miscomprehend, ignore, misinterpret, declare, state, enunciate, express.*

understanding—knowledge, discernment, interpretation, construction, agreement, intellect, intelligence, mind, sense, conception, reason, brains. (*ignorance, misapprehension, misunderstanding, misinterpretation, misconstruction, mindlessness, irrationality*)

unfit—*a.* improper, unsuitable, inconsistent, untimely, incompetent.

unfit—*v.* disable, incapacitate, disqualify, render unfit.

unfortunate—calamitous, ill-fated, unlucky, wretched, unhappy, miserable.

uniform—unvarying, invariable, conformable, homogeneous, consistent, equal, even, alike, unvaried, regular, symmetrical, equable. (*varying, variable, inconformable, incongruous, diverse, heterogeneous, inconsistent, irregular, unsymmetrical, multifarious, multigenous polymorphic, bizarre, eccentric, erratic*)

union—junction, coalition, combination, agreement, harmony, conjunction, concert, league, connection, alliance, confederacy, concord, confederation, consolidation. (*disjunction, separation, severance, divorce, disagreement, discord, disharmony, secession, disruption, multiplication, diversification, division*)

unit—ace, item, part, individal. (*total, aggregate, collection, sum, mass*)

unite—join, combine, link, attach, amalgamate, associate, coalesce, embody, merge, be mixed, conjoin, connect, couple, add, incorporate with, cohere, concatenate, integrate, converge. (*disjoin, sever, dissociate, separate, disamalgamate, resolve, disconnect, disintegrate, disunite, disrupt, divide, multiply, part, sunder, diverge*)

unity—oneness, singleness, individuality, concord, conjunction, agreement, uniformity, indivisibility. (*plurality, multitude, complexity, multiplicity, discord, disjunction, separation, severance, variety, heterogeneity, diversity, incongruity, divisibility*)

universal—all, embracing, total, unlimited, boundless, comprehensive, entire, general, whole, exhaustive, complete. (*partial, local, limited, incomplete, exclusive, particular, inexhaustive, exceptional*)

unreasonable—foolish, silly, absurd, preposterous, immoderate, exorbitant, ridiculous.

upright—vertical, erect, perpendicular, honest, honorable, pure, principled, conscientious, just, fair, equitable. (*inverted, inclined, dishonest, dishonorable, corrupt, unprincipled, unconscientious*)

urge—press, push, drive, impel, propel, force, importune, solicit, animate, incite, instigate, stimulate, hasten, expedite, accelerate, dispatch. (*repress, hold, retain, inhibit, coerce, restrain, cohibit, hinder, retard, discourage, damp, obstruct*)

urgent—pressing, imperative, immediate, importunate, forcible, strenuous, serious, grave, momentous, indeferrible. (*unimportant, insignificant, trifling, trivial, deferrible*)

use—*n.* advantage, custom, habit, practice, service, utility, usage.

use—*v.* employ, exercise, treat, practice, accustom, habituate, inure. (*discard, suspend, ignore, avoid, disaccustom, dishabituate, disinure*)

useful—advantageous, profitable, helpful, serviceable, beneficial, available, adapted, suited, conducive. (*disadvantageous, unprofitable, obstructive, retardative, preventative, antagonistic, hostile, cumbersome, burdensome, unbeneficial, unavailable, inconducive, useless, fruitless, ineffectual*)

usual—common, customary, ordinary, normal, regular, habitual, wonted, accustomed, general. (*uncommon, rare, exceptional, uncustomary, extraordinary, abnormal, irregular, unusual*)

utter—circulate, issue, promulgate, express, articulate, pronounce, speak. (*recall, suppress, repress, hush, stifle, check, swallow*)

utter—extreme, perfect, complete, unqualified, absolute, thorough, consummate, entire, sheer, pure. (*imperfect, incomplete, impure*)

utterly—totally, completely, wholly, quite, altogether, entirely.

V

vacant—empty, leisure, unemployed, unencumbered, unoccupied, void, unfilled, mindless, exhausted. (*full, replenished, business, employed, engaged, occupied, filled, thoughtful*)

vague—general, lax, indefinite, undetermined, popular, intangible, equivocal, unsettled, uncertain, ill-defined, pointless. (*strict, definite, determined, limited, scientific, pointed, specific*)

vain—empty, worthless, fruitless, unsatisfying, unavailing, idle, ineffectual, egotistic, showy, unreal, conceited, arrogant. (*solid, substantial, sound, worthy, efficient, effectual, cogent, potent, unconceited, modest, real*)

valid—strong, powerful, cogent, weighty, sound, substantial, available, efficient, sufficient, operative, conclusive. (*weak, invalid, powerless, unsound, unsubstantial, unavailable, inefficient, insufficient, inoperative, obsolete, effete, superseded, inconslusive*)

value—appreciate, compute, rate, estimate, esteem, treasure, appraise, prize. (*miscompute, misestimate, disesteem, disregard, vilipend, underrate, undervalue, underestimate, despise, contemn, cheapen, vilify*)

vanity—emptiness, unsubstantiality, unreality, falsity, conceit, self-sufficiency, ostentation, pride, worthlessness, triviality. (*substance, solidity, substantiality, reality, truth, modesty, self-distrust, simplicity, unostentatiousness, humility*)

variable—changeable, mutable, fickle, capricious, wavering, unsteady, inconstant, shifting. (*unchanging, unchangeable, immutable, constant, firm, true, fast, stanch, unwavering, steady, unalterable, invariable*)

variation—deviation, alteration, mutation, diversity, departure, change, abnormity, exception, discrepancy. (*continuance, fixity, indivergency, exemplification, law, rule, uniformity, harmony, agreement*)

variety—difference, diversity, medley, miscellany, multiplicity, multiformity, abnormity. (*uniformity, species, type, specimen*)

various—different, diverse, multiform, multitudinous, several, sundry, uncertain, manifold,

diversified. (*one, same, identical, uniform, few, similar*)

vast—waste, wild, desolate, extensive, spacious, widespread, gigantic, wide, boundless, measureless, enormous, mighty, huge, immense, colossal, prodigious, far-reaching. (*narrow, close, confined, frequented, populated, cultivated, tended, tilled, limited, bounded, circumscribed, moderate*)

vehement—violent, impetuous, ardent, burning, fervent, raging, furious, passionate, fervid, urgent, forcible, eager. (*mild, feeble, inanimate, subdued, controlled, unimpassioned, passionless, cold, stoical, gentle, weak, mitigated.*)

vengeance—retribution, retaliation, revenge. (*forgiveness, pardon, condonation, amnesty, grace, remission, absolution, oblivion, indulgence, reprieve*)

venture—speculation, risk, chance, hazard, stake, undertaking, luck, experiment, throw. (*non-speculation, caution, reservation, calculation, certainty, law, method*)

veracity—truth, truthfulness, credibility, exactness, accuracy.

verdict—finding, judgment, answer, opinion, decision, sentence. (*non-declaration, indecision, indetermination*)

verge—tend, bend, slope, incline, approach, approximate, trend, bear. (*decline, deviate, revert, depart, recede, return, back, retrocede*)

verify—establish, confirm, fulfill, authenticate, substantiate, identify, realize, test, warrant, demonstrate. (*disestablish, subvert, fail, falsify, mistake, misrepresent, misstate, disappoint, misdemonstrate*)

versed—skilled, practiced, conversant, acquainted, initiated, indoctrinated, clever, familiar, thoroughly acquainted, proficient. (*unskilled, illversed, unpracticed, inconversant, unfamiliar, uninitiated, ignorant, awkward, strange, unversed, untaught*)

vex—tease, irritate, provoke, plague, torment, tantalize, bother, worry, pester, trouble, disquiet, afflict, harass, annoy. (*soothe, appease, gratify, quiet, please*)

vice—corruption, fault, defect, evil, crime, immorality, sin, badness. (*purity, faultlessness, perfection, virtue, immaculateness, goodness, soundness*)

vicious—corrupt, faulty, defective, bad, morbid, peccant, debased, profligate, unruly, impure, depraved. (*pure, sound, perfect, virtuous, healthy*)

victory—conquest, triumph, ovation, success. (*failure, defeat, frustration, disappointment, abortion, miscarriage, non-succses*)

view—*v.* behold, examine, inspect, explore, survey, consider, contemplate, reconnoitre, observe, regard, estimate, judge. (*ignore, overlook, disregard, misconsider, misinspect, misobserve, misestimate, misjudge*)

view—*n.* sight, vision, survey, examination, inspection, judgment, estimate, scene, representation, apprehension, sentiment, conception, opinion, object, aim, intention, purpose, design, end, light, aspect. (*blindness, occultation, obscuration, darkness, misexamination, deception, error, delusion, misjudgment, misrepresentation, misconception, aimlessness, non-intention*)

vile—cheap, worthless, valueless, low, base, mean, despicable, hateful, bad, impure, vicious, abandoned, abject, sinful, sordid, ignoble, wicked, villainous, degraded, wretched. (*costly, rare, precious, valuable, high, exalted, noble, honorable, lofty, venerable*)

villain—scoundrel, ruffian, wretch.

villainous—base, knavish, depraved, infamous.

vindicate—assert, maintain, uphold, clear, support, defend, claim, substantiate, justify, establish. (*waive, abandon, surrender, forego, disprove, disestablish, neutralize, nullify, destroy, subvert, annul, vitiate*)

violate—ravish, injure, abuse, disturb, hurt, rape, outrage, debauch, break, infringe, profane, transgress, disobey. (*respect, foster, observe, regard, preserve, cherish, protect, obey*)

violence—verhemence, impetuosity, force, rape, outrage, rage, profanation, injustice, fury, infringement, fierceness, oppression. (*lenity, mildness, self-restraint, feebleness, gentleness, respect, forbearance, self-control, observance, obedience, preservation, conservation, protection*)

virtue—power, capacity, strength, force, efficacy, excellence, value, morality, goodness, uprightness, purity, chastity, salubrity. (*weakness, incapacity, inability, inefficacy, badness, corruption, vice, immorality, impurity, unchastity, virulence, malignancy*)

visible—perceptible, apparent, clear, plain, obvious, conspicuous, observable, discernible, palpable, manifest, distinguishable, evident. (*imperceptible, non-apparent, inconspicuous, impalpable, microscopic, invisible, inobservable, concealed, eclipsed, withdrawn, indiscernible, indistinguishable*)

visionary—fanciful, dreamy, chimerical, baseless, shadowy, imaginary, unreal, fabulous, romantic. (*actual, real, truthful, sound, substantial, palpable, unromantic, sober, veritable*)

vivid—bright, brilliant, luminous, resplendent, lustrous, radiant, graphic, clear, lively, animated, stirring, striking, glowing, sunny, bright, scintillant. (*dull, opaque, non-luminous, obscure, rayless, lurid, somber, non-reflecting, dim, dusky, cloudy, nebulous, pale, wan, caliginous*)

volume—size, body, bulk, dimensions, book, work, tome, capacity, magnitude, compass, quantity. (*diminutiveness, tenuity, minuteness, smallness*)

voluntary—deliberate, spontaneous, free, intentional, optional, discretional, unconstrained, willing. (*compulsory, coercive, necessitated, involuntary*)

volunteer—offer, proffer, tend, originate. (*withhold, refuse, suppress*)

voluptuous—sensual, luxurious, self-indulgent, licentious, highly pleasant. (*unsensual, abstinent, self-denying, ascetic, sober*)

vulgar—popular, general, loose, ordinary, public, vernacular, plebeian, uncultivated, unrefined, low, mean, coarse, underbred.   (*strict, scientific, philosophical, restricted, technical, accurate, patrician, select, choice, cultivated, refined, polite, high-bred, stylish, aristocratic*)

W

wages—remuneration, hire, compensation, stipend, salary, allowance. (*gratuity, douceur, premium, bonus, grace*)

wander—ramble, range, stroll, rove, expatiate, roam, deviate, stray, depart, err, swerve, straggle, saunter, navigate, circumnavigate, travel. (*rest, stop, perch, bivouac, halt, lie, anchor, alight, settle, moor, pause, repose*)

want—deficiency, lack, failure, insufficiency, scantiness, shortness, omission, neglect, non-production, absence. (*supply, sufficiency, provision, abundance, production, allowance, supplement, adequacy*)

wanton—wandering, roving, sportive, playful, frolicsome, loose, unbridled, uncurbed, reckless, unrestrained, irregular, licentious, dissolute, inconsiderate, heedless, gratuitous. (*stationary, unroving, unsportive, unplayful, unfrolicsome, joyless, thoughtful, demure, sedate, discreet, staid, self-controlled, well-regulated, formal, austere, purposed, deliberate, cold-blooded, determined*)

warm—blood-warm, thermal, genial, irascible, hot, ardent, affectionate, fervid, fiery, glowing, enthusiastic, zealous, eager, excited, interested, animated. (*frigid, cold, tepid, starved, indifferent, cool, unexcited, passionless*)

warmth—ardor, glow, fervor, zeal, heat, excitement, intensity, earnestness, cordiality, animation, eagerness, vehemence, geniality, sincerity, **passion,** irascibility, emotion, life. (*frigidity, frost, congelation, iciness, coldness, calmness, coolness, indifference, torpidity, insensitiveness, apathy, slowness, ungeniality, insincerity, passionlessness, good-temper,; death*)

waste—ruin, destroy, devastate, impair, consume, squander, dissipate, throw away, diminish, lavish, desolate, pine, decay, attenuate, dwindle, shrivel, wither, wane. (*restore, repair, conserve, preserve, perpetuate, protect, husband, economize, utilize, hoard, treasure, accumulate, enrich, flourish, luxuriate, multiply, augment, develop*)

watchful—vigilant, expectant, wakeful, heedful, careful, observant, attentive, circumspect, wary, cautious. (*unwatchful, invigilant, unwakeful, slumbrous, drowsy, heedless, careless, inobservant, inattentive, uncircumspect, unwary, incautious, distracted*)

weak—feeble, infirm, enfeebled, powerless, debile, fragile, incompact, inadhesive, pliant, frail, soft, tender, milk and water, flabby, flimsy, wishy-washy, destructible, watery, diluted, imbecile, inefficient, spiritless, foolish, injudicious, unsound, undecided, unconfirmed, impressible, wavering, ductile, easy, malleable, unconvincing, inconclusive, vapid, pointless. (*strong, vigorous, robust, muscular, nervous, powerful, tough, stout, lusty, sturdy, compact, adhesive, resistant, fibrous, hard, indestructible, potent, intoxicating, efficient, spirited, animated, wise, sound, judicious, cogent, valid, decided, determined, unwavering, stubborn, unyielding, inexorable, conclusive, irrestible, forcible, telling*)

weaken—debilitate, enfeeble, enervate, dilute, impair, paralyze, attenuate, sap. (*strengthen, invigorate, empower, corroborate, confirm*)

wealth—influence, riches, mammon, lucre, plenty, affluence, abundance, opulence. (*indigence, poverty, scarcity, impecuniosity*)

wear—carry, bear, exhibit, sport, consume, don, waste, impair, rub, channel, groove, excavate, hollow, diminish. (*doff, abandon, repair, renovate, renew, increase, swell, augment*)

weary—fatigued, tired, exhausted, worn, jaded, debilitated, spent, toil-worn, faint. (*fresh, vigorous, recruited, renovated, hearty*)

weave—interlace, braid, intertwine, intermix, plait, complicate, intersect. (*unravel, untwist, disunite, disentangle, extricate, simplify, enucleate, dissect*)

weight—gravity, ponderosity, heaviness, pressure, burden, importance, power, influence, efficacy, consequence, moment, impressiveness. (*lightness, levity, portableness, alleviation, unimportance, insignificance, weakness, inefficacy, unimpressiveness, triviality, worthlessness*)

well—rightly, thoroughly, properly, hale, sound, healthy, hearty. (*wrongly, imperfectly, improperly*)

white—colorless, pure, snowy, unblemished, unspotted, stainless, innocent, clear. (*black, impure*)

whole—total, entire, all, well, complete, sound, healthy, perfect, unimpaired, undiminished, integral, undivided, gross. (*partial, imperfect, incomplete, unsound, sick, impaired, diminished, fractional, divided, sectional*)

wholesome—healthful, salubrious, salutary, salutiferous, beneficial, nutritious, healing. (*unhealthy, unhealthful, insalubrious, insalutary, prejudicial, unwholesome, deleterious, detrimental, morbific*)

whore—harlot, prostitute, courtesan, cyprian, drab, night-walker, street-walker, wench, strumpet, woman of ill-fame, Magdalen, bawd, punk, demirep, woman of the town, huzzy, of the demi monde, fille de joie. (*virgin, pure woman*)

wicked—evil, bad, godless, sinful, immoral, iniquitous, criminal, unjust, unrighteous, irreligious, profane, ungodly, vicious, atrocious, black, dark, foul, unhallowed, nefarious, naughty, heinous, flagitious, abandoned, corrupt. (*good, virtuous, just, godly, moral, religious, upright, honest, pure, honorable, incorrupt, sinless, spotless, immaculate, stainless*)

wild—untamed, undomesticated, uncultivated, uninhabited, desert, savage, uncivilized, unrefined, rude, ferocious, untrained, violent, ferine, loose, disorderly, turbulent, ungoverned, inordinate, disorderly, chimerical, visionary, incoherent, raving, distracted, haggard. (*tame, domesticated, cultivated, inhabited, frequented, populous, civilized, polite, refined, reclaimed, gentle, mild, subdued, regulated, orderly, rational, collected, coherent, sane, sober, sensible, calm, trim*)

wilful—purposed, deliberate, designed, intentional, prepense, premeditated, preconcerted, wayward, refractory, stubborn, self-willed, headstrong. (*undesigned, accidental, unintentional, unpremeditated, docile, obedient, amenable, manageable, deferential, considerate, thoughtful*)

wisdom—knowledge, erudition, learning, enlightenment, attainment, information, discernment, judgment, sagacity, prudence, light. (*ignorance, illiterateness, sciolism, indiscernment, injudiciousness, folly, imprudence, darkness, empiricism, smattering, inacquaintance*)

wit—mind, intellect, sense, reason, understanding, humor, ingenuity, imagination. (*mindlessness, senselessness, irrationality, dullness, stolidity, stupidity, inanity, doltishness, wash, vapidity, platitude, common-place*)

withhold—retain, keep, inhibit, cohibit, stay, restrain, refuse, stint, forbear, detain. (*grant, afford, furnish, provide, allow, permit, encourage, incite, concede, lavish*)

withstand—oppose, resist, confront, thwart, face. (*yield, surrender, submit, acquiesce, countenance, support, encourage, aid, abet, back*)

witness—attestation, testimony, evidence, corroboration, cognizance, corroborator, eye-witness, spectator, auditor, testifier, voucher, ear-witness. (*invalidation, incognizance, refutation, ignorance, alien, ignoramus, stranger*)

wonder—amazement, astonishment, surprise, admiration, phenomenon, prodigy, portent, miracle, sign, marvel. (*inastonishment, indifference, apathy, unamazement, anticipation, expectation, familiarity, triviality*)

wonderful—amazing, astonishing, wondrous, admirable, strange, striking, surprising, awful, prodigious, portentous, marvelous, miraculous, supernatural, unprecedented, startling. (*unamazing, unastonishing, unsurprising, common, every-day, regular, normal, customary, usual, expected, anticipated, calculated, current, natural, unwonderful, unmarvelous*)

word—term, expression, message, account, tidings, order, vocable, signal, engagement, promise. (*idea, conception*)

work—exertion, effort, toil, labor, employment, performance, production, product, effect, result, composition, achievement, operation, issue, fruit. (*effortlessness, inertia, rest, inoperativeness, non-employment, non-performance, non-production, abortion, miscarriage, frustration, neutralization, fruitlessness*)

worldly—terrestrial, mundane, temporal, secular, earthly, carnal. (*heavenly, spiritual*)

) **worry**—harass, irritate, tantalize, importune, vex, molest, annoy, tease, torment, disquiet, plague, fret. (*soothe, calm, gratify, please, amuse, quiet*)

worth—value, rate, estimate, cost, price, merit, desert, excellence, rate. (*inappreciableness, cheapness, worthlessness, demerit*)

worthless—cheap, vile, valueless, useless, base, contemptible, despicable, reprobate, vicious. (*costly, rich, rare, valuable, worthy, useful, honorable, estimable, excellent, noble, precious, admirable, virtuous*)

wrench—wrest, twist, distort, strain, extort, wring.

wretched— miserable, debased, humiliated, fallen, ruined, pitiable, mean, paltry, worthless, vile, despicable, contemptible, sorrowful, afflicted, melancholy, dejected. (*flourishing, prosperous, happy, unfallen, admirable, noble, honorable, worthy, valuable, enviable, joyous, felicitous, elated*)

wrong—unfit, unsuitable, improper, mistaken, incorrect, erroneous, unjust, illegal, inequitable, immoral, injurious, awry. (*fit, suitable, proper, correct, accurate, right, just, legal, equitable, fair, moral, beneficial, straight*)

Y

yearn—long, hanker, crave, covet, desire. (*loathe, revolt, recoil, shudder*)

yet—besides, nevertheless, notwithstanding, however, still, eventually, ultimately, at last, so far, thus far

yield—furnish, produce, afford, bear, render, relinquish, give in, let go, forego, accede, acquiesce, resign, surrender, concede, allow, grant, submit, succumb, comply, consent, agree. (*withdraw, withhold, retain, deny, refuse, vindicate, assert, claim, disallow, appropriate, resist, dissent, protest, recalcitrate, struggle, strive*)

yielding—conceding, producing, surrendering, supple, pliant, submissive, accommodating, unresisting. (*firm, defiant, stiff, hard, unyielding, resisting, unfruitful*)

yoke—couple, conjoin, connect, link, enslave, subjugate. (*dissever, divorce, disconnect, liberate, release, manumit, enfranchise*)

youth—youngster, young, person, boy, lad, minority, adolescence, juvenility.

youthful—juvenile, young, early, fresh, childish, unripe, puerile, callow, immature, beardless. (*aged, senile, mature, decrepit, decayed, venerable, antiquated, superannuated*)

Z

zeal—ardor, interest, energy, eagerness, engagedness, heartiness, earnestness, fervor, enthusiasm. (*apathy, indifference, torpor, coldness, carelessness, sluggishness, incordiality*)

zenith—height, highest point, pinnacle, acme, summit, culmination, maximum. (*nadir, lowest point, depth, minimum*)

zest—flavor, appetizer, gusto, gust, pleasure, enjoyment, relish, sharpener, recommendation, enhancement. (*distaste, disrelish, detriment*)

HOMONYMS

abba, father. abbe, an abbot. abbey, a convent.

able, strong, skillful. Abel, a name.

accidence, rudiments. accidents, unexpected events.

acclamation, applause. acclimation, used to climate.

aching, continued pain. akin, related.

acts, deeds. ax or axe, a tool.

adds, increases. adze or adz, a tool.

adherence, constancy. adherents, followers.

advice, counsel. advise, to give council.

aha, pleasant surprise. ah, surprise. awe, fear.

ail, pain, trouble. ale, a liquor.

air, atmosphere. ere, before. heir, inheritor. are, from the verb TO BE.

aisle, passage. isle, island. I'll, I will.

ait, an island. ate, devoured. eight, a number.

akin, related. aching, continued pain.

ale, liquor. ail, pain, trouble.

all, every one. awl, a tool.

allegation, affirmation. allegation, uniting.

alley, a passage. ally, a friend.

alms, charity. arms, limbs, weapons.

aloud, with noise. allowed, permitted.

altar, for worship. alter, to change.

amend, to make better. amende, retraction.

anker, a measure. anchor, of a vessel.

Ann, a name. an, one

annalist, historian. analyst, analyzer

annalize, to record. analyze, to separate.

ant, insect. aunt, relative.

ante, before. anti, opposed to.

arc, part of a circle. ark, chest, boat.

arches, parts of a circle. archers, bowmen.

are, see air.

arraign, to accuse. **arrange,** to put in order.
arrant, bad. **errand,** message. **errant,** wandering.
arrear, unpaid. **arrier,** rear guard.
artist, professor of art. **artiste,** female artist.
ascent, act of rising. **assent,** consent.
asperate, make rough. **aspirate,** give sound of "h"
asperation, making rough. **aspiration,** ambition.
assistance, help, aid. **assistants,** helpers.
ate, devoured. **ait,** an island. **eight,** a number.
a'te, a goddess. **eighty,** a number.
attendance, waiting on. **attendants,** those who attend.
aught, anything. **ought,** should.
augur, to predict. **auger,** a tool.
aune, a cloth measure. **on,** not off.
aunt, relative. **ant,** insect.
auricle, external ear. **oracle,** counsel.
awe, fear. see **ah** or **aha.**
awed, dreaded. **odd,** uneven.
awl, a tool. **all,** everyone.
axe, a tool. **acts,** deeds.
axes, tools. **axis,** turning line.
aye, yes. **eye,** organ of sight. **I,** myself.

B

bacon, pork. **baken,** baked.
bad, wicked. **bade,** past tense of bid.
bail, security. **bale,** a bundle.
bait, food to allure. **bate,** to lessen.
baize, cloth. **bays,** water, garland, horses.
bald, hairless. **bawled,** cried aloud.
ball, round body, dance. **bawl,** cry aloud.
ballad, song. **ballet,** dance. **ballot,** ticket.
balm, plant, balsam. **barm,** yeast.
banded, united. **bandied,** tossed to and fro.
bans, marriage notice. **bands,** companies.
bare, naked. **bear,** animal, to carry.
bard, poet. **barred,** fastened with a bar.
bark, cry of dog, rind of tree. **barque,** vessel.

baron, nobleman. **barren,** unfruitful.

baroness, baron's wife. **barrenness,** sterility.

base, mean. **base** or **bass,** in music.

bask, to lie in warmth. **basque,** to a lady's dress,

batten, a board, to fatten. **baton,** a staff, a rod. **batting,** cotton in sheets.

baulking, relating to horses. **bocking,** cloth.

baulks, or **bocks,** relating to horses. **box,** case tree.

bay, water, color, tree. **bey,** governor.

beach, sea shore. **beech,** a tree.

bear, an animal, to carry. **bare,** naked.

beat, to strike. **beet,** vegetable.

beau, man of dress. **bow,** in archery.

bee, insect. **be,** to exist.

been, of the verb to be. **bin,** for grain.

beer, malt liquor. **bier,** carriage for the dead.

behoof, advantage. **behoove,** to be fit.

berry, fruit. **bury,** to inter.

berth, sleeping place. **birth,** being born.

better, superior. **bettor,** one who bets.

bey, governor. **bay,** sea, color, tree.

bier, carriage for the dead. **beer,** malt liquor.

bight, of a rope. **bite,** with the teeth.

billed, furnished with a bill. **build,** to erect.

bin, for grain. **been,** of the verb TO BE.

binocle, telescope. **binnacle,** compass box.

birth, coming into life. **berth,** sleeping place.

blew, did blow. **blue,** a color.

bloat, to swell. **blote,** to dry by smoke.

boa, neck wear, a serpent. see **bow.**

boar, swine. **bore,** to make a hole. see **boor.**

board, timber. **bored,** pierced, worried.

bocking, cloth. **baulking,** relating to horses.

bodice, waistcoat. **bodies,** material substances.

bold, courageous. **bowled,** rolled balls.

bole, earth, trunk of tree. see **boll.**

boll, a pod, a ball. **bowl,** basin. see **bole.**

boor or **boar,** a clownish person. see **boar.**

border, outer edge. **boarder,** lodger.

born, come into life. **bourn,** a limit, stream. **borne,** carried.

borough, a town. **burrow,** hole for rabbits.

bow, in archery. **beau,** a man of dress. see **boa.**

bow, to salute, part of ship. **bough** of tree.

boy, male child. **buoy,** floating signal.

braid, to plait. **brayed,** did bray.

brake, to a wheel, a thicket. **break,** opening, to part.

bray, harsh sound. **brae,** broken ground.

breach, a gap, a break. **breech,** part of a gun.

bread, food. **bred,** brought up.

brewed, fermented. **brood,** offspring.

brew, to make malt liquor. **bruise,** to crush.

bridal, belonging to a wedding. **bridle,** a curb.

Briton, native of Britain.   **Britain, England and** Scotland.

broach, to utter. **brooch,** a jewel.

brows, edges. **browse,** to feed.

bruin, a bear. **brewing,** preparing malt liquors.

bruit, noise, report. **brute,** a beast.

build, to erect. **billed,** furnished with a bill.

bun, small cake or bread. **bonne,** a nurse.

buoy, floating signal. **boy,** male child.

burrow, hole for rabbit. **borough,** a town.

bury, to cover with earth. **berry,** a fruit.

but, except, yet. **butt,** cask, to push with head.

buy, see **bye.**

bye, bye the bye. **by,** at, near. **buy,** to purchase.

C

cab, a carriage. **kab,** a Hebrew measure.

cable, rope. **cabal,** party of men.

caddy, a box. **cadi,** a Turkish judge.

Cain, man's name. **cane,** walking stick.

calendar, almanac. **calender,** to polish.

calk, to stop leaks. **cauk** or **cawk,** mineral. **cock,** male bird. **cork,** bark of a tree.

call, to name. **caul,** a membrane.

caller, see **choler.**

caloric, heat. **choleric,** angry.

camera, optical machine. **chimera,** idle fancy.

campaign, time of army in field. see **champaign.**

can, could, tin vessel. **Khan** or **Kan,** a ruler.

candid, fair, open. **candied,** turned to sugar.

cannon, large gun. **canon,** a law, a rule.

canvas, cloth. **canvass,** to solicit, to examine.

canyon, or **canon,** a gorge, a gully. see **cannon.**

capital, upper part, principal. **capitol,** edifice.

carat, weight. **caret,** mark. **carrot,** vegetable.

carol, song of joy. **Carroll,** a name.

cash, money. **cache,** hole for hiding goods.

cask, wooden vessel. **casque,** a helmet.

cast, to throw, to mold. **caste,** rank.

Castile,—ancient Spanish kingdom. **cast steel,** a metal.

castor, a beaver. **caster,** frame for bottles, roller.

catarrh, a disease. **guitar,** musical instrument.

caudal, tail. **caudle,** drink. **coddle,** fondle, parboil.

cauf, fish box. **cough,** effort of lungs.

caught, did catch. **cot,** small bed.

cause, that which produces. **caws,** cries of crows.

cavalier, horseman. **caviller,** a captious person.

cease, to leave off. see **seas.**

cede, to give up. **seed,** germ of plants.

ceil, to cover upper surface. see **seal.**

ceiling, of a room. **sealing,** fastening.

celery, a plant. **salary,** annual payment.

cell, small room. **sell,** to part for a price.

cellar, a room under house, **seller,** one who sells.

censor, critic. **censure,** blame. **censer,** vessel.

census, numbering. **senses,** faculties.

cent, coin. **sent,** caused to go. **scent,** odor. **cense,** tax.

centaury, a plant. **century,** a hundred years.

cerate, a salve. **serrate,** shaped like a saw.

cere, to cover with wax. **seer,** a prophet. **sear,** dry.

cession, yielding. **session,** a sitting.

cetaceous, whale species. **setaceous**, bristly.

chagrin, ill humor. **shagreen**, fish skin.

champaign, open country. **champagne**, a wine.

chance, accident. **chants**, melodies.

chapter, a division. **chapiter**, of a pillar.

chaste, pure. **chased**, pursued car.

chews, masticates. **choose**, to select.

chimera, idle fancy. **camera**, optical instrument.

choir, singers. **quire**, of paper.

choler, anger. **collar**, neck wear. **color**, hue. **caller**, visitor. **collier**, coal digger.

cholera, disease. **colliery**, coal mine.

choleric, angry. **caloric**, heat.

chord, musical sound. **cord**, string.

chronical, a long duration. **chronicle**, history.

chuff, a clown. **chough**, a sea bird.

cilicious, made of hair. **silicious**, flinty.

cingle, a girth. **single**, alone, only one.

cion or **scion**, a sprout. **sion** or **zion**, mountain.

circle, round figure. **sercle**, a twig.

cit, a citizen. **sit**, to rest.

cite, summons. **site**, situation. **sight**, view.

clause, part of a sentence. **claws**, talons.

climb, to ascend. **clime**, climate.

close, to shut, to end **clothes**, garments.

coal, fuel. **cole**, cabbage.

coaled, supplied with coal. **cold**, frigid, not hot.

coals, fuel. **colds**, sickness.

coarse, rough. **course**, route. **corse** or **corpse**, dead body.

coat, garment. **cote**, sheep fold.

cock, male bird. see **calk**.

coddle, to fondle. see **caudal**.

codling, apple. **coddling**, par-boiling.

coffer, money chest. **cougher**, one who coughs.

coffin, box for dead. **coughing**, effect of lungs.

coin, money. **quoin**, wedge.

colation, straining. **collation**, a repast.

colonel, officer. **kernel**, seed in a nut.

color, tint. **culler,** a chooser. see **choler.**

collar, neck wear. see **choler.**

comity, politeness. **committee,** managers.

complacement, civil. **complaisant,** seeking to please.

complacence, satisfaction. **complaisance,** condesension.

compliment, flattery. **complement,** the full number.

concert, entertainment. **consort,** companion.

concur, to agree. **conquer,** to overcome.

confidant, one trusted with secrets. **confident,** having full belief.

consequence, that which follows. **consequents,** deduction.

consonance, concord. **consonants,** letters which are not vowels.

consession, a sitting together. **concession,** a yielding.

coolly, without heat, calmly. **coolie,** E. Indian laborer.

coom, soot. **coomb,** a measure.

coppice, woods. **copies,** imitations.

coquet, to deceive in love. **coquette,** vain girl.

coral, from the ocean. **corol,** a corolla.

cord, string. **chord,** musical sound.

core, inner parts. **corps,** soldiers.

cored, taken from center. see **cord.**

correspondence, interchange of letters. **correspondents,** those who correspond.

cot, small bed. **caught,** did catch.

cough, effort of lungs. **cauf,** fish box.

council, assembly. **counsel,** advice.

courier, messenger. **currier,** preparer of leather.

cousin, relative. **cozen,** to cheat.

coward, one without courage. **cowherd,** one who tends cows. **cowered,** frightened.

crane, a bird, machine, pipe. **crayon,** pencil.

creak, harsh noise. **creek,** steam. **crick,** cramp.

crewel, yarn. **cruel,** savage.

crews, seamen. **cruise,** voyage. **cruse,** a cruet.

critic, judge. **critique,** criticism.

cue, hint, rod, tail. **queue,** Chinaman's hair.

culler, selecter. **color,** a tint, see **choler.**

currant, fruit. **current,** flowing stream.

currier, preparer of leather. **courier,** messenger.

cygnet, a swan. **signet,** a seal.

cymbal, musical instrument. **symbol,** sign.

cypress, a tree. **cyprus,** thin black stuff, an island.

D

dam, wall for stream. **damn,** to doom or curse.

dammed, confined by banks. **damned,** doomed.

dance, to move with music. **daunts,** discourages.

dane, a native of Denmark. **deign,** condescend.

day, time. **dey,** a governor.

days, plural of day. **daze,** to dazzle. **dace,** fish.

dear, beloved, costly. **deer,** an animal.

decease, death. **disease,** sickness.

deformity, defect. **difformity,** variety of form.

deign, to condescend. **Dane,** native of Denmark.

demean, to behave. **demesne,** land.

dents, marks. **dense,** close, compact.

dependents, subordinates. **dependence,** reliance.

depository, place of deposit. **depositary,** a trustee.

depravation, corruption. **deprivation,** loss.

descendent, falling. **descendant,** offspring.

descent, descension. **dissent,** disagreement. **decent,** becoming suitable.

descension, descent. **dissension,** strife.

device, design. **devise,** to contrive.

deviser, contriver. **divisor,** a term used in arithmetic.

dew, moisture. **do,** to perform. **due,** own.

die, to expire, a stamp. **dye,** to color.

dies, expires. **dice,** small cubes.

dire, dreadful. **dyer,** one who dyes.

discous, broad and flat. **discus,** quoit. **discuss,** to argue.

discreet, prudent. **discrete,** separate.

disease, sickness. **decease,** death.
doe, female deer. **dough,** unbaked bread.
does, female deer. **doze,** to slumber.
done, performed. **dun,** a color.
dost, from verb TO BE. **dust,** powdered earth.
drachm, weight. **dram,** small quantity.
draft, bill. **draught,** a drink, a potion.
dual, two. **duel,** combat.
due, owed. **dew,** moisture. **do,** to perform.
dun, color, ask for debt. **done,** finished.
dust, powdered earth. **see dost.**
dye, to color. **die,** to expire, a stamp.
dyer, one who dyes. **dire,** dreadful.
dyeing, staining. **dying,** expiring.

E

earn, to gain by labor. **urn,** a vase.
eight, a number. **see ate.**
eighty, a number. **a'te,** a goddess.
either, one of two. **ether,** volatile fluid.
elicit, to draw out. **illicit,** unlawful.
elision, division. **elysian,** delightful.
elude, to escape from. **illude,** to deceive.
emersion, rising out. **immersion,** going beneath.
empyreal, pure. **imperial,** relating to an emperor.
ere, before. **see air.**
errand, message. **errant,** wandering. **arrant,** bad.
eruption, bursting. **irruption,** sudden invasion.
ether, volatile fluid. **either,** one of two.
ewe, female sheep. **hue,** tint. **yew,** tree. **you,** pronoun.
ewer, vessel for water. **your,** belonging to you.
ewes, sheep. **hues,** colors. **yews,** trees. **use,** to employ.
exercise, work. **exorcise,** to abjure.
eye, organ of sight. **I,** myself. **aye,** yes.

F

fain, pleased. **fane,** temple. **feign,** pretend.
faint, languid. **feint,** pretense.

fair, beautiful, just. fare, price, food.
farther, further. father, male parent. see fother.
fat, animal grease. vat, a cistern.
fated, decreed by fate. see fetid.
faults, defects. false, untrue.
fawn, young deer. faun, woodland deity.
feat, deed,. feet, plural of foot. fete, feast.
feign, pretend. fain, pleased. fane, temple.
feint, pretense. faint, languid.
felloe, rim of wheel. fellow, companion.
ferrule, metallic band. ferule, wooden pallet.
fetid, stinking. feted, honored. see fated.
feud, quarrel. feod, tenure.
fillip, jerk of finger. Philip, man's name.
filter, to strain. philter, love charm.
find, to discover. fined, punished.
fir, tree. fur, animal hair.
fissure, a crack. fisher, fisherman.
fizz, hissing noise. phiz, the face.
flea, insect. flee, to run away.
flew, did fly. flue, chimney.
flour, ground grain. flower, a blossom.
for, because of. fore, preceding. four, 4.
formally, ceremoniously. formerly, time past.
fort, fortified place. forte, peculiar talent.
forth, forward. fourth, 4th.
fother, fodder. see farther.
foul, unclean. fowl, a bird.
franc, French coin. Frank, a name, generous.
frays, quarrels. phrase, parts of a sentence.
freeze, to congeal with cold. frieze, cloth. frees, to set at liberty.
fur, hair on animals. fir, a tree.
fungus, spongy excresence. fungous, growing as fungus.
furs, skins of beasts. furze, a shrub.

G

gable, end of house. gabel, a tax.
gage, a pledge, a fruit. gauge, a measure.

gait, manner of walking. gate, a door.
gala, a show. gayly, in a gay manner.
gall, bile. gaul, a Frenchman.
gamble, to wager. gambol, to skip.
gantlet, punishment. gauntlet, a glove.
genius, talent. genus, a class or order.
gentle, mild. Gentile, one not Jewish.
gesture, posture. jester, merry fellow.
gild, to overflow with gold. guild, a corporation.
gilt, gold on surface. guilt, crime.
glaciers, fields of ice. glaziers, those who set glass.
glare, splendor. glair, white of an egg.
gneiss, rock similar to granite. nice, fine.
gnu, animal. new, not old. knew, understood.
goal, mark. gaol, prison.
goer, one who goes. gore, blood, to pierce.
gourd, a plant. gored, pierced.
grandeur, magnificence. grander, greater.
grate, iron frame. great, large.
grater, a rough instrument. greater, larger.
Greece, country in Europe. grease, fat.
grisly, frightful. grizzly, an animal, gray. gristly,
  cartilaginous.
groan, deep sigh. grown, increased.
grocer, merchant. grosser, coarser.
guana, lizard. guano, manure.
guessed, conjectured. guest, visitor.
guilt, crime. gilt, gold on surface.
guise, appearance. guys, ropes.
guitar, musical instrument. catarrh, disease.

H

hail, ice, to salute. hale, healthy.
hair, of the head. hare, a rabbit.
half, one of two equal parts. halve, to part equally.
hall, large room, a passage. haul, to pull.
hallow, to make holy. halo, circle around sun.
hart, an animal. heart, seat of life.
hay, dried grass. hey, an expression.
heal, to cure. heel, part of foot.

hear, to hearken. **here,** in this place.

heard, did hear. **herd,** a drove.

heir, inheritor. **see air.**

hew, to cut down. **see hue.**

hey, an expression. **hay,** dried grass.

hide, skin to conceal. **hied,** hastened.

hie, to hasten. **high,** lofty, tall.

higher, more lofty. **hire,** to employ.

him, that man. **hymn,** sacred song.

hoa, exclamation. **ho,** cry, stop. **hoe,** tool.

hoard, to lay up. **horde,** tribe.

hoarse, rough voice. **horse,** animal.

hoes, tools. **hose,** stockings, tubing.

hole, cavity. **whole,** all, entire.

holy, pure sacred. **wholly,** completely.

home, dwelling. **holm,** evergreen oak.

honorary, conferring honor. **see onerary.**

hoop, circular, binding. **whoop,** shout, cry.

hour, sixty minutes. **our,** belonging to us.

hue, color. **ewe,** sheep. **you,** yourself. **hew, to cut**
   down. **Hugh,** man's name.

hymn, sacred song. **him,** that man.

I

idol, image. **idle,** unemployed. **idyl,** poem.

I'll, I will. **isle,** island. **aisle,** passage.

illicit, unlawful. **elicit,** to draw out.

illude, to deceive. **elude,** to escape from.

immersion, going beneath. **emersion,** rising out.

imperial, relating to an emperor. **empyreal,** pure.

impostor, pretender. **imposture,** fraud.

incidents, events. **incidence,** a falling on.

incision, cut into. **insition,** grafting.

incite, to urge. **insight,** discernment.

indict, to accuse. **indite,** to dictate.

indicted, accused. **indited,** composed.

indicter, one who indicts. **inditer,** composer.

indiscreet, imprudent. **indiscrete,** not separated.

ingenious, inventive. **ingenuous,** open, artless.

inn, a tavern. in, within.
innocence, purity. innocents, harmless things.
instants, moments. instance, example.
intense, extreme. intents, designs.
intention, purpose. intension, straining.
invade, to infringe. inveighed, censured.
irruption, invasion. eruption, bursting forth.
isle, island. I'll, I will. aisle, passage.

J

jam, preserves. jamb, side of door.
jester, merry fellow. gesture, motions.
Jewry, land of Judea. jury, a set of men.
jointor, plane. jointure, wife's estate.
just, upright. joust, mock, fight.

K

kernel, seed in nut. colonel, officer.
key, for a lock. quay, wharf.
kill, slay, murder. kiln, furnace.
khan, or kan, a ruler. can, to be able, tin vessel.
knag, knot in wood. nag, small horse.
knap, protuberance, noise. nap, short sleep.
knave, rogue. naive, artless. nave, center, hub.
knawed, nibbled. nod, to move the head.
knead, work dough. need, want. kneed, having
    knees.
kneel, rest on knee. neal, to temper.
knew, understood. gnu, animal. new, not old.
knight, title of honor. night, darkness.
knit, unite, weave, frown. nit, insect's egg.
knot, tied. not, word of refusal.
know, understand. no, not so.
knows, understands. nose, organ of smell.

L

lack, to want. lac, gum.
lacks, wants, needs. lax, loose, slack.
lade, to load. laid, placed, produced eggs.
lanch, to dart, let fly. launch, a ship.

237

lane, a road. **lain,** rested.

Latin, language. **latten,** brass.

lea, meadow. **lee,** shelter place.

leach, to filtrate. **leech,** a worm.

lead, metal. **led,** guided.

leaf, part of a plant. **lief,** willingly. **leave,** permission to go away.

leak, a hole. **leek,** a plant.

lean, not fat, to rest, to slant. **lien,** mortgage.

leased, rented. **least,** smallest.

legislator, lawgiver. **legislature,** assembly.

lends, loans. **lens,** optical glass (convex concave).

lesson, task. **lessen,** to diminish.

levee, bank, visit. **levy,** to collect.

liar, falsifier. **lyre,** musical instrument. **lier,** one who lies down.

lie, falsehood. **lye,** liquid.

lief, willingly. see **leaf.**

lien, legal claim. **lean,** not fat, to rest, to slant.

lightning, electricity. **lightening,** unloading.

limb, branch. **limn,** to draw.

lineament, features. **liniment,** ointment.

links, connecting rings. **lynx,** an animal.

liquor, a fluid. **liqueur,** a cordial.

loan, to lend. **lone,** solitary.

loath, unwilling. **loathe,** to feel nausea.

lock, hair, fastening. **loch** or **lough,** lake.

lomp, fish. **lump,** a shapeless mass.

lore, learning. **lower,** bring low.

lose, to miss anything. **loose,** unbound.

low, not high, mean. **lo,** look, see.

lump, a shapeless mass. **lomp,** a fish.

lusern, a lynx. **lucerne,** clover.

lye, liquid. **lie,** falsehood.

lynx, animal. **links,** connecting rings.

lyre, musical instrument. **liar,** falsifier.

M

made, created. **maid,** unmarried woman.

mail, armor, post bag. **male,** masculine.

main, principal. **mane,** hair. **Maine,** a state.

maize, corn. **maze,** intricate. **mace,** spice.

mall, hammer, walk. **maul,** to beat.

manner, method. **manor,** landed estate.

mantel, chimney piece. **mantle,** a cloak.

mare, a female horse. **mayor,** city officer.

mark, visible line. **marque,** a license.

marshal, officer. **martial,** warlike.

marten, an animal. **martin,** a bird.

mead, drink. **meed,** reward. **Mede,** native of Media.

mean, low. **mien,** aspect. **mesne,** middle.

meddle, interfere. **medal,** a token.

meddler, one who meddles. **medlar,** a tree.

message, communication. **messuage,** horse and land.

meter, measurer. **metre** or **meter** in poetry.

mettle, spirit, courage. **metal,** mineral.

mew or **mue,** to melt. **mew,** fowl, enclosure.

mewl, to cry. **mule,** an animal.

mews, cat cries. **muse,** deep thought.

mien, look, aspect. **mean,** low. **mesne,** middle.

milienary, of a thousand. **millinery,** bonnets, etc.

mince, to cut. **mints,** coining places.

minds, faculties, obeys. **mines,** underground works.

miner, worker in mines. **minor,** one underage.

missal, book. **missel,** bird. **missile,** weapon thrown.

mite, insect, small. **might,** power.

mity, having mites. **mighty,** powerful.

moan, lament. **mown,** cut down.

moat, ditch. **mote,** small particle.

mode, manner. **mowed,** cut down.

modal, formal. **model,** a pattern.

more, greater quantity. **mower,** grasscutter.

morn, early in the day. **mourn,** to grieve.

morning, before noon. **mourning,** grief.

mucous, slimy. **mucus,** a fluid.

mue or **mew**, to molt. **mew**, fowl enclosure.
mule, an animal. **mewl**, to cry.
muscat, grape. **musk-cat**, animal. **musket**, gun.
muse, deep thought. **mews**, cat cries.
mustard, plant. **mustered**, assembled.

N

nag, small horse. **knag**, knot in wood.
nap, short sleep. **knap**, protuberance, noise.
naval, nautical. **navel**, center of abdomen.
nave, center hub. **naive**, artless. **knave**, rogue.
nay, no. **neigh**, whinny of a horse.
neal, to temper. **kneel**, to rest on knee.
near, not distant. **ne'er**, never.
need, necessity, want. see **knead**.
neigh, whinny of a horse. **nay**, no.
neither, not either. **nether**, lower.
new, not old. **gnu**, animal. **knew**, understood.
news, fresh accounts. **noose**, slip knot.
nice, fine. **kneiss**, rock similar to granite.
nick, a notch. **niche**, hollow space.
night, darkness. **knight**, title of honor.
nit, insect's egg. **knit**, to unite, to form.
no, not so. **know**, to understand.
nod, to move the head. **knawed**, nibbled.
none, no one. **nun**, female devotee.
noose, slip knot. **news**, fresh accounts.
nose, organ of smell. **knows**, understands.
not, word of refusal. **knot**, a tie.
nun, female devotee. **none**, no one.

O

oar, rowing blade. **o'er**, over. **ore**, mineral.
odd, uneven. **awed**, dreaded.
ode, poem. **owed**, under obligation.
of, belonging to. **off**, denoting separation.
o'er, over. **oar**, paddle. **ore**, mineral.
oh, denoting pain. **O!** surprise. **owe**, indebted.
on, not off. **aune**, a cloth measure.
one, single unit. **won**, gained.

onerary, fit for burdens. see **honorary.**
oracle, counsel. **auricle,** external ear.
order, method. **ordure,** dung, filth.
ordinance, a law. **ordnance,** cannon, etc.
ore, mineral. **o'er,** over. **oar,** paddle.
ottar, oil of roses. **otter,** an animal.
ought, should. **aught,** anything.
our, belonging to us. **hour,** sixty minutes.
owe, to be indebted. see **oh.**
owed, under obligation. **ode,** poem.

P

paced, moved slowly. **paste,** flour and water mixed.
packed, bound in a bundle. **pact,** contract.
pail, bucket. **pale,** whitish.
pain, agony. **pane,** a square of glass.
pair, a couple, two. **pare,** to peel. **pear,** a fruit.
palace, princely home. **pallas,** heathen deity.
palate, organ of taste. **pallette,** artists' board.
    pallet, a bed.
pall, covering for the dead. **Paul,** man's name.
panel, part of door, jury. **pamel,** saddle.
papa, father. **pawpaw,** a fruit.
passable, tolerable. **passible,** with feeling.
pastor, clergyman. **pasture,** meadow.
patience, calmness. **patients,** sick persons.
paw, foot of a beast. **pa,** papa.
paws, beasts' feet. **pause,** stop.
peace, quiet. **piece,** a part. **peas,** vegetable.
peak, the top. **pique,** grudge. **peek,** to peep.
peal, loud sound. **peel,** to pare.
pealing, sounding loudly. **peeling,** rinds.
pear, a fruit. **pair,** a couple, two. **pare,** to peel.
pearl, a precious substance. **purl,** to murmur.
pedal, for the feet. **peddle,** to sell.
peer, nobleman. **pier,** column, wharf.
pencil, writing instrument. **pensile,** suspended.
pendant, flag. **pendent,** hanging.
personal, individual. **personnel,** staff.
phial, or **vial,** bottle. **viol,** violin. **vile,** wicked.

Philip, man's name. **fillip,** jerk of the fingers.
philter, love charm. **filter,** to strain.
phiz, the face. **phizz,** hissing noise.
phrase, expression. see **frays.**
piece, a part. **peace,** quiet. **peas,** vegetable.
pier, a column, wharf. **peer,** nobleman.
pillar, column. **pillow,** headrest.
pistil, part of a flower. **pistol,** firearm.
place, situation. **plaice,** a fish.
plain, clear, simple. **plane,** flat surface, tool.
plaintive, sorrowful. **plaintiff,** accuser.
pleas, arguments. **please,** to delight.
plum, a fruit. **plumb,** perpendicular, leaden weight.
pole, stick, native of Poland. **poll,** the head.
pool, water. **poule** or **pool,** stakes played for.
populace, the people. **populous,** full of people.
pore, opening. **pour,** cause to flow. **poor,** not rich.
poring, looking intently. **pouring,** raining, flowing.
port, harbor. **porte,** Turkish court.
portion, part. **potion,** draught of medicine.
practice, habit. **practice,** to exercise.
praise, commendation. **prays,** entreats, petitions.
  preys, feeds by violence, plunders.
pray, to supplicate. **prey,** plunder.
presence, being present. **presents,** gifts.
pride, self-esteem. **pried,** moved by a lever.
pries, looks into. **prize,** reward. **price,** value.
principal, chief. **principle,** an element.
prints, impressions. **prince,** king's son.
princess, king's daughter. **princes,** king's sons.
prior, previous. **prier,** close inquirer.
profit, gain. **prophet,** a foreteller.
purl, to flow gently. **pearl,** precious substance.

Q

quarts, measure. **quartz,** rock crystal.
quay, wharf. **key,** lock fastener.
queen, king's wife. **quean,** worthless woman.
queue, chinaman's hair. **cue,** hint, rod.

quire, package of paper. **choir,** church singers.
quoin, a wedge. **coin,** money.

R

rabbet, a joint. **rabbit,** small animal.
radical, of first principles. **radicle,** a root.
radish, vegetable. **reddish,** somewhat red.
rain, water. **reign,** rule. **rein,** bridle.
raise, to lift. **rays,** sunbeams. **raze,** to demolish.
raised, lifted. **razed,** demolished.
raiser, one who raises. **razor,** shaving blade.
rancor, hate. **ranker,** coarser.
rap, to strike. **wrap,** to fold.
rapped, struck with quick blows. **wrapped,** enclosed.
rapping, striking **wrapping,** a cover.
read, to peruse. **reed,** a plant.
real, true. **reel,** winding machine, to stagger.
reck, to heed. **wreck,** destruction.
red, color. **read,** perused.
reddish, somewhat red. **radish,** vegetable.
reek, to emit vapor. **wreak,** to inflict.
reign, rule. **rein,** bridle. **rain,** water.
relic, memento. **relict,** a widow.
reseat, to seat again. **receipt,** acknowledgment.
residence, place of abode. **residents,** citizens.
resign, to give up. **re-sign,** to sign again.
rest, quiet. **wrest,** to twist.
retch, to vomit. **wretch,** miserable person.
rheum, thin, water matter. **room,** space.
Rhodes, name of an island. **roads,** highways.
rhumb, vertical circle. **rum,** liquor.
rhyme, harmonical sound. **rime,** hoar frost.
rice, food. **rise,** to ascend.
rifle, gun. **rival,** a competitor.
rigger, rope fixer. **rigor,** severity.
right, correct. **rite,** ceremony. see **write.**
rime, hoar frost. **rhyme,** harmonical sound.
ring, circle, sound. **wring,** to twist.

roads, highways. **Rhodes,** name of an island.
road, way. **rode,** did ride. **rowed,** did row.
roan, color. **rown,** impelled by oars. **Rhone,** river.
roar, loud cry. **rower,** one who rows.
roe, deer. **row,** to impel with oars, a line.
roes, eggs, deer. **rows,** uses oars. **rose,** a flower.
Rome, city in Italy. **roam,** to wander.
rood, a measure. **rude,** rough.
rot, to decay. **wrought,** worked.
rote, memory of words. **wrote,** did write.
rough, not smooth. **ruff,** plaited collar.
rouse, stir up, provoke. **rows,** disturbances.
rout, rabble, disperse. **route,** road.
rude, rough. **rood,** measure.
ruff, collar. **rough,** not smooth.
rung, sounded, a step. **wrung,** twisted.
rum, liquor. **rhumb,** vertical circle.
rye, grain. **wry,** crooked.

S

sail, canvas of a ship. **sale,** traffic.
sailer, vessel. **sailor,** seaman.
salary, annual payment. **celery,** a plant.
sane, sound, in mind. **seine,** fish net, a river.
satire, ridicule. **Satyr,** a sylvan god.
saver, one who saves. **savor,** taste, scent.
scene, a view. **seen,** viewed.
scent, odor. **sent,** caused to go. **cent,** coin.
scion, or **cion.** sprout. **Sion** or **Zion,** a mountain.
scull, oar, boat. **skull,** bone of the head.
sculptor, a carver. **sculpture,** carved work.
sea, ocean. **see,** to perceive.
seal, stamp, animal. **seel,** to lean, to close eyes.
  ceil, to cover the upper surface.
sealing, fastening. **ceiling,** top of a room.
seam, a juncture. **seem,** to appear.
seamed, joined together. **seemed,** appeared.
seas, water. **sees,** looks. **seize,** take hold of. **see**
  cease.

sects, religious bodies. **sex,** male or female.

seed, germ of a plant. **cede,** to give up.

seen, viewed. **scene,** a view.

seer, a prophet. **sear,** to burn. **cere,** wax.

seine, a net, a river. **sane,** sound in mind.

sell, to part for price. **cell,** small room.

seller, one who sells. **cellar,** room.

senior, elder. **seignior,** a title.

sense, feeling. **scents,** odors. **cents,** coins.

senses, faculties. **census,** numberings.

sent, caused to go. **scent,** odor. **cent,** coin.

serf, a slave. **surf,** of the sea.

serge, a cloth. **surge,** a billow.

serrate, shaped like a saw. **cerate,** salve.

session, a sitting. **cession,** a yielding.

set, to place. **sit,** to repose on a seat.

setaceous, bristly. **cetaceous,** whale species

sew, to stitch. **sow,** to plant. **so,** in this manner.

sewer, one who uses a needle. see **sower.**

sewer, a drain. **suer,** one who entreats.

sex, male or female. **sects,** denominations.

shagreen, fish skin. **chagrin,** ill humor.

shear, to clip. **sheer,** to deviate, pure. **shire,** county.

sheath, the case of anything. **sheathe,** to enclose.

shoe, covering for foot. **shoo,** begone.

shoer, fastener of shoes. **sure,** certain.

shone, did shine. **shown,** exhibited.

shoot, to let fly, to kill. **chute,** a fall.

side, edge, margin. **sighed,** did sigh.

sigher, one who sighs. **sire,** father.

sighs, deep breathings. **size,** bulk.

sign, token, mark. **sine,** geometrical term.

signet, a seal. **cygnet,** a swan.

sight, view. **site,** situation. **cite,** to summon.

silicious, flinty. **cilicious,** made of hair.

silly, foolish. **Scilly,** name of islands.

single, alone. **cingle,** a girth.

sink, to fall, a drain. **cinque,** five.

sit, to rest. **cit,** a citizen. see **set.**

skull, bone of the head. **scull,** oar, boat.

slay, to kill. **sley,** weaver's reed. **sleigh,** vehicle.

sleeve, cover for arm. **sleave,** untwisted silk.

slew, killed. **slue,** to turn about. **slough,** bog.

slight, neglect, small. **sleight,** artful trick.

sloe, fruit, animal. **slow,** not swift.

soar, to rise high. **sore,** painful. see **sower.**

soared, ascended. **sword,** a weapon.

sole, part of foot, only. **soul,** spirit of man.

sold, did sell. **soled,** furnished with soles. **souled,** instinct with soul or feeling.

some, a part. **sum,** the whole.

son, a male child. **sun,** luminous orb.

soot, condensed smoke. **suit,** set of things. **suet,** hard fat. **suite,** train of followers.

sooth, truth, reality. **soothe,** to allay.

sorrel, color. **sorel,** a buck in third year.

sow, to scatter seed. see **sew.**

sower, one who sews. **soar,** to fly aloft. see **sewer.**

staid, sober, remained. **stayed,** supported.

stair, steps. **stare,** to gaze.

stake, a post, a wager. **steak,** meat.

stationary, motionless. **stationery,** paper, etc.

steel, metal. **steal,** to thieve.

sticks, pieces of wood. **styx,** a fabulous river.

stile, stairway. **style,** manner.

straight, not crooked. **strait,** narrow pass.

succor, aid. **sucker,** a shoot of a plant, a fish.

suer, one who entreats. **sewer,** a drain.

suite, train of followers. see **soot.**

sum, the whole. **some** a part.

sun, fountain of light. **son,** a male child.

surcle, a twig. **circle,** a round figure.

sure, certain. **shoer,** fastener of shoes.

surf, dashing waves. **serf,** a slave.

surge, a billow. **serge,** cloth.

sutler, trader. **subtler,** more cunning.

suttle, net weight. **subtle,** cunning.

swap, a blow. **swop,** to barter.
symbol, representative. **cymbal,** instrument.

T

tack, changing course of ship. **tact,** skill.
tacks, small nails. **tax,** a tribute.
talc, mineral. **talk,** to converse.
tale, story. **tail,** the hinder part.
talents, abilities. **talons,** claws.
taper, a wax candle. **tapir,** an animal.
tare, a week, allowance. **tear,** to pull to pieces.
tarrier, a delayer. **terrier,** a dog.
taught, instructed. **taut,** tight.
teal, a water fowl. **teil,** a tree.
team, two or more horses. **teem,** to be full.
tear, moisture from eyes. **tier,** a rank, a row.
tear, to pull to pieces. **tare,** weed, allowance.
teas, different kinds of tea. **tease,** to torment.
tenor, course. **tenure,** act of holding.
tense, rigid, form of a verb. **tents,** canvas house.
the, adjective. **thee,** thyself.
their, belonging to them. **there,** in that place.
threw, did throw. **through,** from end to end.
throw, to hurl. **throe,** extreme pain.
thrown, hurled. **throne,** seat of a king.
thy, pronoun. **thigh,** leg just below hip.
thyme, a plant. **time,** duration.
tide, stream, current. **tied,** fastened.
tier, a rank, a row. **tear,** moisture from eyes.
tierce, a cask. **terse,** neat, elegant.
timber, wood. **timbre,** crest, quality.
time, duration. **thyme,** a plant.
tiny, little, small. **tinny,** like tin.
tire of a wheel, weary. **Tyre,** city. **tier,** one who
    ties.
toad, reptile. **toed,** having toes. **towed,** drawn.
toe, part of foot. **tow,** hemp, to drag.
told, related. **tolled,** rang. **toled,** allured.
tole, to allure. **toll,** a tax.
ton, a weight. **tun,** a large cask.

too, denoting excess. **to,** toward. **two,** couple.
track, path. **tract,** short treatise.
tracked, followed. **tract,** region.
travail, to labor with pain. **travel,** to journey.
tray, shallow vessel. **trey,** three of cards.
treatise, discourse. **treaties,** agreement.
tun, a large cask. **ton,** a weight.
two, a couple. **to,** toward. **too,** denoting excess.

U

urn, a vase. **earn,** to gain by labor.
use, to employ. **yews,** trees. **ewes,** sheep.

V

vale, valley. **vail,** a fee. **veil,** to cover.
vane, weathercock. **vein,** blood vessel. **vain,** proud.
veil, a covering for face. **veil,** to cover. **vail,** a fee.
vein, blood vessel. **vane,** weathercock. **vain,** proud.
venal, mercenary. **venial,** pardonable.
Venus, planet. **venous,** relating to the veins.
veracity, truthfulness. **voracity,** greediness.
vial, or **phial,** a bottle. **viol,** violin. **vile,** wicked.
vice, sin, instead of. **vise,** a press.
violate, to transgress. **violet,** a flower.
virtu, love of fine arts. **virtue,** moral goodness.

W

wade, to ford. **weighed,** balanced.
wail, to moan. **wale,** a mark. **whale,** a sea animal.
waist, part of the body. **waste,** destruction.
wait, to stay for. **weight,** heaviness.
waive, to relinquish. **wave,** a billow.
wall, a fence. **wawl,** cat cry.
wane, to decrease. **wain,** a wagon.
want, desire. **wont,** custom, habit.
ware, merchandise. see **wear.**
wart, hard, excrescence. **wort,** beer.
wax, bees' wax, etc. **whacks,** heavy blows.
way, road, manner. **whey,** of milk. **weigh,** to balance.

weak, not strong. **week,** seven days.

weal, happiness. **wheal,** a pustule. see **wheel.**

wear, to impair by use. **ware,** merchandise. **where,**
in which place. **were,** from verb TO BE.

weasel, an animal. **weazel,** thin, weasen.

ween, to think. **wean,** to alienate.

weigh, to balance. **way,** road. **whey** of milk.

weighed, balanced. **wade,** to ford.

weight, heaviness. **wait,** to stay for.

wen, a tumor. **when,** at what time.

were, from verb TO BE. **whir,** turn around with
noise.

wert, from verb TO BE. see **wart.**

wet, moisture. **whet,** to sharpen.

wether, a ram. **weather,** state of air. see **whether.**

whacks, heavy blows. **wax,** bees'-wax, etc.

whale, sea animal. **wail,** to moan. **wale,** a mark.

what, that which. **wot,** to know.

wheel, circular body. **wheal,** a pustule. see **weal.**

when, at what time. **wen,** a tumor.

where, in which place. see **were** and **wear.**

whet, to sharpen. **wet,** moisture.

whether, which of two. see **wether.**

whey, thin part of milk. see **way.**

which, which one. **witch,** a sorceress.

Whig, name of a party. **wig,** false hair.

while, time. **wile,** deceit, fraud.

whine, plaintive noise. **wine,** juice of grapes.

whir, to turn around with noise. see **were.**

whist, a game of cards. **wist,** thought, knew.

whit, small part. **wit,** quickness of fancy.

white, color of snow. **wight,** a being. **wite,** blame.

whither, to which place. **wither,** to fade.

whole, all, entire. **hole,** a cavity.

wholly, completely. **holy,** sacred, pure.

whoop, shout. **hoop,** circular binding.

wig, false hair. Whig, name of a party.

wight, a person. **wite,** blame. **white,** color of sno
wile, deceit, fraud. **while,** time.

wine, juice of grapes. **whine,** plaintive noise.
wist, thought, knew. **whist,** a game of cards.
wit, quickness of fancy. **whit,** small part.
witch, a sorceress. **which,** which one.
wither, to fade. **whither,** to which place.
won, gained. **one,** single, unit.
wont, custom, habit. **want,** desire.
wood, substance of trees. **would,** was willing.
wort, beer, herb. **wart,** hard excrescence.
wot, to know. **what,** that which.
wrap, to fold. **rap,** to strike.
wrapped, covered. **rapped,** struck with quick blows.
wrapping, a cover. **rapping,** striking.
wreak, to inflict. **reek,** to emit vapor.
wreath, anything circled. **wreathe,** to encircle.
wrest, to twist. **rest,** quiet.
wretch, miserable person. **retch,** to vomit.
wring, to twist. **ring,** a circle, a sound.
write, to form letters. **wright,** workman. see **right.**
wrote, did write. **rote,** a memory of words.
wrought, worked. **rot,** to decay.
wrung, twisted. **rung,** sounded.
wry, crooked. **rye,** a grain.

Y

yew, a tree. **you,** person spoken to. **ewe,** a sheep.
    hue, a color. **Hugh,** name.
yews, trees. **use,** employ. **ewes,** sheep.
yolk, yellow of egg. **yoke,** collar for oxen.
your, belonging to you. **ewer,** a vessel for water.